MACHINE LEARNING

FUNDAMENTALS AND APPLICATIONS

MACHINE LEARNING
FUNDAMENTALS AND APPLICATIONS

Ms. Poonam Adhikari

Prof. (Dr.) Birajashis Pattnaik

Mr. Anil Kumar Tanwar

Prof. (Dr.) Basant Kumar Verma

ACADEMIC ENCLAVE

First Edition, 2025

ISBN: 978-93-48642-73-8

Published by
ACADEMIC ENCLAVE
House No. 10/15, Ground Floor,
Block-A, Street No. 14/3, Kamal Vihar,
Kamal Pur, Burari, Delhi-110084
Email: info@academicenclave.com
Mobile: +91-7042423166
Website: www.academicenclave.com

Printed at Replika Press Pvt. Ltd.

Acknowledgment

This book is the result of collective effort, collaboration, and encouragement from a host of individuals and institutions, all of whom played a vital role in its successful completion. First and foremost, I would like to express my heartfelt gratitude to my mentors and professors, whose invaluable guidance and deep insights into machine learning laid the foundation for this work. Special thanks are due to the academic community and peer reviewers who provided critical feedback during the manuscript development. Their suggestions enriched the content and ensured clarity, coherence, and academic rigor throughout the book. I also extend my appreciation to the students and research scholars whose questions and curiosity consistently motivated deeper exploration and clearer articulation of complex ML concepts.

I am immensely thankful to my family and close friends for their unwavering support and patience during the long hours of research, writing, and revision. Their encouragement gave me the strength to persist through the challenges of compiling and organizing such a comprehensive body of knowledge. Finally, I acknowledge the contributions of open-source communities, ML practitioners, and fellow authors whose works have inspired, informed, and supplemented my understanding of this dynamic field. This book stands as a testament to the collaborative spirit of the ML community, and I hope it will, in turn, contribute meaningfully to its continued growth and evolution.

Preface

In the rapidly evolving digital age, Machine Learning (ML) stands as a cornerstone of technological innovation. From personalized recommendations and intelligent virtual assistants to medical diagnosis and autonomous vehicles, ML has redefined the boundaries of what machines can accomplish. Recognizing its transformative potential, this book aims to serve as a comprehensive introduction and practical guide for learners, educators, and professionals who wish to delve into both the theory and real-world applications of machine learning. The inspiration behind this book stems from a growing need to bridge the gap between foundational knowledge and applied skillsets in ML. While numerous resources explore isolated aspects of machine learning, few offer a cohesive journey from fundamental concepts to advanced methodologies in a pedagogically sound manner. This book attempts to fill that gap by integrating conceptual clarity with hands-on examples and use cases drawn from varied domains.

Each chapter is thoughtfully structured to ensure logical progression—starting with the basics of supervised and unsupervised learning, progressing through reinforcement learning, and culminating in deep learning and practical deployments. Readers are introduced not just to algorithms and models, but also to the mathematical and statistical underpinnings that support them, fostering both theoretical understanding and practical intuition. Whether you are a student beginning your journey, a researcher refining your focus, or a practitioner applying ML to solve complex problems, this book is crafted to support your learning. We hope it empowers you to not only comprehend but also innovate in the field of Machine Learning.

Authors

The Authors

Ms. Poonam Adhikari is an accomplished researcher and educator with over six years of experience in academia. Her research journey began at IIT, Ropar, where she specialized in computer vision and natural language processing, making significant contributions to scholarly literature. As the founder of EdVanta AI, a forward-thinking edtech platform, she is dedicated to bridging the gap between academia and industry, empowering the next generation of learners and professionals with essential skills.

Prof. (Dr.) Birajashis Pattnaik, Professor of Mechanical Engineering at Medicaps University, Indore, is a seasoned academic leader with 32 years of experience in education, research, and institutional administration. Holding a Ph.D. from IIT Kharagpur, his expertise spans Quality Control Engineering, Artificial Intelligence (AI), and Micro-Electro-Mechanical Systems (MEMS). He has been instrumental in advancing strategic academic planning, accreditation (NAAC & NBA), campus administration, and global industry-academia collaborations, significantly contributing to research excellence and institutional growth.

Mr. Anil Kumar Tanwar is currently working as a Deputy Manager in the Technology Team (Design) in a South Korea Based company in the Field of Physics with more than fifteen years of professional experience in R&D, Manufacturing, and Quality Engineering with an emphasis on Vacuum Technology, High frequency THz devices: - Design & Development of Electron Sources, Super Conduction Coils, high volume production. Anil has a diverse skill set, with experience as a design engineer on finite element analysis models for various types of Electromagnets for Accelerator, Medical, and Education. His research interests revolve around IOT based devices, Smart devices, & Network Security, Theory of Computation, and Internet of Things (IoT) Mr. Anil also have expertise in the RF components design, Manufacturing, and RF Tests for Accelerators Nuclear Fusion Reactors, He having expertise in various New communication Technologies and processes. Anil holds a Bachelor's degree in Electronics & Communications Engineering from the Sabarmati University Gujrat, India.

Technical Reviewer

Prof. (Dr.) Basant Kumar Verma is currently serving as Professor and Head of the Department of Computer Science and Engineering – Artificial Intelligence and Data Science at Panipat Institute of Engineering and Technology (PIET), Haryana. He holds B.E. and M.E. degrees from BITS Pilani, Rajasthan, and a D.Sc. from The Thames International University, Paris, France. His academic and professional journey reflects his unwavering commitment to excellence and innovation.

CONTENTS

1

FUNDAMENTALS OF MACHINE LEARNING

Introduction

Machine Learning (ML) is a branch of artificial intelligence (AI) that enables computers to learn from data and make predictions or decisions without being explicitly programmed. It is an essential technology driving advancements in various fields, including healthcare, finance, education, and autonomous systems. By analyzing patterns and trends in large datasets, machine learning models can provide insights, automate tasks, and enhance decision-making processes. At its core, machine learning relies on data-driven algorithms that improve their performance over time. These algorithms fall into three primary categories: supervised learning, unsupervised learning, and reinforcement learning. Supervised learning involves training a model using labeled data, where the algorithm learns to map input variables to the correct output. In contrast, unsupervised learning deals with unlabeled data, identifying hidden patterns and structures within datasets. Reinforcement learning, inspired by behavioral psychology, involves learning through trial and error using a system of rewards and penalties.

One of the key components of machine learning is the training process, where a model is exposed to data and adjusts its internal parameters to minimize error. This is typically achieved using techniques such as gradient descent, which optimizes the model by iteratively reducing errors. The quality of training data plays a crucial role in determining the accuracy and effectiveness of the model, making data preprocessing including cleaning, normalization, and feature selection an essential step in the ML pipeline. Machine learning models use various mathematical and statistical concepts, such as probability theory, linear algebra, and optimization, to process and analyze data. Techniques like decision trees, support vector machines, neural networks, and ensemble methods are commonly used for different tasks, ranging from classification and regression to clustering and anomaly detection. Selecting the right model and fine-tuning its parameters significantly impact the performance of an ML system. Another fundamental aspect of machine learning is model evaluation and validation. To ensure that a model generalizes well to new data, it is tested on unseen datasets using performance metrics like accuracy, precision, recall, and F1-score. Overfitting and underfitting are common challenges that arise when a model is either too complex or too simplistic, respectively. Techniques such as cross-validation and regularization help address these issues by optimizing the model's complexity. Machine learning continues to evolve, integrating with deep learning, natural language processing, and big data technologies to create more powerful and intelligent systems. As industries adopt machine learning to enhance automation and decision-making, ethical considerations such as bias, transparency, and data privacy become increasingly important. Understanding the fundamentals of ML lays the foundation for developing innovative solutions that leverage data-driven intelligence to solve complex real-world problems.

Basic Concepts of Machine Learning

Machine Learning (ML) is a branch of artificial intelligence (AI) that enables computers to learn from data and make decisions without being explicitly programmed. It works by developing algorithms that identify patterns in data and improve their performance over time. ML models are trained using vast amounts of data, where they learn from examples and adjust their internal parameters to make accurate predictions. The primary goal of ML is to create systems that can automatically adapt to new data, enabling automation and intelligent decision-making in various fields such as healthcare, finance, and marketing. There are three main types of machine learning: supervised learning, unsupervised learning, and reinforcement learning. In supervised learning, the model learns from labeled data, where input-output pairs are provided to make predictions. Common algorithms include linear regression, decision trees, and neural networks. Unsupervised learning, on the other hand, deals with unlabeled data and focuses on finding hidden patterns, clusters, or associations within datasets, with algorithms like K-means clustering and principal component analysis (PCA). Reinforcement learning is a dynamic learning approach where an agent interacts with an environment, receives feedback in the form of rewards or penalties, and optimizes its actions accordingly widely used in robotics, gaming, and autonomous systems. Machine learning has widespread applications in today's world, revolutionizing industries with automation and intelligent systems. It powers recommendation engines (such as those used by Netflix and Amazon), fraud detection in banking, medical diagnostics, and even self-driving cars. However, ML also faces challenges such as data privacy concerns, biases in training data, and the need for large computational resources. As research progresses, advancements like explainable AI and federated learning are addressing these limitations, making ML more transparent and efficient. Ultimately, machine learning continues to evolve, shaping the future of technology and decision-making.

Definition of Learning Systems

A learning system is any computational system that improves its performance over time by learning from data, experience, or interaction with the environment. Unlike traditional rule-based programming, where explicit instructions are given for every possible scenario, machine learning systems automatically develop models and rules based on observed patterns in data. These systems aim to generalize from past experiences, enabling them to make predictions or decisions when encountering new, unseen situations. In a formal sense, a system is said to learn from experience E concerning some task T and performance measure P if its performance at task T, as measured by P, improves with experience E. For example, an email spam filter learns to distinguish between spam and non-spam emails (Task T) by analyzing labeled examples (Experience E) and improving its accuracy (Performance Measure P) over time.

Goals of Machine Learning

The primary goal of machine learning is to develop intelligent systems that can automatically learn patterns and insights from data without direct human intervention. The objectives of machine learning include:

Pattern Recognition

Pattern recognition is a core goal of machine learning, involving the identification of patterns, trends, or hidden structures within large datasets. By analyzing data, machine learning models can recognize complex relationships that might not be immediately obvious. This goal helps machines identify significant features in datasets such as images, texts, or signals. For example, in computer vision, machine learning algorithms can detect objects, faces, or handwriting. The ability to uncover hidden patterns can lead to better decision-making, such as recognizing fraudulent transactions in finance or classifying diseases in medical diagnoses. Pattern recognition forms the foundation of many advanced applications in artificial intelligence, transforming raw data into actionable insights.

Prediction and Forecasting

Prediction and forecasting are essential aspects of machine learning, where models use historical data to forecast future events or trends. For example, in financial markets, machine learning algorithms analyze past stock prices to predict future market behavior. In weather prediction, they process historical weather patterns to forecast the weather for upcoming days. Machine learning models enable more accurate predictions by learning from vast amounts of data, which would be difficult for humans to analyze manually. By forecasting outcomes, businesses and organizations can make proactive decisions, such as inventory management or predicting customer demand.

Automation and Decision-Making

A critical goal of machine learning is automation and improving decision-making by reducing human involvement in complex processes. Automation allows systems to operate independently based on learned patterns, improving efficiency and reducing human error. For example, machine learning models are used in medical diagnostics, where they can automatically detect anomalies in X-rays or MRI scans, providing faster and more accurate results. Fraud detection systems in banking can automatically flag suspicious activities by analyzing transaction patterns. Machine learning enables decision-making in real time, making systems more responsive and efficient. By reducing human intervention, it not only saves time but also improves scalability in decision-making processes.

Improvement Over Time

One of the remarkable features of machine learning is its ability to improve with experience. As more data becomes available, machine learning models refine their algorithms to enhance performance. This continuous learning process ensures that machine learning systems become more accurate over time. For instance, in a recommendation system like those used by Netflix or Amazon, the more a user interacts with the platform, the better the system becomes at predicting their preferences. This constant refinement leads to models that become increasingly efficient, making them more reliable for decision-making. Machine learning's ability to improve over time makes it a powerful tool for long-term applications.

Adaptability

Adaptability is another key objective of machine learning, which refers to the model's ability to adjust to changing environments or data distributions. In real-world applications, data patterns are constantly evolving, and machine learning systems must be able to adapt accordingly. For instance, in autonomous vehicles, machine learning models must respond to different traffic conditions, weather changes, or unexpected obstacles. Similarly, in customer sentiment analysis, the language and expressions used by consumers may change over time, and the model must adapt to these changes. A system that can adapt to new data ensures that machine learning models remain relevant and effective as external factors evolve. This adaptability is vital for industries that rely on real-time data and dynamic environments.

These goals collectively enable machine learning systems to support various industries by making informed, data-driven decisions, improving efficiency, and providing automation in complex tasks.

Goals and Applications of Machine Learning

Machine learning has widespread applications across multiple industries, transforming the way data is used to drive innovation and efficiency in Figure 1.1. Some key applications include:

Figure 1.1: Goals and Applications of Machine Learning.

Healthcare

Machine learning (ML) is revolutionizing healthcare by improving disease diagnosis, medical image analysis, and personalized treatment recommendations. ML models are trained on vast datasets of patient records, genetic information, and medical images to detect patterns that human experts might overlook. In disease diagnosis, ML assists doctors in identifying conditions like cancer, diabetes, and heart diseases with high accuracy. In medical imaging, ML algorithms enhance the analysis of X-rays, MRIs, and CT scans, enabling faster and more precise detection of abnormalities. Additionally, ML-driven personalized treatment recommendations help tailor medical care based on a patient's unique genetic profile, lifestyle, and medical history, leading to improved treatment outcomes and reduced side effects.

Finance

Banks and financial institutions leverage ML for fraud detection, credit scoring, and algorithmic trading. ML algorithms analyze transaction patterns to detect unusual activities that may indicate fraud, preventing financial crimes in real time. Credit scoring models use ML to assess an individual's creditworthiness by evaluating factors such as transaction history, income, and spending behavior, leading to more accurate loan approvals. Algorithmic trading utilizes ML to analyze market trends, predict stock movements, and execute trades at optimal times. These applications help financial institutions minimize risks, enhance decision-making, and improve overall efficiency in financial operations.

Retail and E-Commerce

Machine learning enhances the retail and e-commerce industry through personalized recommendations, customer behavior analysis, and dynamic pricing. E-commerce platforms like Amazon and Netflix use ML algorithms to analyze user preferences and browsing history to recommend relevant products or content, increasing user engagement. Customer behavior analysis helps businesses understand buying patterns, optimize marketing strategies, and improve inventory management. Dynamic pricing models adjust prices in real time based on demand, competition, and customer willingness to pay, ensuring competitive pricing and maximizing revenue. These ML-driven applications improve customer satisfaction and business profitability.

Autonomous Vehicles

Self-driving cars rely on ML to recognize objects, detect obstacles, and make real-time navigation decisions. ML models process data from sensors, cameras, and LIDAR to identify pedestrians, traffic signals, and road conditions, ensuring safe driving. Object recognition algorithms classify and track moving and stationary objects, helping the vehicle react appropriately to its surroundings. Obstacle detection and avoidance mechanisms enable autonomous vehicles to anticipate and respond to potential hazards. Furthermore, reinforcement learning techniques improve decision-making, allowing self-driving cars to adapt to diverse driving environments and optimize route planning. These advancements contribute to safer and more efficient transportation.

Natural Language Processing (NLP)

Natural language processing (NLP) enables ML-driven applications like chatbots, language translation, and voice assistants. Chatbots powered by ML understand and respond to customer queries in real time, improving customer service efficiency. Language translation models, such as Google Translate, use deep learning to translate text and speech between languages with high accuracy. Voice assistants like Siri and Google Assistant leverage NLP to interpret voice commands, provide information, and execute tasks. Sentiment analysis, text summarization, and document classification are additional NLP applications that enhance communication and information processing, making interactions with technology more seamless and human-like.

Cybersecurity

Machine learning strengthens cybersecurity by detecting anomalies and preventing cyber threats. ML algorithms analyze network traffic and system behaviors to identify patterns associated with malicious activities, such as unauthorized access and malware attacks. Anomaly detection techniques enable proactive threat detection by flagging suspicious activities before they escalate. ML-powered security systems continuously learn from emerging threats, enhancing their ability to recognize new attack patterns. Additionally, ML models assist in fraud prevention by identifying unusual user behaviors in online transactions and login attempts. These capabilities improve cybersecurity defenses, reducing vulnerabilities and ensuring data protection.

Manufacturing and Robotics

In manufacturing and robotics, ML optimizes processes through predictive maintenance, quality control, and industrial automation. Predictive maintenance models analyze machine performance data to anticipate equipment failures, minimizing downtime and maintenance costs. Quality control systems use ML-driven image recognition to detect product defects and ensure high production standards. Industrial automation employs ML algorithms to enhance robotic efficiency, enabling machines to adapt to changing production demands. Additionally, ML-powered supply chain optimization helps manufacturers manage inventory, reduce waste, and streamline logistics. These applications improve operational efficiency, productivity, and cost-effectiveness in manufacturing industries.As machine learning continues to evolve, it plays a crucial role in shaping the future of technology, making systems smarter, more efficient, and capable of solving complex real-world problems.

Aspects of Developing a Learning System

Developing an effective machine learning system involves several critical components that determine the model's ability to learn, generalize, and make accurate predictions. Three essential aspects of building a learning system are training data, concept representation, and function approximation. These elements collectively define how a system learns from experience and applies that learning to new data.

Training Data

Training data is the foundation of any machine learning model, as it provides the necessary information for the system to learn patterns and relationships. The quality, quantity, and diversity of training data significantly impact the model's performance. Training data can be:

Labeled Data (Used in Supervised Learning)

Labeled data plays a crucial role in supervised learning by providing the model with explicit input-output pairs. Each data point includes a predefined label, allowing the model to learn by mapping inputs to corresponding outputs. For example, in image classification, a dataset might contain images labeled as "cat" or "dog," enabling the model to recognize similar patterns in new images. The diversity of labeled data significantly impacts model performance, ensuring that the model generalizes well to different variations of input. If the training data lacks diversity, the model may suffer from overfitting, performing well on training examples but failing on real-world data. A well-balanced dataset with various instances from different contexts improves accuracy and robustness.

Unlabeled Data (Used in Unsupervised Learning)

Unlabeled data is vital in unsupervised learning, where the model identifies hidden patterns and structures without predefined labels. This type of data allows for techniques like clustering and dimensionality reduction, helping the model learn meaningful representations. Since real-world data is often unlabeled, training on diverse, high-quality data ensures that the model can discover useful insights across various domains. If the data lacks variation, the model might form biased or incorrect groupings, limiting its effectiveness. A diverse dataset helps in better generalization, making the model applicable to a wider range of scenarios, such as customer segmentation, anomaly detection, and recommendation systems.

Reinforcement Learning Data

Reinforcement learning data is generated through interactions between an agent and its environment, where rewards or penalties shape the learning process. This type of data is crucial in applications such as robotics, gaming, and autonomous systems. The diversity of experiences collected during training directly influences the model's ability to make optimal decisions. If the data only represents a limited set of actions or environments, the model may struggle to adapt to new situations. A diverse dataset ensures that the agent encounters a wide range of scenarios, allowing it to develop more robust strategies. In reinforcement learning, the balance between exploration (trying new actions) and exploitation (using known strategies) is critical. A well-curated training dataset helps the agent navigate complex environments efficiently, improving its performance and adaptability. Effective training data must be cleaned, preprocessed, and well-structured to minimize noise and bias. Common preprocessing steps include handling missing values, feature scaling, and normalization, ensuring the data is well-suited for the learning algorithm.

Example: Training Data in Image Recognition

Imagine we are developing a facial recognition system. The training dataset should include:

- A diverse set of faces from different ethnicities, ages, and lighting conditions.

- Different angles and facial expressions to improve recognition accuracy.
- Properly labeled images to train the model using supervised learning techniques.

Concept Representation

Concept representation refers to how the learning system structures knowledge within the model. The choice of representation affects how well the model can capture the underlying relationships in the data. Some common ways concepts are represented include:

Logical Representation

Logical representation is a method of expressing knowledge using formal rules and structures that follow logical principles. It is commonly employed in expert systems, where knowledge is encoded using IF-THEN rules. These rules define relationships between different conditions and actions, allowing the system to make decisions based on logical inference. Logical representations can be expressed in propositional logic (which deals with true/false statements) or first-order logic (which includes objects, properties, and relations). For example, an expert system for medical diagnosis might include a rule:

IF a patient has a fever and sore throat, thenit could indicate an infection. Such representations enable machines to perform deductive reasoning, ensuring transparent decision-making processes. However, they struggle with handling uncertainty and require exhaustive rule specification, making them less adaptable to complex, real-world scenarios.

Geometric Representation

Geometric representation encodes knowledge using mathematical structures such as vectors, spaces, and transformations. In machine learning, data points are often represented as vectors in a high-dimensional space, allowing models to learn patterns through geometric relationships. Techniques like linear regression, principal component analysis (PCA), and support vector machines (SVMs) rely on this representation. For instance, in SVM, data points are separated by an optimal hyperplane that maximizes the margin between different classes. Similarly, word embeddings (e.g., Word2Vec) represent words as vectors in a semantic space, capturing their relationships through distances and angles. Geometric representation is powerful because it enables efficient computations, but it may not always capture hierarchical or probabilistic dependencies effectively.

Probabilistic Representation

Probabilistic representation expresses knowledge by modeling uncertainty using probability distributions. Unlike logical representations, which deal with absolute truths, probabilistic methods handle real-world situations where information is incomplete or noisy. Bayesian networks, hidden Markov models (HMMs), and Gaussian mixtures are examples of this approach. Bayesian networks, for example, represent dependencies between variables using a directed graph, where edges indicate probabilistic relationships. Suppose a medical diagnosis system considers symptoms and diseases; a Bayesian network can compute the likelihood of a disease given observed symptoms using Bayes' Theorem. Probabilistic representation is widely used in speech recognition, robotics, and risk assessment, but it can be computationally expensive and require substantial data for accurate modeling.

Neural Representations

Neural representation is based on artificial neural networks (ANNs), which mimic the human brain's structure and function to process information. Unlike rule-based systems, ANNs learn patterns and hierarchies from data without explicit programming. They consist of interconnected neurons arranged in layers, where each neuron applies mathematical transformations to input data. Deep learning architectures, such as convolutional neural networks (CNNs) and transformers, excel in recognizing complex patterns in images, text, and speech. For example, CNNs automatically learn spatial hierarchies in images, making them effective for object detection and medical imaging. Neural representations are highly flexible and powerful but often require large datasets, significant computational resources, and lack interpretability compared to rule-based methods. Selecting the right representation is crucial because it determines how efficiently the model learns and generalizes to new data.

Example: Concept Representation in Speech Recognition

- A speech recognition system converts audio waves into text.
- Waveforms are transformed into numerical features (e.g., frequency, amplitude).
- Neural networks process these features to map sounds to words.
- Hidden Markov Models (HMMs) are often used to represent the sequence of phonemes in speech.

Function Approximation

Function approximation is the process of finding a mathematical function that best maps inputs (features) to outputs (predictions or classifications). Since real-world data is often complex, machine learning models approximate an unknown target function rather than directly computing it. Some common function approximation techniques include:

Linear Models

Linear models are foundational techniques in machine learning and statistics, designed to capture relationships between variables using a straight-line equation. The simplest example is linear regression, which predicts a dependent variable (Y) based on one or more independent variables (X). The mathematical representation is:

$$Y = \beta_0 + \beta_1 X + \epsilon$$

where β0 is the intercept, β1 is the coefficient, and ϵ is the error term. Linear regression assumes a constant rate of change, meaning for every unit increase in X, Y changes by a fixed amount. This makes linear models interpretable and computationally efficient. However, they are limited in capturing complex, nonlinear relationships in data. Despite this, linear models serve as a baseline for more advanced modeling approaches and remain widely used in various fields like finance, economics, and healthcare.

Polynomial and Nonlinear Models

When relationships between variables are nonlinear, a simple straight-line model may not be sufficient. Polynomial regression extends linear models by including higher-degree terms of the independent variable:

$$Y = \beta_0 + \beta_1 X + \beta_2 X^2 + ... + \beta_n X^n + \epsilon$$

This allows the model to capture curved patterns in data, making it more flexible. However, using very high-degree polynomials can lead to overfitting, where the model fits noise rather than the true relationship. Other nonlinear models use transformations, such as logarithmic or exponential functions, to describe relationships that are not well represented by polynomials. More advanced nonlinear models include logistic regression for classification and generalized additive models (GAMs), which allow for nonlinear effects while maintaining interpretability. These models help bridge the gap between simple linear models and highly complex machine learning techniques.

Neural Networks

Neural networks are powerful machine learning models inspired by the structure of the human brain. They consist of layers of interconnected neurons that process and transform data. The simplest type, a feedforward neural network, has an input layer, one or more hidden layers, and an output layer. Each neuron applies a weighted sum of inputs followed by an activation function (e.g., ReLU, sigmoid, or tanh) to introduce nonlinearity:

$$Y = f(WX + b)$$

where W represents weights, b is the bias term, and f is the activation function. With multiple layers, neural networks can learn highly complex, nonlinear relationships that traditional models struggle with. Deep learning models, such as convolutional neural networks (CNNs) for image recognition and recurrent neural networks (RNNs) for sequential data, expand the capabilities of neural networks. However, they require large datasets and substantial computational power. Despite these challenges, neural networks are widely used in modern

AI applications, including speech recognition, autonomous driving, and natural language processing.

Kernel Methods (e.g., SVMs)

Kernel methods, particularly Support Vector Machines (SVMs), are used for classification and regression problems where the data is not linearly separable. SVMs work by finding the optimal hyperplane that maximizes the margin between different classes. However, in complex datasets, a linear hyperplane may not exist.To address this, kernel methods transform data into a higher-dimensional space using a kernel function:

$$K(x_i, x_j) = \phi(x_i) \cdot \phi(x_j)$$

where ϕ maps the data into a higher-dimensional space. Common kernel functions include:

- Polynomial Kernel: Captures polynomial relationships.
- Radial Basis Function (RBF) Kernel: Captures complex patterns by considering the distance between data points.
- Sigmoid Kernel: Similar to neural networks in behavior.

The goal of function approximation is to minimize the error while avoiding overfitting (memorizing the training data) and underfitting (failing to capture patterns). Techniques like regularization, cross-validation, and hyperparameter tuning help optimize function approximation.

Types of Learning

In supervised learning, the model is trained using labeled data. This means that for each input, the corresponding correct output is provided, allowing the model to learn the mapping between input and output. The key features are:

- Use labeled datasets (input-output pairs).
- The model learns from known examples and makes predictions on new data.
- Commonly used for classification and regression problems.

Algorithms Used in Supervised Learning

Supervised learning is a type of machine learning where a model is trained using labeled data, meaning each input in the training dataset has a corresponding correct output in Figure 1.2. The model learns by identifying patterns and relationships between inputs and outputs, adjusting its internal parameters to minimize errors. This approach is commonly used for tasks like classification (e.g., spam detection, medical diagnosis) and regression (e.g., predicting house prices, stock market trends). Algorithms such as decision trees, support vector machines, and neural networks are frequently employed in supervised learning.

The training process involves feeding the model a dataset divided into input features and their correct labels. Using an optimization technique like gradient descent, the model iteratively refines its predictions to improve accuracy. Once trained, the model can make predictions on new, unseen data. However, challenges like overfitting (where the model memorizes training data instead of generalizing) must be addressed through techniques like cross-validation and regularization. Supervised learning plays a crucial role in various real-world applications, including speech recognition, recommendation systems, and fraud detection.

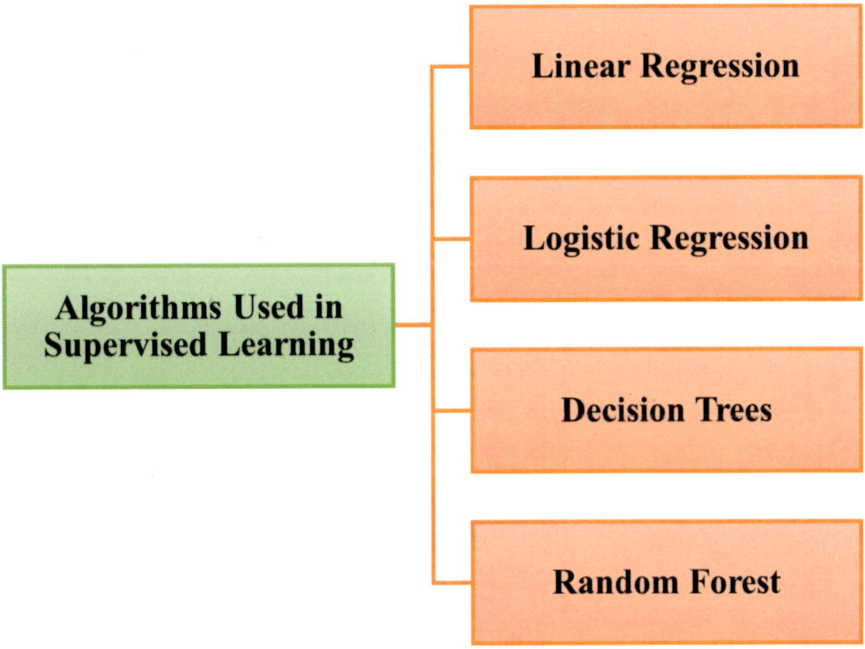

Figure 1.2: Algorithms Used in Supervised Learning.

Linear Regression

Linear Regression is a fundamental supervised learning algorithm used for predictive modeling and data analysis. It establishes a linear relationship between independent variables (features) and a dependent variable (target). The equation of a simple linear regression model is:

$$Y = b_0 + b_1X + \epsilon$$

where Y is the dependent variable, Xis the independent variable, b0is the intercept, b1 is the coefficient, and ϵ is the error term. The model minimizes the sum of squared errors (SSE) using techniques like Ordinary Least Squares (OLS). It is widely used in economics, finance, and healthcare for predicting continuous outcomes such as sales, prices, or scores. However, it assumes linearity, homoscedasticity, and independence of errors, making it less effective for complex datasets with non-linear relationships.

Logistic Regression

Logistic Regression is a classification algorithm that predicts categorical outcomes, particularly binary (0 or 1). Unlike linear regression, it uses the sigmoid function to map predictions between 0 and 1:

$$P(Y=1) = \frac{1}{1+e^{-(b_0+b_1X)}}$$

Here, P(Y=1) represents the probability that the dependent variable belongs to class 1. The model applies a threshold (e.g., 0.5) to decide class labels. Logistic regression is widely used in spam detection, medical diagnosis, and fraud detection. It supports multinomial and ordinal logistic regression for multi-class problems. However, it assumes a linear relationship between independent variables and the log-odds of the outcome, limiting its performance on non-linear datasets.

Decision Trees

Decision Trees are non-parametric, supervised learning models used for both classification and regression. They work by recursively splitting the dataset into subsets based on feature values, forming a tree-like structure. The tree consists of:

- Root Node: Represents the entire dataset.
- Decision Nodes: Represent feature-based splits.
- Leaf Nodes: Represent final predictions.

Common splitting criteria include Gini Impurity and Entropy (Information Gain) for classification and Mean Squared Error (MSE) for regression. Decision trees are easy to interpret and useful in medical diagnosis and risk assessment. However, they tend to overfit, which can be mitigated through pruning and ensemble methods.

Random Forest

Random Forest is an ensemble learning technique that combines multiple decision trees to enhance accuracy and robustness. It operates using bagging (Bootstrap Aggregation), where:

- Multiple decision trees are trained on random subsets of the data.
- The final prediction is obtained by averaging (regression) or majority voting (classification).

Random Forest reduces overfitting compared to individual decision trees and is effective in handling large datasets with missing values and noise. It is widely used in medical diagnostics, stock market predictions, and image recognition. However, it is computationally expensive and may lack interpretability.

Support Vector Machines (SVM)

SVM is a powerful supervised learning algorithm used for both classification and regression. It finds an optimal hyperplane that maximizes the margin between different classes in high-dimensional space.

- In linear SVM, the hyperplane is a straight line separating two classes.
- In non-linear SVM, the model uses kernel functions (e.g., Polynomial, Radial Basis Function) to transform data into a higher dimension for better separation.

SVM is widely used in image classification, text categorization, and bioinformatics. It performs well with small and high-dimensional datasets but is computationally expensive for large datasets.

Neural Networks

Neural Networks are inspired by the human brain and consist of interconnected layers of neurons. A typical Artificial Neural Network (ANN) has:

- Input Layer: Takes raw data features.
- Hidden Layers: Perform complex computations and feature extraction.
- Output Layer: Produces the final prediction.

Each neuron applies an activation function (e.g., ReLU, Sigmoid, Softmax) to introduce non-linearity. Variants include Convolutional Neural Networks (CNNs) for image processing and Recurrent Neural Networks (RNNs) for sequential data. Neural networks excel in tasks like speech recognition, natural language processing, and autonomous driving but require large datasets and significant computational power.

Unsupervised Learning

Unsupervised learning is a type of machine learning where a model is trained on data without predefined labels. Unlike supervised learning, which relies on labeled examples, unsupervised learning algorithms analyze input data to uncover hidden patterns, structures, or relationships. These models work by grouping similar data points (clustering) or reducing dimensionality to extract essential features. Common techniques include k-means clustering, hierarchical clustering, and principal component analysis (PCA), which help in data exploration, anomaly detection, and feature extraction. One of the main advantages of unsupervised learning is its ability to handle large amounts of unstructured data without human intervention. It is widely used in applications such as customer segmentation, fraud detection, and recommendation systems. For example, in market research, businesses use clustering algorithms to identify customer segments based on purchasing behavior, allowing for targeted marketing strategies. Despite its benefits, unsupervised learning can be challenging as it requires interpreting the discovered patterns correctly and determining the optimal number of clusters or features without explicit guidance. The key features are:

- Uses unlabeled datasets.
- The model finds hidden structures and groups in data.
- Commonly used for clustering and association rule mining.

Algorithms Used in unsupervised learning

Unsupervised learning algorithms are used to analyze and cluster unlabeled data, discovering hidden patterns and structures without explicit supervision. Common algorithms include K-Means Clustering, which partitions data into K clusters based on similarity; Hierarchical Clustering, which creates a tree-like structure of nested clusters; DBSCAN (Density-Based Spatial Clustering of Applications with Noise), which groups points based on density and identifies outliers; and Gaussian Mixture Models (GMM), which assumes data is generated from multiple Gaussian distributions. Principal Component Analysis (PCA) and t-SNE (t-Distributed Stochastic Neighbor Embedding) are dimensionality reduction techniques used for feature extraction and visualization. Autoencoders, a type of neural network, are also used in unsupervised learning for anomaly detection and feature learning.

K-Means Clustering

K-Means Clustering is an unsupervised machine learning algorithm used for partitioning a dataset into K distinct, non-overlapping clusters. It operates by initializing K cluster centroids and iteratively assigning data points to the nearest centroid based on Euclidean distance. The centroids are then recalculated as the mean of the assigned points. This process repeats until centroids stabilize or a predefined number of iterations is reached. K-Means is widely used in customer segmentation, anomaly detection, and image segmentation. However, it has limitations such as sensitivity to initial centroid placement and difficulty in handling non-spherical clusters. Optimizations like K-Means++ improve centroid initialization, reducing convergence time and improving cluster quality.

K-Means Clustering Example

Let's consider an example of customer segmentation for a retail store in Table 1.1.

Scenario

A retail store wants to categorize its customers based on their purchasing behavior. The store collects data on customers, including:

- Annual Income ($)

- Spending Score (1-100) (a measure of how much they spend)

The goal is to segment customers into groups so that the store can target each group with different marketing strategies.

Steps in K-Means Clustering

- Choose the number of clusters (K): Suppose the store decides to divide customers into 3 groups (K=3).
- Randomly initialize K centroids: Three points (centroids) are chosen randomly as the initial cluster centers.
- Assign customers to the nearest centroid: Each customer is assigned to the closest centroid based on Euclidean distance.
- Recalculatecentroids: The mean of all points in each cluster is computed to update the centroids.
- Repeatsteps3 and 4 untilconvergence: This process continues until centroids stop moving significantly.

Table 1.1: Dataset and Clustering Result.

Customer	Annual Income ($)	Spending Score	Cluster
A	15,000	85	1 (High Spenders)
B	80,000	20	2 (Moderate Spenders)
C	50,000	50	3 (Average Spenders)
D	18,000	90	1 (High Spenders)
E	90,000	15	2 (Moderate Spenders)

Interpretation

- Cluster 1 (High Spenders): Low income but high spending scores (young customers, impulse buyers).
- Cluster 2 (Moderate Spenders): High income but low spending scores (wealthy customers but cautious spenders).
- Cluster 3 (Average Spenders): Middle-range customers with balanced income and spending.

This segmentation helps the store target high spenders with premium deals, moderate spenders with loyalty programs, and average spenders with promotions.

Hierarchical Clustering

Hierarchical Clustering is a method of clustering that builds a hierarchy of clusters either using a bottom-up (agglomerative) or top-down (divisive) approach. The agglomerative method starts with each data point as its own cluster and merges the closest clusters iteratively, while the divisive approach begins with all data points in one cluster and splits them iteratively. The output is represented as a dendrogram, which helps visualize the merging process. A key advantage of hierarchical clustering is that it does not require specifying the number of clusters in advance. However, it is computationally expensive, especially for large datasets. It is widely used in genetics, social network analysis, and document clustering.

Hierarchical Clustering Example

Let's consider an example of document clustering for news articles.

Scenario:

A news agency wants to group similar articles into categories such as Sports, Politics, and Technology based on their content in Table 1.2. The agency uses Hierarchical Clustering to achieve this.

Steps in Hierarchical Clustering:

- Collect the dataset: The agency collects news articles and converts them into numerical representations (word frequency, TF-IDF, or embeddings).

Choose the approach:

- Agglomerative (bottom-up): Each article starts as its own cluster, and similar articles are merged iteratively.
- Divisive (top-down): All articles start in one cluster and are split iteratively.

Table 1.2: Dataset and Clustering Result.

Article	Topic Keywords	Cluster
A	"Goal, match, football, score"	Sports
B	"Election, government, policy"	Politics
C	"AI, machine learning, robotics"	Technology
D	"Player, championship, tournament"	Sports
E	"President, debate, law"	Politics

Suppose we use Agglomerative Clustering.

- Compute the similarity (distance) between articles: A distance matrix is created based on text similarity (e.g., cosine similarity or Euclidean distance).
- Merge the closest clusters iteratively: At each step, the two most similar clusters are merged.
- Generate a dendrogram: A dendrogram is created to visualize the merging process.

- Decide the number of clusters: By cutting the dendrogram at an appropriate level, we obtain distinct article clusters.

Dendrogram Interpretation

- If we cut the dendrogram at 3 clusters, we get Sports, Politics, and Technology groups.
- The height of merging in the dendrogram indicates how similar or different clusters are.

Principal Component Analysis (PCA)

Principal Component Analysis (PCA) is a dimensionality reduction technique used to transform high-dimensional data into a smaller set of linearly uncorrelated features called principal components. It works by computing the covariance matrix, extracting its eigenvectors, and ranking them based on the corresponding eigenvalues. The first few principal components capture the maximum variance in the data. PCA is commonly used in machine learning for noise reduction, visualization of high-dimensional data, and speeding up computational processes. Despite its effectiveness, PCA assumes linear relationships and may discard information by reducing dimensionality, which can sometimes impact model accuracy.

Principal Component Analysis (PCA) Example

Scenario: Handwritten Digit Recognition (MNIST Dataset)

Imagine you are working on a machine learning project to classify handwritten digits (0-9) using the MNIST dataset. This dataset consists of 28×28 grayscale images (total 784 features per image). However, training a model on 784 features is computationally expensive and may contain redundant information in Table 1.3.

Goal:

- Reduce the dimensionality of the dataset while preserving as much useful information as possible.

Steps in PCA for Dimensionality Reduction

1. Standardizing the Data

PCA works best when the data is normalized (zero mean, unit variance). Each pixel value is transformed so that it has a mean of 0 and a standard deviation of 1.

2. Compute the Covariance Matrix

The covariance matrix captures relationships between different pixel intensities. If two pixels have a high covariance, they vary together and contain redundant information.

3. Calculate Eigenvalues & Eigenvectors

- Eigenvectors represent the principal components (PCs) (new directions in feature space).
- Eigenvalues indicate how much variance each PC captures.

4. Choose Top Principal Components

- Rank PCs by their eigenvalues.
- Select the top k components that explain most of the variance.

Example: Reducing 784 features to 50 components while retaining ~95% of the variance.

5. Project the Data onto the New Feature Space

- Each image is now represented in a lower-dimensional space (e.g., 50D instead of 784D).

Table 1.3: PCA on MNIST Dataset.

Original Features (Pixels)	After PCA (Reduced Features)
784	50
784	40
784	30

Apriori Algorithm

The Apriori Algorithm is a rule-based learning technique used for mining frequent itemsets in transactional datasets. It is widely applied in market basket analysis to identify associations between products. The algorithm follows the principle that if an itemset is frequent, its subsets must also be frequent. It consists of two main steps: candidate generation, where frequent itemsets are identified iteratively, and rule generation, where strong association rules are derived based on minimum support and confidence thresholds. While effective for small datasets, Apriori suffers from high computational complexity for large datasets due to its exponential growth in candidate sets.

Apriori Algorithm Example

Scenario: Market Basket Analysis

A supermarket wants to analyze customer purchasing behavior to find frequent item sets and generate association rules in Table 1.4. This helps them decide which products to place together or offer in combo deals.

Table 1.4: Dataset (Transaction Data)

Transaction ID	Items Purchased
1	Milk, Bread, Butter
2	Milk, Bread
3	Bread, Butter
4	Milk, Butter
5	Milk, Bread, Butter, Eggs

Step 1: Find Frequent Itemsets

Using minimum support = 50% (appears in at least 3 transactions):

- {Milk} → 4 times
- {Bread} → 4 times
- {Butter} → 4 times
- {Milk, Bread} → 3 times
- {Milk, Butter} → 3 times
- {Bread, Butter} → 3 times

Step 2: Generate Association Rules

Using minimum confidence = 70%, we get rules like:

- {Milk} → {Bread} (Support: 3/5, Confidence: 3/4 = 75%)

Customers who buy Milk often buy Bread.

- {Bread} → {Butter} (Support: 3/5, Confidence: 3/4 = 75%)

If someone buys Bread, they likely buy Butter too.

- {Milk, Bread} → {Butter} (Support: 3/5, Confidence: 3/3 = 100%)

Customers buying both Milk and Bread always buy Butter.

Business Use:

- Place Milk & Bread together to increase sales.
- Offer discounts on Butter when customers buy Bread.

Autoencoders (Neural Networks)

Autoencoders are a type of artificial neural network used for unsupervised learning, particularly in dimensionality reduction, feature learning, and anomaly detection. They consist of an encoder, which compresses the input into a lower-dimensional representation, and a decoder, which reconstructs the original input from this representation. The network is trained to minimize the reconstruction error. Variants like variational autoencoders (VAEs) and sparse autoencoders enhance performance for generative tasks and feature extraction. Autoencoders are widely used in image compression, denoising, and fraud detection. However, they require careful tuning and may struggle with capturing complex data distributions without sufficient training data.

Autoencoders Example: Image Denoising

Scenario:

You have noisy images and want to remove the noise while preserving the original structure.

Steps:

- Encoder: Compresses the noisy image into a lower-dimensional representation.
- Bottleneck Layer: Learns the essential features of the image.
- Decoder: Reconstructs the image from the compressed representation, removing noise in the process.

Example:

- Input: A noisy handwritten digit image (e.g., from the MNIST dataset).
- Output: A cleaned version of the digit after passing through the autoencoder.

Key Differences Between Supervised and Unsupervised Learning

Supervised learning is ideal when labeled data is available and the goal is prediction.Unsupervised learning is used when exploring unknown patterns and structures in data.Both types play a crucial role in various applications like artificial intelligence, business analytics, healthcare, and more.

Table 1.5: Comparison between Supervised and Unsupervised Learning.

Feature	Supervised Learning	**Unsupervised Learning**
Data Type	Labeled data	Unlabeled data
Goal	Predict outcomes based on past examples	Identify patterns and structures
Common Tasks	Classification, Regression	Clustering, Association
Output	Defined categories or continuous values	Hidden patterns or groupings
Example	Spam detection, stock price prediction	Customer segmentation, anomaly detection

Overview of Classification in Machine Learning

Classification in machine learning is a supervised learning technique used to categorize data into predefined classes or labels. The algorithm is trained on a dataset containing input features and corresponding class labels, allowing it to learn patterns and make predictions on new, unseen data. Common classification algorithms include decision trees, support vector machines (SVM), k-nearest neighbors (KNN), and neural networks. Classification problems can be binary (e.g., spam detection: spam or not spam) or multi-class (e.g., classifying different species of flowers). Performance evaluation metrics such as accuracy, precision, recall, and F1-score are used to assess the effectiveness of a classification model. Classification techniques can be broadly divided into linear and non-linear models. Linear models, like logistic regression, work well when classes are separable using a straight-line boundary, while non-linear models, such as random forests and deep learning, can capture complex relationships in data. Advanced techniques like ensemble learning (e.g., boosting and bagging) enhance classification accuracy by combining multiple models. Applications of classification are widespread, including medical diagnosis, sentiment analysis, fraud detection, and image recognition. As data quality and feature selection play a crucial role in classification performance, techniques like feature engineering and dimensionality reduction are often used to optimize models. To build a robust classification model, understanding the following key aspects dataset splitting is crucial. When working with a classification problem, the dataset is typically divided into three parts:

Training Dataset

The training dataset is the largest portion of the dataset, typically covering 60-80% of the total data. It plays a crucial role in teaching a machine learning model how to recognize patterns and relationships between input features (independent variables) and output labels (dependent variables). The algorithm processes this data to adjust its internal parameters (weights and biases in neural networks) to minimize prediction errors. For example, in a spam email classification model, the training dataset consists of thousands of emails labeled as "spam" or "not spam." The model learns from these examples by identifying key patterns, such as frequent words, email structure, and sender information. If words like "lottery" or "free money" frequently appear in spam emails, the model adjusts its parameters to give higher weight to such words when classifying future emails.

During training, the model continuously updates itself by minimizing the error through techniques like gradient descent. However, an overtrained model may become too specific to the training data, leading to poor performance on unseen data (overfitting). Therefore, additional datasets (validation and test datasets) are required to ensure the model generalizes well.

Validation Dataset

The validation dataset is a separate portion of data, typically 10-20% of the total dataset, and is used during training to fine-tune hyperparameters like learning rate, number of layers, or activation functions. It helps monitor the model's performance to ensure it generalizes well and does not overfit the training data.For instance, in an image classification model that identifies dog breeds, the training dataset helps the model learn basic patterns. However, to enhance accuracy, we must adjust certain hyperparameters like the number of convolutional layers or dropout rates. The validation dataset assists in this process by providing feedback on how the model performs on unseen data during training.A key use of the validation dataset is early stoppingif the model's performance on the validation dataset starts to decline while still improving on the training dataset, it indicates overfitting. Training is then halted to avoid learning unnecessary noise. Another example is in speech recognition systems, where the validation dataset helps optimize model parameters to distinguish accents and background noise better. Without a validation set, the model might seem perfect on training data but fail in real-world applications.

Test Dataset

The test dataset is another 10-20% of the total dataset, but unlike the validation dataset, it is used only after training is complete. Its primary purpose is to evaluate the final model's performance on completely unseen data and estimate how well it generalizes. For example, consider a fraud detection system for credit card transactions. After training and fine-tuning using validation data, the model is tested on an independent dataset consisting of transactions not seen before. If the model correctly identifies fraudulent and genuine transactions with high accuracy, it indicates strong generalization. If not, it suggests that the model either overfitted the training data or needs better features.

Another example is in medical diagnosis, where a model is trained to detect pneumonia from chest X-rays. The test dataset includes X-ray images from different hospitals and patient demographics. If the model performs well across diverse data, it indicates robustness. Otherwise, it may require further training on more varied data. A test dataset is critical because it acts as a final benchmark before deploying the model in real-world applications. If test performance significantly differs from validation performance, it suggests issues in model generalization, requiring further improvements.

Overfitting

Overfitting occurs when a machine learning model learns not just the underlying pattern in the training data but also the noise and random fluctuations. This makes the model highly specialized to the training data, leading to excellent performance on it but poor generalization to new, unseen data. Overfitting happens when a model is too complex for the given dataset, meaning it has too many parameters relative to the amount of training data. For example, imagine a model trained to classify emails as spam or not spam. If the model memorizes specific words and email structures rather than understanding general characteristics of spam emails, it may misclassify new emails that slightly differ from the training set.

This means the model has high accuracy on the training set but fails when tested on new emails.

Mitigation Strategies

- Regularization (L1/L2): Adds a penalty for overly complex models, preventing excessive reliance on specific details.
- Dropout layers (for neural networks): Randomly drops neurons during training to avoid dependency on specific pathways.
- Pruning (for decision trees): Removes less important branches to simplify the tree.
- Increasing training data size: More data helps in generalizing patterns.
- Early stopping: Stops training when validation accuracy starts decreasing, preventing unnecessary complexity.

Underfitting

Underfitting happens when a model is too simple to capture the underlying patterns in the data. This means it performs poorly on both the training and test sets, indicating that it has not learned enough from the data. This usually occurs when the model lacks complexity, has too few parameters, or has been overly regularized. For example, suppose we are trying to predict house prices using a linear regression model with only one feature—square footage. If the actual price depends on multiple factors like location, number of bedrooms, and age of the house, a simple model may fail to capture these relationships, leading to poor predictions. This is a classic case of underfitting.

Mitigation Strategies

- Increasing model complexity: Using deeper neural networks or more complex models like decision trees instead of simple linear regression.
- Adding more relevant features: Including important variables in the dataset to improve predictive power.
- Reducing regularization: If regularization is too strong, it can suppress useful patterns in the data, so lowering it can help.

Striking a balance between overfitting and underfitting is key to building a robust machine learning model that generalizes well to new data.

Steps in Classification Workflow

Data Collection & Preprocessing

Data collection is the first and most crucial step in the classification workflow. It involves gathering relevant data from various sources, such as databases, online repositories, sensors, or user inputs. The quality of the collected data significantly impacts the model's performance. Once the data is collected, preprocessing ensures that it is clean and suitable for model training. This involves several key tasks:

- **Cleaning:** Removing duplicate entries, correcting inconsistencies, and filtering out irrelevant data.
- **Handling Missing Values:** Filling in missing values using techniques like mean/mode imputation, interpolation, or removing incomplete rows if necessary.
- **Feature Engineering:** Creating new features or modifying existing ones to enhance the model's predictive power. This may include normalization (scaling numerical values), encoding categorical variables, and extracting useful insights from raw data.

Example

Suppose we are building a classification model to detect spam emails. The dataset contains emails with text content, sender information, and metadata. Preprocessing would involve:

- Removing special characters and stop words from text data.
- Converting email text into numerical features using TF-IDF or word embeddings.
- Handling missing sender details by imputing common values.
- By preparing the data effectively, we improve the model's ability to make accurate predictions.

Dataset Splitting

Dataset splitting ensures that a classification model is trained, validated, and tested properly. It prevents overfitting and ensures the model generalizes well to unseen data. The dataset is typically divided into three subsets:

- Training Set (60-80%): Used to train the model.
- Validation Set (10-20%): Used for hyperparameter tuning and model selection.
- Test Set (10-20%): Used to evaluate the final model's performance.

Example

Consider a medical dataset used to classify whether a patient has diabetes. If we have 10,000 records:

- 7,000 records are used for training.
- 1,500 records are used for validation.
- 1,500 records are kept for testing.

Using separate datasets ensures that the model does not memorize training data and performs well on unseen cases.

Model Selection

Model selection involves choosing an appropriate classification algorithm based on the dataset's characteristics. The choice depends on factors like dataset size, feature complexity, and interpretability requirements. Common classification algorithms:

- Decision Trees: Simple and interpretable but prone to overfitting.
- Support Vector Machines (SVM): Effective for high-dimensional data.
- Neural Networks: Suitable for complex datasets but require large amounts of data.
- Random Forest: An ensemble method that improves accuracy and reduces overfitting.

Example

For a sentiment analysis task on customer reviews, a Naïve Bayes classifier might be ideal due to its efficiency with text data. However, if the dataset has a complex structure with multiple patterns, a Neural Network or Random Forest may be more suitable. Selecting the right model helps balance accuracy, interpretability, and computational efficiency.

Training & Hyperparameter Tuning

Once the model is selected, it undergoes training, where it learns patterns from the training data. The model's parameters are adjusted using optimization techniques like gradient descent.Hyperparameter tuning involves optimizing parameters that control the learning process, such as:

- Learning rate
- Number of layers and neurons (for neural networks)
- Depth of a decision tree
- Number of estimators in a Random Forest

Example

In an image classification task, we train a Convolutional Neural Network (CNN). Hyperparameter tuning involves adjusting the learning rate, dropout rate, and number of convolutional layers to improve accuracy. Fine-tuning hyperparameters ensures the model generalizes well and avoids overfitting.

Evaluation

Model evaluation measures how well the classifier performs on the test set. Key performance metrics include:

- Accuracy: Percentage of correctly classified instances.
- Precision: The proportion of true positive predictions among all positive predictions.
- Recall: The proportion of actual positive instances correctly identified.
- F1-score: The harmonic means of precision and recall.

Example

For a fraud detection system, where false negatives are critical, recall is more important than accuracy. If the model achieves:

- Precision: 85%
- Recall: 92%
- F1-score: 88%

It indicates a well-balanced model. By evaluating performance metrics, we determine whether the model meets the required accuracy and reliability.

Deployment & Monitoring

Once the model performs well, it is deployed for real-world use. Deployment involves integrating the model into applications, APIs, or cloud services. However, models can degrade over time due to data drift. Continuous monitoring ensures sustained performance through:

- Retraining: Updating the model with new data.
- Logging and Alerts: Detecting anomalies in predictions.
- Performance Audits: Regularly assessing model accuracy.

Example

A credit card fraud detection model deployed in a banking system needs constant monitoring. If fraud trends change over time, retraining the model with fresh data ensures it remains effective. By maintaining the model post-deployment, we ensure long-term accuracy and reliability.

Classification Families

Classification families are broad groups of classification techniques used to categorize data, objects, or concepts based on their characteristics. These families are commonly used in machine learning, data science, and various scientific disciplines. The major classification families include supervised learning, where labeled data is used to train models like decision trees, support vector machines, and neural networks; unsupervised learning, which clusters data without predefined labels using techniques like k-means and hierarchical clustering; and semi-supervised learning, which combines aspects of both by using a small amount of labeled data to guide classification. In addition to these, classification families also include rule-based classification, where expert-defined rules determine the categories, and probabilistic classification, which assigns probabilities to different class memberships using algorithms like Naïve Bayes. Another important family is ensemble classification, which improves accuracy by combining multiple classifiers, such as in random forests and boosting methods. These families serve diverse applications, from medical diagnosis and fraud detection to natural language processing and recommendation systems. Here's a breakdown of the classification families you listed:

Linear Discriminative Models

Linear discriminative models are a class of machine learning models that aim to distinguish between different categories in a dataset using a linear decision boundary. They assume that the data points belonging to different classes can be separated by a straight line in two dimensions or a hyperplane in higher dimensions. These models are particularly effective when the classes exhibit a linear relationship in the feature space. One of the fundamental principles of linear discriminative models is to find the optimal decision boundary that minimizes classification errors. This is typically achieved through mathematical techniques such as maximizing the margin between classes or minimizing a loss function that penalizes incorrect classifications. Common examples of linear discriminative models include Linear Discriminant Analysis (LDA) and Support Vector Machines (SVM) with a linear kernel. A key advantage of these models is their efficiency and interpretability. Because they rely on simple mathematical functions, they can be trained and evaluated quickly, making them suitable for large datasets. Additionally, the decision boundary is easy to understand, which aids in model explainability. However, their primary limitation is that they struggle with non-linearly separable data—cases where classes are intertwined in complex ways. In such scenarios, non-linear models or feature transformations are required to improve performance.

Example: Logistic Regression

A common example of a linear discriminative model is logistic regression. Suppose we are classifying whether an email is spam or not based on features such as the presence of certain words, the sender's reputation, and the length of the email. Logistic regression fits a linear function to these features and predicts probabilities of belonging to each class. If the probability crosses a threshold (e.g., 0.5), the email is classified as spam; otherwise, it is not spam.

Limitations

While these models are easy to interpret and computationally efficient, they may struggle when data is not linearly separable. For example, if spam emails cluster in a non-linear manner within the feature space, a linear decision boundary will not effectively separate them. In such cases, non-linear discriminative models or kernel methods are used to improve classification accuracy.

Non-Linear Discriminative Models

Non-linear discriminative models are advanced classification techniques that extend linear models by incorporating non-linearity into their decision boundaries. Unlike linear models, which separate data using a straight line or hyperplane, non-linear discriminative models can learn complex patterns and relationships in data. This is crucial for handling real-world problems where data is rarely perfectly separable using linear boundaries. One widely used approach to introducing non-linearity is the kernel trick in Support Vector Machines (SVMs). Instead of transforming data manually, the kernel function maps it into a higher-dimensional space where a linear separator can be applied. Popular kernels include polynomial, radial basis function (RBF), and sigmoid kernels. These functions enable SVMs to capture intricate patterns in data. Another approach involves polynomial feature transformations, where input features are expanded using polynomial terms, allowing traditional linear classifiers to model more complex relationships. This increases the expressiveness of models but also the risk of overfitting. More sophisticated non-linear discriminative models include neural networks, which use multiple layers of interconnected neurons to learn hierarchical features. Deep learning models, such as convolutional neural networks (CNNs) and recurrent neural networks (RNNs), excel in tasks like image recognition and natural language processing.

Example: *Support Vector Machines (SVM) with Kernel Trick*

A Support Vector Machine (SVM) with a Radial Basis Function (RBF) kernel can separate non-linearly distributed data. Imagine classifying different plant species based on leaf shape and size. If a linear boundary fails, an RBF kernel SVM can project data into a higher-dimensional space where a linear decision boundary can then separate the species effectively.

Limitations

While non-linear models handle complex decision boundaries, they require more computational power and hyperparameter tuning. For example, choosing the right kernel and its parameters (like gamma in an RBF kernel) significantly affects performance. Additionally, they are harder to interpret compared to linear models.

Decision Trees

A decision tree is a supervised machine learning algorithm used for classification and regression tasks. It models decisions based on input features, splitting data recursively into subgroups to achieve the best separation of classes or predictions. The result is a tree-like structure where internal nodes represent features, branches signify decision rules, and leaf nodes correspond to output labels or values.

Example: *Predicting Loan Approval*

A bank may use a decision tree to determine whether to approve a loan based on factors like credit score, income, and debt. The first split might be on credit score (above or below a threshold). If high, another split might check income level, and so on. Each path through the tree represents a decision rule leading to an approval or rejection.

Limitations

Decision trees are prone to overfitting, especially when they grow too deep. A deep tree memorizes training data instead of generalizing. Pruning or using ensemble methods (like Random Forests) helps mitigate overfitting. Another drawback is their sensitivity to small changes in data, which can lead to different structures.

Probabilistic Models

Probabilistic models classify instances by estimating probability distributions. They can be:

- **Discriminative models**: Estimate P(y|X), the probability of a class given input features.
- **Generative models**: Estimate P(X|y) and P(y), learning how data is generated per class.

Example: *Naïve Bayes for Spam Detection*

Naïve Bayes assumes features are **conditionally independent** given a class. For spam classification, it calculates:

- P(spam)and P (not spam)from prior email statistics.
- P(X|spam) for features like the presence of "free" or "money." Using Bayes' Theorem, it predicts the probability of an email being spam.

Limitations

Naïve Bayes assumes independence among features, which may not always hold. Despite this, it performs surprisingly well in text classification and sentiment analysis.

Nearest Neighbor Models

Nearest Neighbor models are a type of instance-based learning algorithm used for classification and regression tasks. These models do not assume an underlying data distribution but rely on the similarity between data points to make predictions. The fundamental idea behind Nearest Neighbor models is that similar data points exist in close proximity in a given feature space. When a new data instance needs to be classified, the model searches for the most similar points in the training dataset and assigns a label based on the labels of these nearest neighbors. This is often done using distance metrics such as Euclidean distance, Manhattan distance, or Minkowski distance. The choice of distance metric significantly impacts model performance, as it determines how similarity is measured. A key advantage of Nearest Neighbor models is their simplicity and adaptability to various data distributions. However, they have some drawbacks, such as high computational cost for large datasets since they require storing all training data and recalculating distances for every new instance. Additionally, they are sensitive to noise and irrelevant features, making preprocessing techniques like feature scaling and dimensionality reduction essential for improved accuracy. Despite these challenges, Nearest Neighbor models remain popular in pattern recognition, recommendation systems, and anomaly detection applications.

Example: *Image Classification*

A KNN classifier can classify images based on pixel similarity. If a new image is given, KNN finds the K most similar images in the dataset and assigns the majority class label.

Limitations

KNN is computationally expensive for large datasets since it must store and compare every instance. Additionally, it performs poorly in high-dimensional spaces (curse of dimensionality) where distances become less meaningful.

K-Nearest Neighbors (KNN) Algorithm

The K-Nearest Neighbors (KNN) algorithm is one of the most widely used Nearest Neighbor models. It is a non-parametric, instance-based learning algorithm that classifies a new data point based on the majority vote of its K closest neighbors in the training dataset. The KNN classification process follows these steps:

- Choose K – Select the number of nearest neighbors (K).
- Calculate Distances – Compute the distance between the new data point and all points in the training dataset using a chosen metric (e.g., Euclidean distance).
- Select K Nearest Neighbors – Identify the K points that are closest to the new data instance.
- Majority Voting – Assign the class label based on the most common class among the K neighbors.

For KNN regression, instead of majority voting, the algorithm takes the average (or weighted average) of the K nearest neighbors' target values.The choice of K is crucial; a small K (e.g., 1) can lead to overfitting, whereas a large K may result in underfitting. KNN is easy to implement and works well for small to medium-sized datasets but becomes computationally expensive for large datasets. To improve efficiency, optimizations such as KD-Trees and Ball Trees are used for faster nearest neighbor searches.

Summary

Machine learning has emerged as a crucial technology, driving advancements across various domains by enabling systems to learn from data and improve performance without explicit programming. The fundamental aspects of learning systems involve training data, concept representation, and function approximation, which together form the basis for developing intelligent models. The two primary types of learning supervised and unsupervised offer different approaches to extracting patterns from data. Supervised learning leverages labeled data to train models, while unsupervised learning discovers hidden structures without predefined labels. A key application of supervised learning is classification, where datasets are split into training, validation, and test sets to ensure model generalization and avoid issues like overfitting. Classification techniques fall into various families, including linear and non-linear discriminative models, decision trees, probabilistic methods, and nearest neighbor approaches. Each technique has its strengths and is chosen based on the problem requirements and dataset characteristics. As machine learning continues to evolve, understanding its foundational principles is essential for developing robust and efficient learning systems. By selecting appropriate learning paradigms and classification methods, researchers and practitioners can build models that drive innovation and solve complex real-world problems across industries.

Exercise Questions

- Define a learning system.
- What are the main goals of machine learning?
- List three common applications of machine learning.
- What are the key aspects involved in developing a learning system?
- Differentiate between supervised and unsupervised learning.
- What is the role of training data in a learning system?
- Explain the importance of a validation dataset in classification tasks.
- What is overfitting, and how does it affect a machine learning model?
- Name and briefly describe two types of classification families.
- How does a nearest neighbor classifier make predictions?

2

ADVANCED TECHNIQUES IN MACHINE LEARNING: FROM FUNDAMENTALS TO OPTIMIZATION

Machine learning has revolutionized the way we process and analyze data, enabling automation, predictive modeling, and artificial intelligence-driven solutions. While traditional machine learning techniques lay the groundwork for data-driven decision-making, advanced methodologies refine these processes, improving accuracy, efficiency, and adaptability. From deep learning architectures to meta-learning and reinforcement learning, advanced techniques push the boundaries of what machines can achieve. A solid understanding of fundamental machine learning concepts, including supervised, unsupervised, and reinforcement learning, serves as the backbone for exploring more sophisticated models. Basic algorithms like linear regression, decision trees, and k-means clustering provide essential insights into data patterns. However, as datasets grow in complexity and scale, traditional approaches often face limitations in performance, scalability, and generalization. This has led to the emergence of more advanced techniques that enhance model capabilities.

One key area of advancement is deep learning, which utilizes artificial neural networks to model complex data representations. Convolutional neural networks (CNNs) excel in image recognition, while recurrent neural networks (RNNs) and transformers drive natural language processing breakthroughs. The advent of generative adversarial networks (GANs) and self-supervised learning further showcases the power of deep learning in generating and understanding data without extensive human intervention. Beyond deep learning, optimization techniques play a crucial role in refining machine learning models. Gradient-based methods like Adam and RMSprop enhance convergence speed, while meta-learning strategies allow models to learn from previous experiences. Techniques such as hyperparameter tuning, Bayesian optimization, and evolutionary algorithms enable fine-tuning of models for optimal performance.

These strategies contribute to reducing computational costs and improving real-world applicability.

Another critical advancement is the integration of explainability and fairness in machine learning models. As AI systems become more complex, understanding model decisions and mitigating biases is essential for ethical AI deployment. Techniques like SHAP values, LIME, and counterfactual explanations help improve transparency, ensuring machine learning applications remain interpretable and accountable. Additionally, federated learning and privacy-preserving machine learning techniques address security concerns by enabling decentralized learning without compromising sensitive data.In this exploration of advanced machine learning techniques, we bridge the gap between foundational concepts and optimization-driven methodologies. From deep learning architectures to reinforcement learning and model interpretability, mastering these advanced approaches equips researchers and practitioners with the tools necessary to build cutting-edge AI solutions. As machine learning continues to evolve, embracing these techniques will be crucial in tackling increasingly complex challenges across various industries.

Logistic Regression

Logistic regression is a statistical method used for binary classification problems (i.e., when the target variable has two possible outcomes). It predicts the probability that a given input belongs to a particular class using the logistic (sigmoid) function. Unlike linear regression, which predicts continuous values, logistic regression outputs probabilities, which can then be converted into class labels (e.g., 0 or 1, True or False).

Mathematical Representation

The logistic regression model is based on the sigmoid function:

$$P(Y = 1|X) = \frac{1}{1 + e^{-(\beta_0 + \beta_1 X_1 + \beta_2 X_2 + \ldots + \beta_n X_n)}}$$

where:

- P(Y=1|X)is the probability of the target class (1).
- β0is the intercept.
- β_1, β_2,...,βnare the coefficients for input features X_1,X_2,...,X_n.
- e is the Euler's number (≈ 2.718).

Python Example: Predicting Whether a Student Passes or Fails an Exam

We will use scikit-learn to train a logistic regression model on a small dataset.

Step 1: Import Libraries

```
import numpy as np
import pandas as pd
from sklearn.model_selection import train_test_split
from sklearn.linear_model import LogisticRegression
from sklearn.metrics import accuracy_score
# Sample data: [Hours Studied, Previous Scores]
X = np.array([[1, 50], [2, 55], [3, 65], [4, 70], [5, 75],
        [6, 80], [7, 85], [8, 90], [9, 95], [10, 98]])
# Pass (1) or Fail (0)
y = np.array([0, 0, 0, 0, 0, 1, 1, 1, 1, 1])
# Split data into train and test sets
X_train, X_test, y_train, y_test = train_test_split(X, y, test_size=0.2, random_
state=42)
# Train logistic regression model
model = LogisticRegression()
model.fit(X_train, y_train)
# Predict on test data
y_pred = model.predict(X_test)
# Check accuracy
accuracy = accuracy_score(y_test, y_pred)
print(f"Accuracy: {accuracy * 100:.2f}%")
# Predict for a new student who studied 6 hours and scored 78 previously
new_student = np.array([[6, 78]])
prediction = model.predict(new_student)
print(f"Prediction for new student: {'Pass' if prediction[0] == 1 else 'Fail'}")
```

Explanation

- We create a dataset with study hours and previous scores as input features.
- We define pass/fail (1 or 0) as the output.
- We split the dataset into training and testing sets.
- We train a Logistic Regression model.
- We make predictions and check the accuracy.

- We test the model on a new student's data.

Expected Output

- *Accuracy (varies based on data split)*
- Prediction: If a student studies 6 hours and scores 78, the model predicts whether they pass or fail.

Perceptron

A Perceptron is one of the simplest types of artificial neural networks, primarily used for binary classification problems. It is a type of linear classifier that takes multiple inputs, applies weights, sums them, and passes the result through an activation function.

A perceptron consists of:

Inputs (X1,X2,...,Xn) – Feature values.

Weights (W1,W2,...,Wn) – Adjustable parameters.

Bias (b) – A constant that helps adjust the decision boundary.

Summation Function – Computes the weighted sum:

$$Z = \sum W_i X_i + b$$

Activation Function (Step Function) – Applies a threshold to determine the output:

$$Y = \begin{cases} 1, & \text{if } Z \geq 0 \\ 0, & \text{if } Z < 0 \end{cases}$$

Example: Perceptron for AND Logic Gate

The AND gate truth in Table 2.1.

Step 1: Define Inputs and Outputs

Table2.1: The AND gate truth

Input X1	Input X2	Output Y
0	0	0
0	1	0
1	0	0
1	1	1

Step 2: Choose Initial Weights and Bias

We set:

$W_1=1$

$W_2=1$

$b=-1.5$

Step 3: Apply Perceptron Formula

For each input combination, we compute:

$$Z = W_1X_1 + W_2X_2 + b$$

Case **(0,0):** $Z= (1\times0) +(1\times0) -1.5=-1.5 \Rightarrow Y=0$

Case **(0,1):** $Z= (1\times0) +(1\times1) -1.5=-0.5 \Rightarrow Y=0$

Case **(1,0):** $Z= (1\times1) +(1\times0) -1.5=-0.5 \Rightarrow Y=0$

Case **(1,1):** $Z= (1\times1) +(1\times1) -1.5=0.5 \Rightarrow Y=1$

The perceptron can successfully learn simple problems like AND, OR.It cannot learn non-linearly separable problems like XOR.Training involves adjusting weights using the perceptron learning rule.

Exponential Family

The Exponential Family is a broad class of probability distributions that can be expressed in the general form:

$$f(x \mid \theta) = h(x) \exp\left(\eta(\theta)^T T(x) - A(\theta)\right)$$

Where:

x is the random variable,

θ is the parameter (or parameters) of the distribution,

h(x) is the base measure (sometimes called the carrier function),

T(x) is the sufficient statistic,

η(θ) is the natural parameter or canonical parameter,

A(θ) is the log partition function (ensures normalization).

Key Properties

General Form: Many common distributions (Gaussian, Bernoulli, Poisson, etc.) can be written in this form.

Sufficiency: The function T(x) is a sufficient statistic for θ, meaning that it captures all information about the parameter.

Convexity: The function A(θ) is convex, leading to nice statistical properties in estimation.

Natural Parameter Space: Transforming parameters into the natural parameter η simplifies calculations.

Example: Bernoulli Distribution

The Bernoulli distribution models a binary outcome (success/failure), where X∈ {0,1} with probability mass function:

$$P(X = x \mid p) = p^x (1-p)^{1-x}, \quad x \in \{0,1\}, \quad 0 < p < 1$$

Writing in Exponential Family Form:

Comparing with the general exponential family form:

$$f(x \mid \theta) = h(x) \exp\left(\eta(\theta) T(x) - A(\theta)\right)$$

$\log \frac{p}{1-p}$ **we identify:**

- Natural Parameter:
- Sufficient Statistic: T(x)=x
- Base Measure: h(x)=1 (since it doesn't depend on p)
- Log Partition Function: A(θ)=log(1+e^{η}), ensuring normalization.

Thus, rewriting:

$$P(X = x) = \exp\left(x \log \frac{p}{1-p} - \log(1 + e^{\log \frac{p}{1-p}})\right)$$

$\eta = \log \frac{p}{1-p}.$ This confirms that the Bernoulli distribution belongs to the Exponential Family with natural parameter

Generative Learning Algorithms

Generative Learning Algorithms are a class of machine learning models that attempt to understand the underlying probability distribution of data. These algorithms model how data is generated rather than simply mapping inputs to outputs. Unlike discriminative models that focus solely on decision boundaries, generative models aim to capture the full joint probability distribution P(X,Y), which allows them to generate new, realistic samples..

Example: *Classifying Emails as Spam or Not Spam*

```
from sklearn.datasets import load_digits
from sklearn.model_selection import train_test_split
from sklearn.naive_bayes import GaussianNB
from sklearn.metrics import accuracy_score
# Load dataset (digits classification as an example)
```

```
digits = load_digits()
X, y = digits.data, digits.target
# Split into training and test sets
X_train, X_test, y_train, y_test = train_test_split(X, y, test_size=0.2, random_state=42)
# Initialize and train the model
gnb = GaussianNB()
gnb.fit(X_train, y_train)
# Predict on test data
y_pred = gnb.predict(X_test)
# Compute accuracy
accuracy = accuracy_score(y_test, y_pred)
print(f"Accuracy: {accuracy:.2f}")
```

Key Takeaways

- Generative models learn the probability distribution of each class and generate new samples.
- Naïve Bayes assumes feature independence and is widely used for text classification (e.g., spam detection).
- More complex generative models like GANs and VAEs are used for image generation, text synthesis, and deep learning applications.

Types of Generative Learning Algorithms

Naïve Bayes Classifier

Naïve Bayes is a probabilistic generative learning algorithm based on Bayes' theorem. It assumes that features in a dataset are conditionally independent given the class label, which is why it is termed "naïve." Despite this strong assumption, Naïve Bayes performs remarkably well in various real-world applications like spam detection, sentiment analysis, and document classification. The algorithm calculates the posterior probability of a class given the input features using Bayes' theorem:

$$P(C|X) = \frac{P(X|C)P(C)}{P(X)}$$

where C is the class, and X represents the features. The likelihood P(X|C) is modeled as the product of the probabilities of individual features under the assumption of independence.

There are different variations of Naïve Bayes based on the data distribution:

- **Gaussian Naïve Bayes:** Assumes normal distribution of numerical features.
- **Multinomial Naïve Bayes:** Suitable for text classification.
- **Bernoulli Naïve Bayes:** Works with binary features.

Despite its simplicity, Naïve Bayes is computationally efficient, requires minimal training data, and provides interpretable results. However, its main limitation is the independence assumption, which may not hold true in all real-world scenarios, leading to suboptimal performance when features are highly correlated.

Gaussian Mixture Models (GMM)

Gaussian Mixture Models (GMM) are a powerful tool for clustering, where the goal is to group similar data points together. GMM assumes that the data is generated from a mixture of several Gaussian distributions, each representing a different cluster. Each Gaussian distribution in the model is characterized by its mean, covariance, and weight, which dictate the cluster's center, spread, and size, respectively. Unlike k-means clustering, which assigns each data point to a single cluster, GMM allows for soft assignments, where each point has a probability of belonging to each cluster. This flexibility allows GMM to model more complex cluster shapes, making it especially useful for datasets where the boundaries between clusters are not well-defined. The Expectation-Maximization (EM) algorithm is typically used to estimate the parameters of the GMM, iteratively improving the model's fit to the data by maximizing the likelihood of the observed data under the assumed mixture. Mathematically, GMM represents the probability of a data point X as:

$$P(X) = \sum_{i=1}^{k} \pi_i \mathcal{N}(X|\mu_i, \Sigma_i)$$

where k is the number of Gaussian components, π_i represents the mixture weight, μ_i is the mean, and Σ_i is the covariance matrix of the ith Gaussian distribution.

The Expectation-Maximization (EM) algorithm is commonly used to estimate the parameters of GMM. The process involves:

- Expectation (E) step: Assigning probabilities to data points for belonging to each Gaussian component.
- Maximization (M) step: Updating the parameters (μ,Σ,π) to maximize the likelihood.

GMM is widely used for applications like speech recognition, anomaly detection, and image segmentation. Unlike k-means, it provides a probabilistic clustering approach, allowing for soft clustering, where a point can belong to multiple clusters with different probabilities. However, it may struggle with high-dimensional data due to increased computational complexity.

Hidden Markov Models (HMM)

Hidden Markov Models (HMMs) are statistical models used for analyzing sequential or time-series data. They are built upon the principle that the system being modeled is assumed to be a Markov process with hidden (unobservable) states. Each hidden state has an associated probability distribution over possible observable output. Transitions between hidden states are governed by a set of probabilities, typically represented in a transition matrix, and the process is memoryless, meaning the next state depends only on the current state. HMMs are particularly useful for tasks such as speech recognition, bioinformatics, and financial modeling, where the goal is to infer the sequence of hidden states based on the observable data. The model is trained using algorithms like the Expectation-Maximization (EM) method or the Baum-Welch algorithm, which iteratively optimize the model's parameters to best fit the observed sequence. An HMM is defined by:

- States (S) – A set of hidden states.
- Observations (O) – The visible symbols associated with each state.
- Transition probabilities (A) – The probability of moving from one state to another.
- Emission probabilities (B) – The probability of observing a symbol given a state.
- Initial probabilities (π) – The probability of starting in each state.

The probability of an observation sequence is computed using algorithms such as:

- Forward Algorithm: Computes the probability of observing a sequence given the model.
- Viterbi Algorithm: Finds the most likely sequence of hidden states.

HMMs are widely used in speech recognition (e.g., Google Voice, Siri), handwriting recognition, and bioinformatics (e.g., DNA sequence modeling). However, they assume a fixed number of states and have difficulty capturing long-range dependencies, which limits their application to highly complex sequential data.

Generative Adversarial Networks (GANs)

Generative Adversarial Networks (GANs) are a class of generative models that use deep learning techniques to create high-quality synthetic data, such as images, audio, and text. Proposed by Ian Goodfellow in 2014, GANs consist of two neural networks: a generator and a discriminator. The generator creates fake data, while the discriminator attempts to distinguish between real and generated data. The two networks are trained together in a competitive process, where the generator continuously improves its ability to produce realistic data, and the discriminator refines its ability to identify fake data. This adversarial training process leads to the generator producing data that is increasingly indistinguishable from real-world examples. GANs have gained significant attention for their ability to generate photorealistic images, enhance image resolution, and even generate new content in various fields such as art, gaming, and medicine. Their versatility has led to numerous applications in diverse industries, GANs consist of two neural networks:

- **Generator (G):** Generates synthetic data similar to the real dataset.
- **Discriminator (D):** Differentiates between real and fake data.

The two networks play a minimax game:

- The generator tries to create data that can fool the discriminator.
- The discriminator learns to distinguish real data from fake data.

Mathematically, the objective function is:

$$\min_{G} \max_{D} V(D,G) = \mathbb{E}_{x \sim p_{data}}[\log D(x)] + \mathbb{E}_{z \sim p_z}[\log(1 - D(G(z)))]$$

where x is real data, z is random noise, and G(z) is generated data.

GANs are used in various applications:

- Image generation (e.g., deepfake videos, artistic style transfer).
- Data augmentation for training deep learning models.
- Super-resolution (enhancing low-resolution images).

Despite their success, GANs suffer from instability during training, mode collapse (where the generator produces limited variations), and require large amounts of training data.

Variational Autoencoders (VAEs)

Variational Autoencoders (VAEs) are a type of generative model used to learn complex data distributions and generate new samples. Unlike traditional autoencoders, VAEs incorporate a probabilistic framework by learning the distribution of latent variables instead of directly learning a fixed latent representation. The model consists of an encoder, which maps input data to a distribution over the latent space, and a decoder, which reconstructs the input from the latent representation. The key innovation of VAEs is the use of a variational inference technique to approximate the true posterior distribution, ensuring that the latent space is continuous and structured. The model is trained by maximizing a lower bound on the likelihood of the data, balancing reconstruction accuracy and the regularization of the latent space. VAEs have been widely used in image generation, anomaly detection, and semi-supervised learning, enabling the generation of novel data samples that resemble the original dataset.

VAEs consist of:

- Encoder Network: Maps input data X to a latent variable Z, represented as a probability distribution.
- Latent Space: A compressed probabilistic representation of the data.
- Decoder Network: Reconstructs the original data from Z.

Unlike standard autoencoders, VAEs impose a probability distribution (typically Gaussian) on the latent space. The key idea is to optimize the variational lower bound:

$$\mathcal{L} = \mathbb{E}_{q(z|x)}[\log p(x|z)] - D_{KL}(q(z|x)||p(z))$$

where q(z|x) is the encoder's approximation of the posterior distribution, p(z) is the prior, and D_{KL} is the Kullback-Leibler divergence.

While VAEs offer structured latent representations and efficient sampling, they may generate blurry images compared to GANs due to their probabilistic nature. Training stability can also be challenging, requiring careful tuning of the loss function.

Gaussian Discriminant Analysis

Gaussian Discriminant Analysis (GDA) is a probabilistic classification technique that utilizes Bayes' theorem to classify data points. It assumes that the features within each class are normally distributed (i.e., follow a Gaussian distribution). GDA is a generative model, meaning it models the distribution of each class separately by estimating the parameters (mean and covariance) of the Gaussian distribution for each class. Once the parameters are learned from the training data, GDA computes the posterior probability for each class and classifies a new data point based on the highest probability. The model also assumes that the classes share the same covariance matrix (in the case of Linear Discriminant Analysis, or LDA), or they can have different covariance matrices. GDA is useful in problems where class distributions are well-approximated by Gaussian distributions, such as in pattern recognition, medical diagnosis, and text classification tasks.

1. Mathematical Formulation

Given a dataset with feature vector $x \in R^n$ and labels $y \in \{0,1\}$, GDA assumes:

The conditional probabilityP(x|y=k) follows a multivariate normal distribution:

$$P(x|y=k) = \frac{1}{(2\pi)^{n/2}|\Sigma_k|^{1/2}} e^{-\frac{1}{2}(x-\mu_k)^T \Sigma_k^{-1}(x-\mu_k)}$$

Where:

- μk is the mean vector for class k,
- Σk is the covariance matrix.

The prior probability of each class is:

$$P(y = k) = \phi_k$$

Whereϕk is the proportion of class k in the dataset.

Using Bayes' theorem, the posterior probability is:

$$P(y = k|x) = \frac{P(x|y = k)P(y = k)}{P(x)}$$

The decision rule assignsx to the class with the highest posterior probability.

Example

Let's implement a simple example of GDA on a synthetic dataset.

Example: Classifying Two Gaussian-Distributed Classes

```
import numpy as np
import matplotlib.pyplot as plt
from sklearn.discriminant_analysis import QuadraticDiscriminantAnalysis as QDA
# Generate synthetic data
np.random.seed(42)
n_samples = 100
# Class 0 (Gaussian with mean -2, std 1)
X0 = np.random.normal(loc=-2, scale=1, size=(n_samples, 2))
y0 = np.zeros(n_samples)
# Class 1 (Gaussian with mean 2, std 1)
X1 = np.random.normal(loc=2, scale=1, size=(n_samples, 2))
y1 = np.ones(n_samples)
# Combine dataset
X = np.vstack((X0, X1))
y = np.hstack((y0, y1))
# Train Gaussian Discriminant Analysis (QDA)
qda = QDA()
```

```
qda.fit(X, y)
# Generate grid for decision boundary visualization
xx, yy = np.meshgrid(np.linspace(-5, 5, 200), np.linspace(-5, 5, 200))
Z = qda.predict(np.c_[xx.ravel(), yy.ravel()])
Z = Z.reshape(xx.shape)
# Plot the decision boundary
plt.contourf(xx, yy, Z, alpha=0.3)
plt.scatter(X0[:, 0], X0[:, 1], label="Class 0", edgecolors='black')
plt.scatter(X1[:, 0], X1[:, 1], label="Class 1", edgecolors='black')
plt.legend()
plt.title("Gaussian Discriminant Analysis (QDA)")
plt.show()
```

Main Points

- Gaussian Discriminant Analysis (GDA) assumes that each class follows a multivariate Gaussian distribution.
- The decision boundary can be linear (LDA) or quadratic (QDA) depending on whether the covariance matrices are shared or not.
- It is useful for problems where the assumption of normality holds and performs well in low-data scenarios.

Naive Bayes

Naïve Bayes is a simple and efficient probabilistic machine learning algorithm based on Bayes' Theorem, which describes the probability of a class given observed features. It is primarily used for classification tasks and works by applying Bayes' rule to predict the class of a given data point. The key assumption of Naïve Bayes is that the features (or attributes) are conditionally independent, which simplifies the computation. While this assumption is rarely true in real-world data, the algorithm often performs surprisingly well in practice, especially for text classification, spam filtering, and sentiment analysis. The Naïve Bayes classifier calculates the posterior probability for each class, selecting the class with the highest probability. It is computationally efficient, particularly suitable for large datasets, and works well with both categorical and continuous data. Despite its simplicity, Naïve Bayes is a powerful model when independence assumptions hold or when high-dimensional data is involved.

Bayes' Theorem:

$$P(A|B) = \frac{P(B|A) \cdot P(A)}{P(B)}$$

where:

- $P(A|B)$ = Probability of event A happening given B
- $P(B|A)$ = Probability of event B happening given A
- $P(A)$ = Prior probability of A
- $P(B)$ = Prior probability of B

Example: *Spam Email Classification*

Let's classify whether an email is Spam or Not Spam based on words in Table 2.2.

Step 1: Training Data

Table 2.2: Training data set.

Email	Contains "Win"	Contains "Prize"	Spam?
E1	Yes	Yes	Yes
E2	No	Yes	No
E3	Yes	No	No
E4	Yes	Yes	Yes

From this, we compute probabilities.

Step 2: Probability Calculation

P(Spam)=2/4=0.5

P (Not Spam) =2/4=0.5

Now, we calculate conditional probabilities:

P(Win|Spam) =2/2=1

P(Prize|Spam) =2/2=1

P(Win|Not Spam) =1/2=0.5

P(Prize|Not Spam) =1/2=0.5

Step 3: Classifying a New Email

Suppose a new email contains "Win" and "Prize". We calculate:

$$P(Spam|Win, Prize) \propto P(Win|Spam) \cdot P(Prize|Spam) \cdot P(Spam)$$

=1×1×0.5=0.5

$$P(Not\ Spam|Win, Prize) \propto P(Win|Not\ Spam) \cdot P(Prize|Not\ Spam) \cdot P(Not\ Spam)$$

=0.5×0.5×0.5=0.125

Since0.5>0.125, the email is classified as Spam.

Naïve Bayes is widely used in spam filtering, sentiment analysis, and text classification because of its simplicity and efficiency. However, it assumes independence among features, which may not always be accurate.

Support Vector Machines: Optimal hyper plane and Kernels

Support Vector Machines (SVMs) operate on the principle of constructing an optimal hyperplane that maximizes the margin between different classes in a given dataset. The optimal hyperplane is determined by selecting the decision boundary that ensures the greatest separation between support vectorsthe critical data points that influence the classification. This margin maximization enhances the model's generalization capability, reducing the risk of overfitting while improving predictive performance. To handle non-linearly separable data, SVM employs kernel functions, which map input features into a higher-dimensional space where linear separation becomes feasible. Common kernel functions include the linear kernel, polynomial kernel, radial basis function (RBF), and sigmoid kernel, each tailored to different data distributions. By utilizing the kernel trick, SVM efficiently computes transformations without explicitly performing high-dimensional computations, thereby maintaining computational efficiency while enhancing classification accuracy.

Optimal Hyperplane in SVM

The main goal of SVM is to find a hyperplane that best separates data into different classes while maximizing the margin between them. A hyperplane is a decision boundary that separates different classes in an n-dimensional space. Mathematically, it is represented as:

$w \cdot x + b = 0$

where:

w is the weight vector (normal to the hyperplane),

x is the input feature vector,

b is the bias term.

Maximizing the Margin

The margin is the distance between the support vectors (closest data points to the hyperplane) and the hyperplane.

The optimal hyperplane is the one that maximizes this margin.

The margin is given by:

$$\text{Margin} = \frac{2}{||w||}$$

To find this optimal hyperplane, we solve the convex optimization problem:

$$\min_{w,b} \frac{1}{2}||w||^2$$

subject to:

where y_i represents the class labels (+1 or −1).

This optimization problem is solved using Lagrange multipliers and Quadratic Programming.

Kernel Trick in SVM

Support Vector Machines (SVM) are effective for linearly separable data, where data points can be divided by a straight line or hyperplane. However, in real-world scenarios, most data is non-linearly separable. To address this, SVM uses the kernel trick, a technique that transforms the input data into a higher-dimensional space, where it becomes easier to separate the data points with a hyperplane. The kernel function computes the inner product between data points in this higher-dimensional space without explicitly calculating their transformation, saving computation time. Common kernel functions include the linear, polynomial, and radial basis function (RBF) kernels. By applying the kernel trick, SVM can create complex decision boundaries and effectively classify non-linearly separable data. This makes SVM a powerful tool for a variety of applications, including classification and regression tasks, in domains such as image recognition, bioinformatics, and text mining.

Kernel Trick

Instead of working in the original feature space, we map the data to a higher-dimensional space where it becomes linearly separable. The kernel function K (x_i ,x_j) computes the dot product in this higher-dimensional space without explicitly transforming the data.

$$K(x_i, x_j) = \phi(x_i) \cdot \phi(x_j)$$

Where$\phi(x)$ is the transformation function mapping inputs to a higher-dimensional space.

Types of Kernel Functions

- Linear Kernel (for linearly separable data):

$$K(x_i, x_j) = x_i \cdot x_j$$

- Polynomial Kernel (maps data to a polynomial feature space):

$$K(x_i, x_j) = (x_i \cdot x_j + c)^d$$

dis the degree of the polynomial.

- Radial Basis Function (RBF) Kernel (popular for non-linear problems):

$$K(x_i, x_j) = \exp\left(-\frac{||x_i - x_j||^2}{2\sigma^2}\right)$$

σcontrols the spread of the function.

- Sigmoid Kernel (similar to neural networks' activation functions):

$$K(x_i, x_j) = \tanh(\alpha x_i \cdot x_j + c)$$

Model Selection and Feature Selection

Model selection and feature selection are critical steps in developing efficient machine learning models. Model selection involves choosing the most suitable algorithm for a given problem, based on the data characteristics and task requirements. Common algorithms include decision trees, support vector machines, and neural networks. The goal is to find the model that best captures the underlying patterns in the data, ensuring good generalization and minimizing overfitting. Feature selection, on the other hand, focuses on selecting the most relevant input variables (features) that contribute to the model's predictive power. By eliminating irrelevant or redundant features, feature selection helps improve model accuracy, reduce computational complexity, and prevent overfitting. Techniques such as recursive feature elimination, mutual information, and regularization are commonly used for feature selection. Together, model and feature selection optimize the learning process, enabling the development of more efficient and effective machine learning systems.

Model Selection

Model selection is a crucial step in machine learning, where the goal is to choose the most appropriate model for a given dataset and task, such as classification or regression. This process involves evaluating several potential models based on performance metrics like accuracy, precision, recall, F1-score, or mean squared error. Interpretability is also an important factor, especially in fields like healthcare or finance, where understanding model decisions is critical. Additionally, computational efficiency must be considered, especially when dealing with large datasets or real-time applications. The choice of model may also depend on domain-specific requirements, such as the need for robustness, scalability, or handling imbalanced data. Model selection often involves cross-validation, grid search, and hyperparameter tuning to ensure the model generalizes well to unseen data. Ultimately, the best model balances performance, complexity, and practical considerations for the given task and dataset.

Steps in Model Selection

Define the Problem

The first step in model selection is defining the problem, as it determines the type of machine learning algorithm to use. This involves understanding whether the task is classification, regression, clustering, anomaly detection, or reinforcement learning. In classification problems, the goal is to assign labels to input data (e.g., spam detection), while regression predicts continuous values (e.g., stock prices). Clustering is used in unsupervised learning to group similar data points without predefined labels. Accurately defining the problem helps in identifying relevant features, selecting appropriate evaluation metrics, and deciding on preprocessing techniques. Moreover, understanding the problem scope ensures that business objectives and constraints are considered. For instance, in healthcare applications, model interpretability might be crucial, whereas in financial forecasting, predictive accuracy takes priority. Without a clear problem definition, model selection becomes arbitrary and may lead to poor performance, misinterpretation of results, or ineffective deployment in practical applications.

Choose Candidate Models

Once the problem is defined, the next step is to choose potential models that align with the dataset and task. Different machine learning algorithms have unique strengths and weaknesses. For classification, common models include logistic regression, decision trees, support vector machines (SVMs), random forests, and neural networks. For regression, options include linear regression, ridge regression, decision trees, and deep learning models. Clustering problems may use K-means, hierarchical clustering, or DBSCAN. Selecting candidate models involves considering factors like data size, feature types, interpretability, and computational complexity. For instance, if the dataset is small, simpler models like logistic regression may perform well, whereas deep learning models are ideal for large, high-dimensional datasets. It is beneficial to experiment with multiple models, as different algorithms may perform better based on data patterns and distribution. Thus, an informed selection of candidate models lays the foundation for efficient training and evaluation.

Split Data

A crucial step in model selection is splitting the dataset into distinct subsets for training, validation, and testing. This ensures that the model is evaluated fairly and generalizes well to new data. Typically, the dataset is divided into three parts:

- Training Set: Used to train the model and learn patterns from data. It comprises the largest portion (e.g., 60-80% of data).
- Validation Set: Helps in tuning hyperparameters and selecting the best model by evaluating intermediate results. Usually around 10-20% of the data.

- Test Set: Evaluates final model performance on unseen data, ensuring it generalizes well. It is typically 10-20% of the dataset.

This division prevents overfitting, where a model memorizes training data but performs poorly on new inputs. Additionally, stratified sampling is used for imbalanced datasets to maintain label distribution across sets. Proper data splitting is essential for reliable model assessment and selection.

Train Models

Training models involves feeding the training dataset into different machine learning algorithms to learn patterns and relationships. This process includes adjusting model parameters to minimize error and improve accuracy. The training phase varies based on the chosen algorithm. For instance, in supervised learning, models learn from labeled data, while in unsupervised learning, they detect patterns in unlabeled datasets. Deep learning models require extensive training with multiple iterations, often using GPUs for efficiency. Hyperparameters such as learning rate, tree depth, and the number of neurons in neural networks significantly impact training quality. Proper feature selection, data preprocessing, and normalization improve model training by reducing noise and computational complexity. Additionally, regularization techniques like L1/L2 regularization prevent overfitting. The training process must be carefully monitored to avoid excessive computation while ensuring optimal performance. Training multiple models allows comparison and aids in selecting the best-performing one based on evaluation metrics.

Evaluate Performance

Evaluating model performance is crucial to determining its effectiveness. Different metrics are used based on the type of problem:

- Classification: Accuracy, Precision, Recall, F1-score, ROC-AUC
- Regression: Mean Squared Error (MSE), Root Mean Squared Error (RMSE), R-squared
- Clustering: Silhouette Score, Davies-Bouldin Index

Each metric provides insights into different aspects of model behavior. For instance, accuracy is useful when classes are balanced, but F1-score is preferable in imbalanced datasets. Regression models are assessed using RMSE, which measures prediction errors. Comparing these metrics across models helps in selecting the most effective one. However, real-world applications require trade-offs; for example, in medical diagnoses, higher recall is prioritized over precision to minimize false negatives. Additionally, performance evaluation should be done on validation and test datasets to ensure generalizability. Poor evaluation can lead to selecting a model that performs well on training data but fails in real-world scenarios.

Use Cross-Validation

Cross-validation is a statistical technique used to assess a model's performance and prevent overfitting. The most common method is k-fold cross-validation, where the dataset is divided into k subsets (folds). The model is trained on k-1 folds and tested on the remaining fold, repeating the process k times. This approach ensures that every data point gets tested once, leading to a more reliable performance estimate.

Types of cross-validation

- K-Fold: Divides data into k subsets, commonly k=5 or k=10.
- Stratified K-Fold: Maintains class proportions across folds, useful for imbalanced datasets.
- Leave-One-Out (LOO): Uses one sample as a test set and the rest for training.

Cross-validation reduces bias and variance, providing a more generalized model evaluation. It helps in tuning hyperparameters and comparing models fairly. Without cross-validation, models may perform well on training data but fail to generalize. This technique ensures that the final model selection is based on robust performance, improving real-world applicability.

Compare and Select the Best Model

After evaluating multiple models, the final step is selecting the best one based on various criteria. These include:

- Performance Metrics: Models are compared using accuracy, precision, recall, RMSE, or other relevant metrics.
- Computational Efficiency: Some models require extensive resources, making them impractical for deployment.
- Interpretability: Simpler models like decision trees may be preferred in industries where explanations are needed (e.g., healthcare, finance).
- Business Constraints: Real-world applications consider budget, deployment feasibility, and scalability.

Selecting the best model involves balancing trade-offs between accuracy, complexity, and real-world usability. In some cases, ensemble methods (e.g., bagging, boosting) may be used to combine multiple models for improved performance. The final model should undergo additional testing to validate its performance before deployment. Model selection is not a one-time process; it may require revisiting as new data and business needs evolve. Thus, a well-documented, systematic approach ensures that the chosen model delivers optimal results in practical applications.

Common Model Selection Techniques

Grid Search

Grid Search is a traditional hyperparameter optimization technique that performs an exhaustive search over a specified set of hyperparameter values. It systematically evaluates all possible combinations within a predefined grid to determine the best-performing configuration for a given model. This approach ensures that no potential combination is overlooked, making it effective for small to medium-sized parameter spaces. However, Grid Search can be computationally expensive, especially when dealing with high-dimensional data or models with numerous hyperparameters. Despite its inefficiency, it remains a popular choice because of its simplicity and thoroughness. Typically, it is implemented using tools such as GridSearchCV from Scikit-learn, which automates the process of cross-validation. The main advantage of Grid Search is its ability to guarantee finding the optimal combination within the defined search space. However, for larger datasets and complex models, alternative methods like Random Search or Bayesian Optimization are often preferred due to their efficiency and speed.

Random Search

Random Search is a hyperparameter tuning technique that selects random combinations of hyperparameters from a predefined range instead of exhaustively evaluating all possibilities. This approach is more efficient than Grid Search because it does not require evaluating every combination, making it particularly useful for large search spaces. Studies have shown that Random Search often finds good hyperparameter settings faster than Grid Search, especially when only a few hyperparameters significantly impact model performance. It is widely used in machine learning and deep learning tasks, with implementations available in libraries such as Scikit-learn and TensorFlow. One key advantage of Random Search is its flexibility, as it allows practitioners to allocate a fixed computational budget rather than being constrained by a grid. However, the downside is that it does not guarantee the absolute best hyperparameter combination, but it provides a good trade-off between performance and computational efficiency in many real-world applications.

Bayesian Optimization

Bayesian Optimization is an advanced hyperparameter tuning technique that leverages probabilistic models to efficiently explore the search space. Unlike Grid Search and Random Search, which evaluate hyperparameters without considering past results, Bayesian Optimization builds a surrogate model, typically a Gaussian Process, to predict performance and guide the search toward promising regions. This approach significantly reduces the number of required evaluations, making it computationally efficient for complex models with expensive training processes. It balances exploration and exploitation, ensuring that the search focuses on optimal areas while still considering new possibilities. Popular implementations include BayesOpt and Hyperopt, which integrate seamlessly with machine learning frameworks. While Bayesian Optimization generally outperforms traditional methods in terms of efficiency, it requires more expertise to implement correctly and may struggle with very high-dimensional parameter spaces. Nevertheless, it is widely used in fields such as deep learning and reinforcement learning, where training costs are high, and efficiency is crucial.

Automated Machine Learning (AutoML)

Automated Machine Learning (AutoML) refers to a set of tools and techniques that automate the process of model selection, hyperparameter tuning, and feature engineering. Solutions like TPOT, H2O AutoML, and Google AutoML use algorithms to explore different models and configurations, selecting the best-performing option with minimal human intervention. This approach democratizes machine learning by enabling non-experts to build and deploy models effectively. AutoML techniques often incorporate methods such as evolutionary algorithms, Bayesian Optimization, and reinforcement learning to optimize model performance efficiently. One major advantage of AutoML is its ability to reduce the time and expertise required for model selection, making it particularly valuable for businesses and researchers who lack deep knowledge in machine learning. However, AutoML tools can be computationally expensive and may not always provide interpretable results, as they prioritize performance over understanding. Despite this, AutoML continues to gain popularity as an efficient and accessible approach to machine learning model selection.

Feature Selection

Feature selection is a critical step in machine learning that involves choosing the most relevant features (variables) from a dataset to improve model performance. The goal is to remove irrelevant, redundant, or less important features that do not significantly contribute to predictive accuracy. By selecting the right features, models become more interpretable, computational costs decrease, and the risk of overfitting is reduced. Overfitting occurs when a model learns noise in the data rather than the actual pattern, leading to poor generalization on new data. Feature selection also helps in dealing with the curse of dimensionality, where an excessive number of features can complicate training and lead to suboptimal results. Effective feature selection techniques can enhance the efficiency of machine learning models, ensuring they are both accurate and resource-efficient. These methods fall into three main categories: filter methods, wrapper methods, and embedded methods, each offering different approaches to selecting the best features.

Filter Methods

Filter methods are a type of feature selection technique that evaluates the relevance of features based on their statistical properties rather than their interaction with a specific machine learning model. These methods are computationally efficient and work independently of algorithms, making them useful for preprocessing data before applying any predictive model. They rank features based on various statistical metrics, allowing users to select the most informative ones. By using filter methods, datasets can be significantly reduced in size while maintaining relevant information, improving both model efficiency and interpretability. These methods are particularly useful when dealing with high-dimensional datasets where analyzing all features is computationally expensive. Some popular filter methods include correlation coefficients, chi-square tests, and mutual information measures. These techniques help identify redundant or irrelevant features, preventing them from negatively impacting model performance. Filter methods are commonly used in domains like text classification, bioinformatics, and financial modeling where large feature spaces are present.

Example of Feature Selection

Correlation Coefficient

The correlation coefficient is a widely used filter method for feature selection that measures the statistical relationship between two variables. It quantifies the degree to which a feature is linearly related to the target variable. A high correlation (either positive or negative) indicates that a feature is strongly related to the target and may be valuable for the model. Conversely, features with low correlation may be irrelevant and can be removed to improve model efficiency. One common approach is to eliminate highly correlated features to avoid redundancy, as features that exhibit strong correlation with each other often provide overlapping information. Pearson's correlation coefficient is a popular measure for continuous data, while Spearman's rank correlation is used for ordinal data. By selecting only relevant and non-redundant features, correlation-based feature selection helps simplify models, reduce computational cost, and enhance interpretability without compromising accuracy. This method is commonly applied in domains such as finance, healthcare, and social sciences.

Chi-Square Test

The chi-square test is a statistical method used for feature selection, particularly effective for categorical data. It measures the independence between a feature and the target variable to determine whether they have a significant relationship. The test works by comparing the observed frequencies of different feature values with their expected frequencies under the assumption of independence. A high chi-square statistic indicates a strong dependency between the feature and the target variable, making it a valuable predictor. Conversely, features with low chi-square values contribute little to prediction and can be removed. This method is widely used in applications such as text classification, image recognition, and medical diagnosis where categorical features play a crucial role. Since the chi-square test does not depend on a machine learning model, it is efficient for preprocessing datasets before training. By filtering out irrelevant features, it helps improve model accuracy and reduces the risk of overfitting.

Mutual Information

Mutual information is a filter-based feature selection method that measures the dependency between features and the target variable. Unlike correlation, which only captures linear relationships, mutual information can identify both linear and nonlinear dependencies. It quantifies how much information a feature contributes to predicting the target variable, with higher values indicating stronger relationships. This method is particularly useful in cases where interactions between variables are complex and cannot be captured by traditional statistical tests. Mutual information is widely applied in fields such as natural language processing, bioinformatics, and finance, where datasets often contain intricate relationships between variables. By selecting features with high mutual information scores, models can be optimized to focus on the most informative inputs while discarding redundant or irrelevant data. This reduces dimensionality, speeds up computation, and enhances model generalization. Mutual information-based feature selection ensures that machine learning models extract meaningful patterns, leading to improved predictive performance.

Wrapper Methods

Wrapper methods are a type of feature selection technique that iteratively add or remove features to optimize model performance. These methods use a machine learning algorithm to evaluate the effectiveness of different subsets of features. Unlike filter methods, which rely on statistical techniques, wrapper methods assess feature subsets based on model performance metrics such as accuracy or error rate. Since they involve training multiple models, they tend to be computationally expensive but often yield high-performing feature sets. Examples of wrapper methods include:

- Recursive Feature Elimination (RFE): This method recursively removes the least significant features and re-evaluates model performance until an optimal subset remains.
- Forward Selection: It starts with no features and progressively adds the most important ones based on model performance.
- Backward Elimination: This method begins with all features and systematically removes the least significant ones.
- Wrapper methods are particularly useful for small to medium-sized datasets where computational cost is manageable.

Embedded Methods

Embedded methods integrate feature selection directly into the model training process, making them more efficient than wrapper methods. These methods select the most important features while the model learns, reducing computational cost compared to wrapper approaches. They strike a balance between the simplicity of filter methods and the effectiveness of wrapper methods by leveraging model-specific techniques to identify relevant features. Examples of embedded methods include:

- Lasso (L1 Regularization): This method applies L1 regularization, which penalizes less important feature coefficients and shrinks them to zero, effectively removing irrelevant features. It is particularly useful for high-dimensional datasets.
- Decision Tree-based Methods: Algorithms such as Random Forest and XGBoost automatically assess feature importance by evaluating how much each feature contributes to reducing model impurity. Features with higher importance scores are retained, while less significant ones can be discarded.

Embedded methods are widely used because they efficiently balance performance and feature selection without requiring extensive model retraining.

Model Selection with Grid Search & Cross-Validation

It will compare multiple models (Logistic Regression, Random Forest, and SVM) using Grid Search with Cross-Validation.

Code

```
import numpy as np
import pandas as pd
from sklearn.model_selection import train_test_split, cross_val_score, GridSearchCV
from sklearn.ensemble import RandomForestClassifier
from sklearn.svm import SVC
from sklearn.linear_model import LogisticRegression
from sklearn.metrics import accuracy_score
# Load dataset (Using Breast Cancer dataset as an example)
from sklearn.datasets import load_breast_cancer
data = load_breast_cancer()
X, y = data.data, data.target
# Split dataset into training and testing sets
```

```
X_train, X_test, y_train, y_test = train_test_split(X, y, test_size=0.2, random_state=42)
# Define models and hyperparameters
models = {
    "Logistic Regression": LogisticRegression(),
    "Random Forest": RandomForestClassifier(),
    "SVM": SVC ()
}
# Perform cross-validation and evaluate models
for name, model in models.items():
    scores = cross_val_score(model, X_train, y_train, cv=5)
    print(f"{name}: Mean Accuracy = {np.mean(scores):.4f}")
# Hyperparameter tuning using GridSearchCV for the best model (Random Forest example)
param_grid = {
    "n_estimators": [50, 100, 200],
    "max_depth": [None, 10, 20],
    "min_samples_split": [2, 5, 10]
}
grid_search = GridSearchCV(RandomForestClassifier(), param_grid, cv=5, scoring='accuracy')
grid_search.fit(X_train, y_train)
# Best Model
best_model = grid_search.best_estimator_
y_pred = best_model.predict(X_test)
print(f"Best Random Forest Model Accuracy: {accuracy_score(y_test, y_pred):.4f}")
```

Feature Selection Techniques

Feature selection is crucial to eliminate irrelevant or redundant features.

(A) Filter Method: Select Features Based on Correlation

Python code

```
import seaborn as sns
import matplotlib.pyplot as plt
```

```
# Compute correlation matrix
corr_matrix = pd.DataFrame(X, columns=data.feature_names).corr()
# Plot heatmap of correlations
plt.figure(figsize=(12,8))
sns.heatmap(corr_matrix, annot=False, cmap="coolwarm", linewidths=0.5)
plt.title("Feature Correlation Matrix")
plt.show()
# Remove highly correlated features (correlation > 0.9)
corr_threshold = 0.9
upper = corr_matrix.where(np.triu(np.ones(corr_matrix.shape), k=1).astype(bool))
to_drop = [column for column in upper.columns if any(upper[column] >corr_threshold)]
print(f"Dropping highly correlated features: {to_drop}")
X_filtered = pd.DataFrame(X, columns=data.feature_names).drop(columns=to_drop)
```

Wrapper Method: Recursive Feature Elimination (RFE)

Python code

```
from sklearn.feature_selection import RFE
# Use RFE with RandomForestClassifier
rfe = RFE(RandomForestClassifier(n_estimators=100), n_features_to_select=10)
X_rfe = rfe.fit_transform(X, y)
# Selected features
selected_features = np.array(data.feature_names)[rfe.support_]
print(f"Selected Features using RFE: {selected_features}")
```

Embedded Method: Feature Selection Using Lasso (L1 Regularization)

Python code

```
from sklearn.linear_model import Lasso
# Lasso for feature selection
lasso = Lasso(alpha=0.01)
lasso.fit(X, y)
```

```
# Select important features
selected_features_lasso = np.array(data.feature_names)[lasso.coef_ != 0]
print(f"Selected Features using Lasso: {selected_features_lasso}")
```

Combining Classifiers

Combining classifiers is a technique in machine learning where multiple models are used together to improve prediction accuracy and robustness. Instead of relying on a single classifier, ensemble methods such as bagging, boosting, and stacking aggregate predictions from multiple models, reducing variance and bias. Bagging (e.g., Random Forest) trains multiple instances of the same model on different subsets of data and averages their predictions, while boosting (e.g., AdaBoost, Gradient Boosting) sequentially trains models by giving more weight to misclassified instances. Stacking, on the other hand, involves training a meta-classifier to combine the predictions of multiple base classifiers. These ensemble methods help enhance generalization and mitigate the weaknesses of individual models. Evaluating learning algorithms is crucial to selecting the best model for a given problem. Performance metrics such as accuracy, precision, recall, F1-score, and area under the ROC curve (AUC-ROC) help assess classifier effectiveness. Additionally, cross-validation techniques, like k-fold cross-validation, ensure that evaluation is not biased due to a specific data split. Overfitting and underfitting must also be considered when evaluating models—overfitting occurs when a model learns noise instead of patterns, while underfitting happens when it fails to capture underlying trends. Proper evaluation allows for a balanced trade-off between bias and variance, leading to more reliable and generalizable machine learning models. Here's a breakdown of each concept:

Bagging (Bootstrap Aggregating)

Bagging, or Bootstrap Aggregating, is an ensemble learning technique designed to improve the accuracy and robustness of predictive models. It involves generating multiple subsets of the original dataset through bootstrapping, where samples are randomly drawn with replacement. Each subset is then used to train an independent model, typically of the same type, such as decision trees. Since each model learns from a slightly different dataset, they develop unique decision boundaries, reducing the likelihood of overfitting to noise in the training data. Once all models are trained, their predictions are aggregated, commonly through averaging for regression or majority voting for classification. The key advantage of bagging lies in its ability to reduce variance while maintaining predictive power. High-variance models, like decision trees, tend to overfit the training data, capturing noise rather than true patterns. By averaging multiple models trained on different subsets, bagging smooths out individual model errors, leading to a more generalizable and stable final prediction. Random Forest, a widely used ensemble method, is a prime example of bagging applied to decision trees. By incorporating randomness in both data selection and feature selection, bagging ensures a more diverse set of models, making it a powerful tool in improving machine learning model performance.

Process of Bagging

Bootstrap Sampling

Bootstrap Sampling is a fundamental step in the bagging process, which aims to improve model stability and performance by generating multiple distinct training subsets. In this method, a number of samples are randomly selected from the original dataset with replacement. As a result, some individual data points can appear several times within one subset, while others may not be included at all. This randomness introduces variation between the subsets, allowing the subsequent models to learn different aspects of the data distribution. Each sample serves as a unique representation of the underlying patterns present in the complete dataset, ensuring that the overall variance is captured during training. The practice of drawing with replacement differentiates bootstrap sampling from simple random sampling. By using bootstrap sampling, practitioners create diverse training sets that help reduce overfitting, enhance robustness, and ultimately lead to more reliable ensemble predictions when combined together. This technique significantly boosts performance.

Training Base Models

Training base models is a critical stage in the bagging approach, where each bootstrap sample is used to independently train a weak learner. Typically, a decision tree is chosen as the weak learner due to its simplicity and capacity to capture complex patterns in data. Each model is exposed to a slightly different subset of the training data, resulting in unique learning experiences and error patterns. This independent training process allows the models to develop varied perspectives on the same problem, thereby reducing bias and variance when aggregated. By focusing on distinct data portions, each model is able to learn specific characteristics without being overwhelmed by the complete dataset. This strategy not only speeds up the training process by working in parallel but also increases the resilience of the overall system to overfitting. The combination of these individually trained models forms a robust ensemble. This innovative approach enhances prediction consistency.

Combining Predictions

Combining predictions is the final step in bagging, where the outputs from all individually trained, base models are aggregated to produce a final result. For regression problems, this aggregation typically involves averaging the predictions, which helps to smooth out any variability or noise from individual models. For classification tasks, a majority voting mechanism is commonly employed, where the class that appears most frequently among the predictions is chosen as the final outcome. This method of combining predictions leverages the diversity of models to improve overall accuracy and reliability. By integrating multiple perspectives, the ensemble is less likely to be swayed by errors or anomalies present in any single-model output. This robust approach ultimately results in more stable and generalizable predictions that outperform those of single-model alternatives. By thoughtfully combining each model's individual judgment with an ensemble strategy, bagging transforms isolated insights into a collective intelligence that significantly enhances prediction performance.

Example: Bagging is effective in reducing variance without increasing bias. A common example is Random Forest, which applies bagging to decision trees, improving generalization and robustness.

Boosting (AdaBoost)

Boosting is an ensemble learning technique designed to improve the accuracy of weak classifiers by sequentially training multiple models, each correcting the errors of the previous ones. Unlike bagging, which builds models independently, boosting assigns more weight to misclassified instances, ensuring subsequent models focus on difficult cases. This process continues iteratively, combining the outputs of all models to form a strong classifier with improved predictive performance. AdaBoost (Adaptive Boosting) is a widely used boosting algorithm that assigns adaptive weights to training samples, increasing the influence of misclassified instances in each iteration. It combines multiple weak learners, typically decision stumps, by adjusting their contributions based on their performance. The final model is a weighted sum of all weak classifiers, ensuring higher accuracy and robustness against overfitting. AdaBoost is commonly used in tasks like image recognition, fraud detection, and text classification.

Process:

- Train weak classifiers: The process begins by training a weak model, such as a decision stump (a single-level decision tree), on the dataset. Since the model is weak, it may not classify all samples correctly.
- Reweight incorrectly classified samples: The samples that were misclassified by the first model are assigned higher weights. This ensures that the next model gives more attention to these difficult cases, improving its performance.
- Combine models: Multiple weak models are combined, and their weighted predictions determine the final decision. This iterative process results in a strong classifier that improves accuracy significantly.

AdaBoost (Adaptive Boosting)

AdaBoost, short for Adaptive Boosting, is a machine learning ensemble technique designed to improve the accuracy of weak classifiers. It works by iteratively adjusting the weights of training data points, ensuring that more attention is given to those that were misclassified in previous iterations. The algorithm starts with an initial weak classifier and progressively refines it by training subsequent models on the misclassified samples. By assigning higher weights to incorrectly classified data points, AdaBoost compels each new weak learner to focus on the most challenging cases. This process continues until a strong classifier is formed through a weighted combination of all weak models. AdaBoost is particularly effective for reducing bias and variance, making it a popular choice for classification problems. However, it is sensitive to noisy data and outliers, as they receive increased weight during training. It is widely used in applications such as face recognition, spam filtering, and fraud detection.

Example: AdaBoost, Gradient Boosting, XG-Boost are popular boosting algorithms.

Evaluating and Debugging Learning Algorithms

Evaluation Metrics

Evaluating learning algorithms requires robust metrics to measure their performance effectively. These metrics help determine how well a model generalizes to unseen data and identify areas for improvement. Some of the most commonly used evaluation metrics include accuracy, precision, recall, and F1-score. Accuracy is the simplest metric, measuring the proportion of correctly classified instances out of the total predictions. However, accuracy alone can be misleading, especially in imbalanced datasets where one class significantly outweighs another. Therefore, precision and recall are used to provide a deeper understanding of model performance. Precision measures how many of the predicted positive cases are truly positive, while recall calculates how many of the actual positive cases were correctly predicted. The F1-score is the harmonic mean of precision and recall, balancing both metrics to provide a single performance measure. These metrics are essential for evaluating classification models and ensuring their reliability in real-world applications.

Accuracy

Accuracy is a fundamental evaluation metric used to measure the proportion of correctly predicted instances in a dataset. It is calculated as the ratio of correct predictions to the total number of predictions made by the model. Accuracy is a useful metric when dealing with balanced datasets, where the distribution of classes is nearly equal. However, in cases where the dataset is highly imbalanced, accuracy may give a false impression of model performance. For example, in a medical diagnosis system where 95% of cases are non-diseased, a model that always predicts "no disease" would achieve 95% accuracy but would fail to identify actual diseased cases. This limitation makes it necessary to complement accuracy with other metrics like precision, recall, and F1-score. Despite its limitations, accuracy remains a widely used evaluation metric in various machine learning applications, providing a quick and simple way to assess overall model performance.

Precision

Precision is a crucial evaluation metric used to measure the reliability of positive predictions made by a model. It is calculated as the ratio of true positive predictions to the total number of positive predictions (true positives + false positives). A high precision score indicates that the model has a low rate of false positives, meaning that when it predicts a positive class, it is likely to be correct. Precision is particularly important in scenarios where false positives are costly or undesirable. For instance, in email spam detection, if a classifier incorrectly labels important emails as spam (false positives), it can cause significant inconvenience. Precision helps ensure that only genuinely relevant instances are classified as positive. However, focusing solely on precision can reduce the number of actual positive cases identified, making it necessary to consider recall and F1-score alongside precision to achieve a well-balanced model performance.

Recall

Recall, also known as sensitivity or true positive rate, measures the model's ability to correctly identify actual positive instances. It is calculated as the ratio of true positive predictions to the total number of actual positive cases (true positives + false negatives). A high recall score indicates that the model successfully captures most of the positive cases, minimizing false negatives. Recall is crucial in applications where missing a positive instance has serious consequences. For example, in medical diagnosis, failing to detect a disease (false negatives) can be life-threatening. Similarly, in fraud detection, an undetected fraudulent transaction can lead to financial losses. While maximizing recall ensures that fewer positive cases are missed, it may come at the cost of increasing false positives. Therefore, recall is often balanced with precision to provide a more comprehensive measure of model performance, typically using the F1-score.

F1-Score

The F1-score is a performance metric that combines precision and recall into a single value using their harmonic mean. It is particularly useful when there is an imbalance between the importance of precision and recall. The formula for the F1-score is:

Confusion Matrix: A table used to describe the performance of a classification algorithm, showing true positives, true negatives, false positives, and false negatives.

$$F1 = 2 \times \frac{\text{Precision} \times \text{Recall}}{\text{Precision} + \text{Recall}}$$

A high F1-score indicates a good balance between precision and recall, meaning the model is neither too lenient in classifying positives nor too strict in avoiding false positives. The F1-score is commonly used in classification problems, especially when the dataset is imbalanced, as it provides a more meaningful measure of performance than accuracy alone. In scenarios such as fraud detection, medical diagnosis, and spam filtering, the F1-score ensures that both the correctness of positive predictions and the ability to identify actual positives are well-balanced, leading to more reliable model performance.

Cross-Validation

Cross-validation is a statistical technique used to evaluate the performance and generalizability of a machine learning model. It works by dividing the dataset into multiple subsets, known as folds, to ensure that the model is trained and tested on different data partitions. The most common type of cross-validation is k-fold cross-validation, where the data is split into k subsets. The model is trained on k-1 folds and tested on the remaining fold, and this process is repeated k times, with a different fold used for validation each time. The results are then averaged to obtain a more reliable estimate of model performance. This technique helps to mitigate issues like overfitting, where the model performs well on training data but poorly on unseen data, and underfitting, where the model is too simple to capture patterns. Cross-validation ensures that the model generalizes well and performs consistently across different datasets.

Debugging Algorithms

Debugging algorithms is a critical step in ensuring machine learning models function correctly and efficiently. It involves systematically identifying and fixing errors, inefficiencies, and incorrect assumptions within the algorithm. The debugging process typically starts with understanding the expected behavior and comparing it with actual outputs. Key debugging techniques include examining the loss function, checking data preprocessing steps, and verifying the correctness of feature engineering. Using visualization tools like confusion matrices, histograms, and scatter plots can also help identify patterns or inconsistencies in the data. Step-by-step execution of the algorithm, along with logging intermediate outputs, can highlight unexpected values or calculations. Automated debugging tools and unit tests further aid in catching issues early. A structured approach, such as the scientific method—forming hypotheses, testing them, and iterating—is essential for debugging effectively. Additionally, seeking external perspectives, like code reviews or discussing with peers, can provide new insights into resolving complex algorithmic problems.

Bias vs. Variance

Bias and variance are fundamental concepts in machine learning that influence a model's ability to generalize to new data in Table 2.3. A high-bias model, often referred to as underfitting, fails to capture the complexity of the data and performs poorly on both training and test datasets. This happens when the model is too simplistic, such as using linear regression for a highly nonlinear relationship. On the other hand, a high-variance model overfits the training data, capturing noise rather than meaningful patterns. Such models perform well on training data but generalize poorly to unseen data, leading to poor test performance. The ideal model achieves a balance between bias and variance, known as the bias-variance tradeoff. Techniques to reduce bias include using more complex models, feature engineering, and increasing model parameters. Reducing variance can be achieved by regularization methods, cross-validation, and increasing training data. Understanding bias and variance helps in fine-tuning models for better generalization.

Table 2.3: Comparing Bias vs. Variance.

Aspect	High Bias (Underfitting)	High Variance (Overfitting)
Definition	Model is too simple and fails to capture patterns in data.	Model is too complex and captures noise in data.
Model Performance on Training Data	Poor (high error)	Excellent (low error)
Model Performance on Test Data	Poor (high error)	Poor (high error due to overfitting)
Cause	Insufficient complexity, few features, incorrect model choice	Excessive complexity, too many features, model memorizes training data
Example Models	Linear regression on nonlinear data, simple decision tree	Deep neural networks without regularization, complex decision trees
Impact on Generalization	Fails to learn meaningful patterns, cannot generalize	Learns too many details from training data, leading to poor generalization
How to Reduce Bias?	Use more complex models, feature engineering, increase parameters	-
How to Reduce Variance?	-	Regularization (L1/L2), cross-validation, increasing training data
Bias-Variance Tradeoff	Increasing complexity reduces bias but increases variance	Simplifying the model reduces variance but increases bias

Model Complexity

Model complexity plays a crucial role in machine learning, directly affecting a model's performance and generalization ability. A complex model, such as a deep neural network with many layers or a decision tree with too many splits, may fit the training data perfectly but fail to generalize to new data, leading to overfitting. Conversely, an overly simple model, such as a linear regression model for non-linear data, may fail to capture important patterns, leading to underfitting. The key to optimal performance is finding the right level of complexity. Techniques like cross-validation, regularization (L1 and L2 penalties), and pruning decision trees help control complexity. Additionally, evaluating metrics such as training and validation accuracy can indicate whether the model is too complex or too simple. Hyperparameter tuning, such as adjusting the number of layers in a neural network or the depth of a decision tree, can also help optimize model complexity.

Learning Curves

Learning curves are valuable diagnostic tools in machine learning, providing insight into how well a model learns over time or with increasing data. A learning curve plots training error and validation error as a function of training iterations or dataset size. When a model underfits, both training and validation errors remain high, indicating that the model is too simple to capture the underlying patterns in the data. In contrast, if a model overfits, the training error will be very low while the validation error remains high, indicating poor generalization. By analyzing learning curves, one can determine whether adding more training data, increasing model complexity, or adjusting regularization is necessary. If the training and validation errors converge, the model has a good fit. However, if they remain far apart, the model requires adjustment. Learning curves are crucial for diagnosing issues and improving model performance in supervised learning tasks.

Classification Errors

Classification errors occur when a machine learning model incorrectly labels a given instance. These errors arise when the predicted class does not match the actual class, leading to inaccurate results. Classification errors are common in supervised learning models, where the goal is to assign labels based on learned patterns. In classification problems, errors can be broadly categorized into false positives and false negatives, which impact model performance in various ways. The severity of classification errors depends on the application domain. For instance, in spam detection, misclassifying a spam email as non-spam can be a minor inconvenience. However, in critical applications like medical diagnosis, fraud detection, and security systems, classification errors can lead to significant consequences. Reducing classification errors requires fine-tuning the model using better training data, adjusting thresholds, and optimizing algorithms to achieve a balanced trade-off between sensitivity and specificity. Evaluating classification errors helps improve model accuracy and reliability.

False Positive (Type I Error)

A false positive, also known as a Type I error, occurs when a model incorrectly classifies a negative instance as positive. In other words, the model predicts the presence of a characteristic or condition when it is actually absent. This type of error is particularly critical in domains like medical testing, where a false positive may lead to unnecessary stress, further tests, and unwarranted treatments. For example, if a cancer detection model incorrectly classifies a healthy individual as having cancer, the patient may undergo unnecessary medical procedures, causing physical, emotional, and financial strain. Similarly, in fraud detection, a false positive could flag a legitimate transaction as fraudulent, leading to inconvenience for users. To mitigate false positives, models can be trained with better datasets, improved feature selection, and optimized thresholds. Balancing precision and recall is essential to reducing Type I errors while maintaining a model's effectiveness.

False Negative (Type II Error)

A false negative, or Type II error, occurs when a model incorrectly classifies a positive instance as negative. This means the model fails to detect a condition or characteristic that is actually present. False negatives are often more critical than false positives, especially in high-risk applications like healthcare and security. For example, in cancer detection, a false negative means the model fails to identify a patient with cancer, delaying diagnosis and treatment, potentially leading to severe health consequences. In security systems, a false negative could allow a threat, such as an unauthorized person or malware, to go undetected, compromising safety. False negatives can also be problematic in fraud detection, where undetected fraudulent transactions can cause financial losses. To minimize false negatives, models need better training data, fine-tuned parameters, and increased sensitivity. Adjusting thresholds and using ensemble methods can improve model performance and reduce Type II errors.

Impact on the Model

Classification errors, particularly false positives and false negatives, significantly impact the effectiveness of a machine learning model. The consequences of these errors depend on the application. In scenarios like medical diagnostics, false negatives are more dangerous because missing a serious disease can lead to fatal consequences. Conversely, in spam filtering, a false positive (classifying a legitimate email as spam) may be an inconvenience but is not life-threatening. In fraud detection, false positives may cause unnecessary transaction blocks, frustrating users, while false negatives allow fraudulent activities to proceed undetected, leading to financial losses. Striking a balance between minimizing both types of errors is crucial for model optimization. Techniques such as adjusting classification thresholds, enhancing feature selection, and using ensemble learning can help reduce errors. Proper evaluation metrics like precision, recall, and F1-score should be used to assess model performance and determine the trade-off between false positives and false negatives.

Reducing Classification Errors

Improving Data Quality

One of the most crucial steps in reducing classification errors is improving data quality. Poor-quality data can introduce noise, missing values, and inconsistencies that degrade model performance. To ensure high-quality data, it is essential to remove noise by identifying and eliminating irrelevant or redundant information. Handling missing values is another vital step—techniques like imputation, deletion, or using algorithms that tolerate missing data can improve classification results. Proper data preprocessing, including normalization, standardization, and encoding categorical variables, ensures that data is in a suitable format for machine learning models. Outlier detection techniques, such as Z-score, IQR, or clustering-based methods, help refine the dataset by removing extreme values that may bias the model. Data augmentation and synthetic data generation can also enhance data quality when dealing with limited datasets. By focusing on these techniques, classification errors can be significantly reduced, leading to improved model accuracy and reliability.

Feature Selection/Engineering

Feature selection and engineering play a critical role in reducing classification errors by ensuring that only the most relevant and informative features are used for model training. Feature selection helps eliminate redundant or irrelevant features, which can introduce noise and lead to overfitting. Techniques like Recursive Feature Elimination (RFE), mutual information, and principal component analysis (PCA) can help identify the most important features. On the other hand, feature engineering involves creating new features that enhance the model's ability to distinguish between classes. This can include transformations, polynomial features, domain-specific feature creation, or aggregating information from multiple sources. Properly engineered features can highlight patterns in data that would otherwise remain hidden, improving classification accuracy. Additionally, encoding categorical variables effectively (e.g., one-hot encoding, target encoding) and scaling numerical features appropriately help the model generalize better. Well-designed features make learning more efficient, reducing classification errors and improving predictive performance.

Tuning Hyperparameters

Hyperparameter tuning is a vital process in reducing classification errors, as it optimizes the model's configuration for better generalization and accuracy. Hyperparameters are parameters that govern how a model learns, such as learning rate, regularization strength, number of hidden layers, and kernel functions. Selecting appropriate hyperparameters prevents issues like overfitting or underfitting. Methods such as grid search, random search, and Bayesian optimization help identify the best combination of hyperparameters. Cross-validation is commonly used to evaluate different hyperparameter settings and ensure they work well across different data subsets. Advanced techniques like AutoML or neural architecture search can automate hyperparameter tuning, making the process more efficient. Regularization techniques, such as L1/L2 penalties, dropout, and batch normalization, also contribute to controlling model complexity and reducing errors. By fine-tuning hyperparameters carefully, classification models can achieve optimal performance, minimizing misclassifications and enhancing predictive accuracy.

Summary

Machine learning encompasses a diverse set of classification techniques, each with unique strengths and applications. Logistic regression is a fundamental probabilistic model used for binary classification, while the Perceptron serves as an early neural network model capable of learning linearly separable data. The Exponential family provides a broad mathematical framework that underpins various probabilistic models, including those used in Generative learning algorithms, such as Gaussian Discriminant Analysis (GDA) and Naïve Bayes. GDA assumes class-conditional normal distributions, whereas Naïve Bayes relies on conditional independence assumptions, making it efficient for high-dimensional data.On the discriminative side, Support Vector Machines (SVMs) optimize the optimal hyperplane for maximum class separation, with kernels extending their power to non-linear data. Model selection and feature selection are crucial for improving generalization, balancing bias-variance trade-offs, and avoiding overfitting. Ensemble learning techniques like Bagging and Boosting improve model performance. AdaBoost, a boosting algorithm, sequentially adjusts model weights to enhance weak learners. Proper evaluation and debugging of learning algorithms through metrics such as accuracy, precision, recall, and ROC curves is vital for assessing classification performance. Understanding these concepts is essential for developing robust machine learning models, ensuring efficiency, accuracy, and adaptability across various real-world applications.

Exercise Questions

- What is the key assumption behind logistic regression, and how does it estimate probabilities?
- How does the perceptron algorithm update its weights during training?
- What is the exponential family of distributions, and why is it useful in machine learning?
- How do generative learning algorithms differ from discriminative learning algorithms?

- What are the assumptions made by Gaussian Discriminant Analysis (GDA) for classification?
- Why is the Naive Bayes classifier considered "naive," and in what type of applications does it perform well?
- How does the concept of the optimal hyperplane help in classification using SVMs?
- What is the role of the kernel trick in SVM, and how does it enable handling non-linearly separable data?
- How does the AdaBoost algorithm improve classification performance using weak learners?
- What is precision, recall, and F1-score, and how are they used to evaluate classification errors?

3

UNSUPERVISED LEARNING AND PROBABILISTIC MODELS

Unsupervised learning is a crucial branch of machine learning where algorithms analyze and interpret data without predefined labels. Unlike supervised learning, which relies on labeled datasets for training, unsupervised learning models uncover hidden structures and patterns in raw data. This learning paradigm is essential for applications such as clustering, anomaly detection, and dimensionality reduction, enabling data-driven decision-making in various domains, including healthcare, finance, and artificial intelligence. One of the primary techniques in unsupervised learning is clustering, where data points are grouped based on similarities without prior knowledge of categories. Algorithms such as K-Means, hierarchical clustering, and Gaussian Mixture Models (GMMs) help identify meaningful clusters within datasets. Another critical aspect is dimensionality reduction, where methods like Principal Component Analysis (PCA) and t-Distributed Stochastic Neighbor Embedding (t-SNE) simplify complex datasets while preserving essential information. These techniques are widely used in data visualization and feature selection. Probabilistic models play a fundamental role in unsupervised learning by leveraging probability distributions to represent uncertainties in data. Instead of making deterministic classifications, these models infer the likelihood of data belonging to different groups. Bayesian networks, Markov models, and Gaussian Mixture Models (GMMs) are some of the most commonly used probabilistic models in unsupervised learning. These models excel in applications such as natural language processing, image recognition, and fraud detection.

Gaussian Mixture Models (GMMs) are particularly useful in clustering because they assume data points are generated from multiple Gaussian distributions. Unlike K-Means, which assigns each data point to a single cluster, GMMs provide probabilistic assignments, allowing for soft clustering. Expectation-Maximization (EM) is a widely used algorithm to optimize the parameters of GMMs, making them effective in scenarios where data distributions overlap. Another important probabilistic approach is Hidden Markov Models (HMMs), which are widely used in sequence-based data analysis, such as speech recognition, bioinformatics, and financial modeling. HMMs model systems with hidden states, using probability distributions to capture temporal dependencies in sequential data. By estimating the probabilities of transitions between states, HMMs enable powerful applications in time-series forecasting and language modeling. The combination of unsupervised learning and probabilistic models provides a powerful framework for analyzing complex, high-dimensional data. By leveraging statistical inference, these models enhance pattern recognition, anomaly detection, and generative modeling. As machine learning continues to evolve, the integration of unsupervised learning with probabilistic approaches will remain a cornerstone of artificial intelligence, driving advancements in automation, decision-making, and predictive analytics.

Unsupervised Learning: Clustering

Unsupervised learning is a type of machine learning where algorithms are given data without predefined labels or categories. The goal is for the model to find hidden patterns, structures, or relationships within the data. One of the most common techniques in unsupervised learning is clustering, which involves grouping data points based on their similarity. In clustering, the algorithm identifies natural clusters or segments within the data, where points in the same cluster are more similar to each other than to those in different clusters. Popular clustering algorithms include K-means, hierarchical clustering, and DBSCAN. Clustering is widely used in various applications, such as customer segmentation, anomaly detection, image recognition, and market research. It helps to reveal insights and structure in large, unlabeled datasets, making it a powerful tool for exploratory data analysis and pattern discovery.

Clustering

Clustering is a fundamental technique in machine learning and data science used to group similar data points together. It helps in discovering patterns and structures within a dataset by organizing data into clusters, where objects in the same cluster share common characteristics. Unlike classification, clustering is an unsupervised learning approach, meaning that it does not rely on predefined labels. Instead, it identifies hidden relationships in the data based on similarity measures such as Euclidean distance, cosine similarity, or statistical distribution. Clustering is widely applied in various fields, including marketing, healthcare, finance, and computer vision. Some of the most common clustering algorithms include K-Means, DBSCAN, and hierarchical clustering. The selection of an appropriate algorithm depends on the dataset size, shape, and distribution. Effective clustering can improve decision-making processes, optimize business strategies, and provide deeper insights into complex data patterns, making it an essential tool in modern data analytics.

Customer Segmentation

Customer segmentation is one of the most common applications of clustering, allowing businesses to divide their customer base into meaningful groups based on shared characteristics. These characteristics may include demographics, purchasing behavior, interests, and engagement levels. By identifying different customer segments, businesses can develop targeted marketing strategies, personalize customer experiences, and improve customer retention. For instance, e-commerce companies use clustering to group customers based on their shopping habits, helping them recommend relevant products. Financial institutions use it to classify clients into different risk categories for credit assessment. Clustering techniques such as K-Means and Gaussian Mixture Models (GMM) are commonly employed for customer segmentation, enabling companies to maximize profitability and enhance customer satisfaction. Effective segmentation helps in resource allocation, pricing strategies, and the development of new products based on consumer needs. Overall, clustering provides a data-driven approach to understanding customer behavior and tailoring business strategies accordingly.

Anomaly Detection

Anomaly detection, also known as outlier detection, is a critical application of clustering used to identify unusual patterns in data. Anomalies are data points that deviate significantly from the expected behavior, often indicating fraud, errors, or critical events. Clustering algorithms, such as DBSCAN and hierarchical clustering, help in detecting anomalies by identifying data points that do not belong to any well-defined cluster. In cybersecurity, anomaly detection is used to detect network intrusions or fraudulent transactions. In healthcare, it helps identify rare diseases by analyzing patient records. Manufacturing industries use it for predictive maintenance, detecting equipment failures before they occur. By separating normal patterns from irregularities, clustering-based anomaly detection enhances security, improves operational efficiency, and minimizes risks. The ability to recognize outliers in large datasets makes clustering an essential tool for fraud detection, fault diagnosis, and other critical applications where identifying deviations is crucial.

Image Segmentation

Image segmentation is a technique used in computer vision to divide an image into meaningful regions or segments based on similarities in color, texture, or intensity. Clustering plays a vital role in this process by grouping pixels with similar characteristics together. One of the most commonly used clustering algorithms for image segmentation is K-Means, which partitions an image into distinct regions based on pixel intensity. This technique is widely applied in medical imaging to identify tumors, in autonomous driving for object detection, and in facial recognition systems. Segmentation helps in extracting relevant information from images, improving accuracy in machine perception and analysis. Advanced methods such as mean-shift clustering and hierarchical clustering further enhance segmentation precision. By enabling automated and efficient image processing, clustering-based segmentation contributes to advancements in medical diagnostics, surveillance systems, and digital image enhancement, making it an essential component of modern computer vision applications.

Document Categorization

Document categorization, also known as text clustering, is the process of grouping similar documents together based on their content. Clustering is widely used in organizing large collections of textual data, such as news articles, research papers, or customer reviews. Algorithms like K-Means and Latent Dirichlet Allocation (LDA) help in clustering documents based on word frequencies and semantic similarity. This technique is highly valuable in search engines, topic modeling, and recommendation systems. For instance, clustering enables automatic organization of emails into categories such as promotions, social updates, or spam. In academic research, it helps in grouping papers by subject areas, facilitating easier retrieval of relevant information. Businesses use document clustering for sentiment analysis, customer feedback categorization, and trend analysis. With the rapid growth of digital content, clustering-based document categorization plays a crucial role in managing and extracting insights from unstructured textual data efficiently.

Common clustering techniques include:

K-Means Clustering

K-Means is one of the most widely used clustering algorithms due to its simplicity and efficiency. It works by partitioning a dataset into K clusters, where each data point is assigned to the cluster with the nearest centroid. The algorithm starts with randomly placed centroids, assigns points to the nearest cluster, and then iteratively updates the centroids based on the mean of assigned points. This process continues until convergence, typically when the centroids no longer change significantly. K-Means performs well with spherical clusters of similar sizes but struggles with complex shapes or varying densities. It requires the user to predefine K, which can be challenging if the optimal number of clusters is unknown. Popular techniques like the Elbow Method and Silhouette Score help determine the best K. K-Means is commonly applied in customer segmentation, anomaly detection, and document clustering, making it a fundamental tool in unsupervised learning.

Expectation-Maximization (EM) Algorithm

The Expectation-Maximization (EM) algorithm is a probabilistic clustering technique used when data follows a latent variable model. Unlike K-Means, which assigns points to clusters in a hard manner, EM operates in a soft clustering approach, meaning each point has a probability of belonging to multiple clusters. The algorithm iterates between two steps: Expectation (E-step), where it computes the probability distribution over cluster assignments, and Maximization (M-step), where it updates model parameters to maximize the likelihood. EM is particularly useful when dealing with uncertain or incomplete data, making it a key method in missing data imputation, natural language processing, and gene expression analysis. While EM can be powerful, it is computationally expensive and may converge to local optima rather than the global best solution. Proper initialization and multiple runs can help mitigate this issue. Its ability to handle overlapping clusters makes it preferable over hard clustering methods in various real-world applications.

Mixture of Gaussians (GMM)

The Gaussian Mixture Model (GMM) is an extension of the EM algorithm that assumes data is generated from a mixture of multiple Gaussian distributions. Each Gaussian component represents a cluster, characterized by parameters such as mean, covariance, and weight. The EM algorithm is used to estimate these parameters iteratively. Unlike K-Means, which assigns points to clusters based on distance, GMM provides a probabilistic assignment, meaning each data point has a likelihood of belonging to multiple clusters. This makes GMM suitable for complex and overlapping datasets. It is widely used in image segmentation, speaker recognition, anomaly detection, and bioinformatics. However, GMM requires careful selection of the number of Gaussian components and is computationally more expensive than K-Means. It is sensitive to initialization, so techniques like k-means++ or multiple random starts are often employed to improve convergence. Despite these challenges, GMM provides a more flexible and powerful approach to clustering.

Hierarchical Clustering

Hierarchical clustering builds a nested structure of clusters, forming a tree-like dendrogram that represents the relationships between data points. It operates in two main ways: Agglomerative (bottom-up), where each data point starts as its own cluster and progressively merges with the nearest clusters, and Divisive (top-down), where all data points begin in a single cluster and are recursively split. Unlike K-Means and GMM, hierarchical clustering does not require predefining the number of clusters. Instead, users can cut the dendrogram at a desired level to extract meaningful clusters. It is particularly useful for taxonomy classification, social network analysis, and genomic data organization. While it provides interpretable results, it is computationally expensive ($O(n^2)$ complexity) and struggles with large datasets. Additionally, choosing the right linkage method (single, complete, or average) significantly impacts the clustering outcome. Hierarchical clustering is preferred when understanding cluster relationships is as important as the clusters themselves.

DBSCAN (Density-Based Spatial Clustering)

DBSCAN (Density-Based Spatial Clustering of Applications with Noise) is a powerful clustering algorithm that groups points based on density rather than distance. It defines clusters as dense regions of data points separated by lower-density areas, making it effective for detecting arbitrary-shaped clusters and identifying outliers (noise). DBSCAN uses two parameters: epsilon (ε), which defines the radius of neighborhood search, and minPts, the minimum number of points required to form a dense region. Unlike K-Means and hierarchical clustering, DBSCAN does not require specifying the number of clusters in advance and can automatically detect noise points. It is particularly useful for geospatial analysis, anomaly detection, and image segmentation. However, DBSCAN struggles with datasets of varying densities and high-dimensional data, where defining ε becomes difficult. Despite these challenges, its ability to discover clusters of varying shapes and its robustness to outliers make it a popular choice in real-world applications.

K-Means Clustering

K-Means is a widely used unsupervised machine learning algorithm for clustering, where a dataset is partitioned into K clusters based on similarity. The goal of K-Means is to minimize the variance within each cluster, ensuring that data points within the same cluster are as similar as possible. The algorithm iteratively assigns data points to clusters and updates the cluster centers (centroids) to achieve an optimal grouping. It is efficient and scales well with large datasets, making it a popular choice in applications such as image segmentation, customer segmentation, anomaly detection, and pattern recognition. However, K-Means assumes that clusters are spherical and of similar sizes, which may not always be the case in real-world datasets. The choice of K (number of clusters) significantly impacts the results, and various methods like the Elbow Method or Silhouette Score are used to determine an optimal value. Despite some limitations, K-Means remains a fundamental tool in data clustering tasks.

Mathematical Formulation

The objective of K-Means is to minimize the sum of squared distances of each point from its cluster center:

$$J = \sum_{i=1}^{K} \sum_{x \in C_i} ||x - \mu_i||^2$$

Where:

x represents a data point

μi is the centroid of clusterCi

$||x-\mu i||^2$ is the squared Euclidean distance

Algorithm Steps

- Initialize: The algorithm begins by randomly selecting K initial centroids from the dataset. These centroids act as the starting cluster centers, and their placement can affect the final results. Some improved initialization methods, such as K-Means++, help choose better initial centroids to enhance convergence.

- Assign Clusters: Each data point is assigned to the cluster whose centroid is the closest, using a distance metric like Euclidean distance. This ensures that similar data points are grouped together.
- Update Centroids: The centroid of each cluster is recalculated by taking the mean (average) of all the points assigned to that cluster. This step shifts the centroids to better represent the underlying data distribution.
- Repeat: Steps 2 and 3 are repeated iteratively until either the centroids stop changing significantly or a predefined number of iterations is reached. The final clusters are formed once the algorithm converges.

Expectation-Maximization (EM) Algorithm

The Expectation-Maximization (EM) algorithm is a powerful iterative technique used in statistical inference, particularly in cases where data exhibits hidden or latent structures. It is commonly applied in clustering problems, missing data imputation, and density estimation. The EM algorithm is particularly useful when direct maximization of the likelihood function is complex due to incomplete data. By alternating between two stepsExpectation (E-step) and Maximization (M-step)it refines parameter estimates iteratively. The algorithm is widely used in Gaussian Mixture Models (GMMs), Hidden Markov Models (HMMs), and various machine learning applications. It assumes that observed data is generated from underlying latent variables that arc initially unknown. Unlike other clustering algorithms like k-means, which use hard assignments, EM provides probabilistic soft assignments, making it more flexible. The algorithm guarantees convergence to a local maximum of the likelihood function, making it a reliable choice for many real-world applications, including natural language processing and bioinformatics.

Algorithm Steps

The Expectation-Maximization (EM) algorithm follows a systematic iterative process to refine parameter estimates. It begins by initializing parameters randomly, such as cluster means and variances in a clustering context. The process consists of two main steps:

- Initialization: The algorithm starts with arbitrary parameter values, assuming an initial model for the underlying distribution. These parameters can be means, variances, or mixture weights, depending on the problem.
- Expectation Step (E-Step): In this step, the algorithm computes the probability of each data point belonging to different clusters based on the current parameter estimates. These probabilities serve as soft assignments of data points to clusters.

- Maximization Step (M-Step): Using the probabilities computed in the E-step, the algorithm updates the parameters to maximize the likelihood of observed data. This step ensures a better model fit.
- Iteration: Steps 2 and 3 are repeated until the algorithm converges, meaning that parameter updates become negligible.

Mixture of Gaussians (GMM)

A Gaussian Mixture Model (GMM) is a probabilistic approach used in clustering and density estimation. Unlike traditional clustering methods such as K-Means, which assigns each data point to a single cluster, GMM assumes that data is generated from a mixture of multiple Gaussian distributions. Each Gaussian component represents a cluster, characterized by a mean (center), covariance (shape), and mixing coefficient (weight). This flexibility allows GMM to model complex datasets with overlapping clusters more accurately than K-Means, which only forms spherical clusters. The Expectation-Maximization (EM) algorithm is commonly used to estimate GMM parameters iteratively. EM optimizes the probability distribution of data belonging to different Gaussian components by alternating between expectation (assigning probabilities to clusters) and maximization (adjusting parameters for better fit). GMM is widely used in pattern recognition, anomaly detection, speech processing, and computer vision, where data distribution is non-linear and requires a more sophisticated clustering technique.

Mathematical Formulation

GMM models a dataset as:

$$p(x) = \sum_{i=1}^{K} \pi_i \mathcal{N}(x|\mu_i, \Sigma_i)$$

Where:

πi is the mixing coefficient (weight) of the ith Gaussian

$N(x|\mu i,\Sigma i)$is the Gaussian distribution with mean μi and covariance matrixΣi

K is the number of Gaussian components

Algorithm Steps (Using EM)

Initialize

The first step in the Expectation-Maximization (EM) algorithm is initialization. This involves setting initial values for three key parameters: the means, covariances, and mixing coefficients of the Gaussian components in a mixture model. The choice of these initial values significantly impacts the convergence and accuracy of the EM algorithm. Means can be initialized randomly or using methods like k-means clustering. Covariances, which represent the spread of each component, are often initialized as identity matrices or small random positive-definite matrices. Mixing coefficients, which define the proportion of each Gaussian component in the dataset, are initialized such that they sum to one. Poor initialization can lead to slow convergence or local optima, making this step crucial for the algorithm's success. Various heuristics and refinements, such as multiple restarts or using data-driven initializations, can improve the performance of the EM algorithm by providing a better starting point.

Expectation (E-Step)

In the Expectation (E) step, the algorithm calculates the probability that each data point belongs to each Gaussian component, given the current parameter estimates. This probability is derived using Bayes' theorem and is often referred to as the "responsibility" of a Gaussian component for a particular data point. Mathematically, it is computed using the posterior probability, which is the likelihood of the data point given the Gaussian parameters, weighted by the mixing coefficient and normalized across all components. This step essentially soft-assigns data points to different clusters rather than making hard assignments, as in k-means clustering. The computed probabilities serve as the weights for the subsequent Maximization step. The accuracy of these assignments improves as the algorithm iterates, leading to refined parameter estimates. A well-executed E-step ensures that the model correctly captures the underlying structure of the data, enabling effective updates in the next phase.

Maximization (M-Step)

The Maximization (M) step follows the E-step by updating the model parameters—means, covariances, and mixing coefficients—based on the probability assignments computed previously. The new means are calculated as weighted averages of the data points, where the weights are the responsibilities determined in the E-step. Similarly, the covariance matrices are updated by computing the weighted variance of each component, ensuring that they accurately reflect the spread of data points assigned to them. The mixing coefficients are also updated to represent the relative proportion of data points assigned to each Gaussian component. This step ensures that the model parameters move closer to the optimal values that maximize the likelihood of the observed data. The M-step effectively refines the clusters by shifting the Gaussian distributions to better fit the dataset. By iteratively improving parameter estimates, the algorithm enhances its ability to model complex data distributions.

Repeat Until Convergence

The Expectation-Maximization algorithm iterates between the E-step and M-step until convergence is reached. Convergence typically occurs when the changes in the parameter values or the overall log-likelihood of the model become negligible between successive iterations. Several stopping criteria can be used, such as setting a threshold for the difference in log-likelihood values or limiting the number of iterations. Since the EM algorithm guarantees non-decreasing likelihood at each step, it eventually stabilizes at a local maximum or saddle point. However, due to the possibility of local optima, multiple runs with different initializations may be necessary for achieving the best solution. Additionally, practical techniques like early stopping, regularization, or constraints on covariance matrices can help improve robustness. When the algorithm converges, the final parameter values represent the optimal Gaussian mixture model that best explains the given dataset, making EM a powerful approach for clustering and density estimation.

ComparisonK-Means vs. EM vs. GMM

K-Means is a fast, hard-clustering algorithm that assigns each data point to one cluster, assuming spherical clusters with equal variance, making it effective for simple, well-separated clusters in Table 2.4. The Expectation-Maximization (EM) algorithm, on the other hand, is a soft-clustering approach that assigns probabilities to cluster memberships and is more flexible but computationally intensive. The Gaussian Mixture Model (GMM) is an extension of EM that models' data using multiple Gaussian distributions, allowing for ellipsoidal clusters and greater adaptability. While K-Means is distance-based and minimizes variance, GMM and EM use probabilistic models and likelihood maximization. Though K-Means is faster, EM and GMM offer higher flexibility for complex datasets.

Table2.4: Comparison K-Means vs. EM vs. GMM

Feature	**K-Means**	**EM Algorithm**	**GMM**
Clustering Type	Hard (one point per cluster)	Soft (probabilistic assignment)	Soft (probabilistic assignment)
Cluster Shape	Spherical (equal variance)	Can be flexible	Can be ellipsoidal
Speed	Fast	Slower	Slower (uses EM)
Flexibility	Limited	High	High
Mathematical Basis	Minimizes variance (distance-based)	Maximizes likelihood	Probabilistic Gaussian modeling

Factor Analysis (FA)

Factor Analysis (FA) is a statistical technique used to identify underlying relationships among observed variables by assuming that they are influenced by a smaller number of unobserved latent factors along with some random noise. It helps in reducing data dimensionality while preserving essential patterns, making it useful in research areas where complex variables need to be understood in a simplified manner. FA works by extracting common factors that explain the shared variance among variables, differentiating them from unique variances caused by measurement errors or other external influences. This method is widely applied in psychology, social sciences, and market research to uncover hidden structures in data. In psychology, FA is used to identify fundamental personality traits or cognitive abilities from survey responses. Social scientists use it to analyze social attitudes, behaviors, and demographic patterns. In market research, it helps businesses segment consumers based on purchasing behaviors, preferences, and brand perceptions. By revealing latent factors, FA enhances data interpretation, aiding researchers in drawing meaningful conclusions and improving predictive modeling.

Objective: Identify underlying latent variables (factors) that explain observed variables' correlations.

Mathematical Model

$X=LF+\epsilon$

Where:

X = Observed variables (data)

L = Factor loadings (relationship between factors and observed variables)

F = Latent factors

ϵ = Error term

Factors are not necessarily independent. It models the covariance between observed variables. Requires assumptions about factor structure (e.g., number of factors).Uses techniques like Maximum Likelihood Estimation (MLE) or Principal Axis Factoring.

Principal Component Analysis (PCA)

Principal Component Analysis (PCA) is a widely used dimensionality reduction technique that transforms high-dimensional data into a lower-dimensional space while preserving as much variance as possible in Figure 3.1. It does this by identifying new orthogonal axes, known as principal components, which capture the directions of maximum variance in the data. The first principal component accounts for the highest variance, followed by the second, and so on, with each subsequent component being uncorrelated with the previous ones. This transformation helps in simplifying complex datasets, improving computational efficiency, and reducing noise while retaining essential patterns. PCA is extensively used in various fields, including exploratory data analysis, image compression, and pattern recognition. In exploratory data analysis, PCA helps visualize high-dimensional data by projecting it into two or three principal components, making it easier to interpret. In image compression, it reduces data redundancy by keeping only the most significant components, thereby decreasing storage and processing requirements. Additionally, PCA is applied in pattern recognition tasks, such as facial recognition and medical diagnostics, where it enhances feature extraction by eliminating irrelevant variations, leading to better classification and clustering performance.

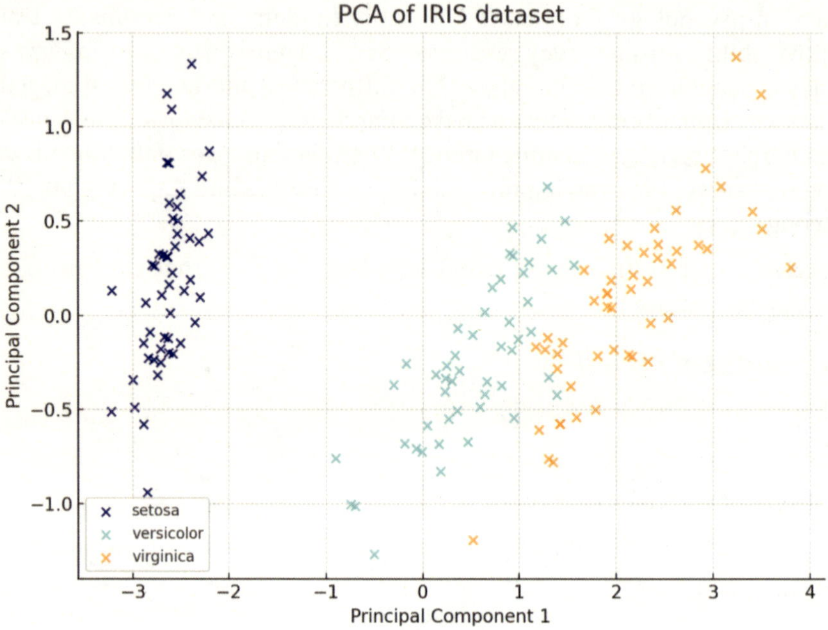

Figure 3.1: Graph on Principal Component Analysis (PCA).

Objective: Reduce the dimensionality of data while preserving as much variance as possible.

Mathematical Model:

X=WZ

Where:

X = Original data matrix

W = Projection matrix (eigenvectors of covariance matrix)

Z = Transformed data (principal components)

Components are uncorrelated (orthogonal).Each principal component captures maximum variance in the data. PCA does not assume an underlying data model. Based on eigenvalue decomposition (EVD) or singular value decomposition (SVD).

Independent Component Analysis (ICA)

Independent Component Analysis (ICA) is a computational method used to separate a set of mixed signals into their original, independent sources without prior knowledge of those sources. It assumes that the observed signals are linear mixtures of statistically independent components, making it particularly useful in Blind Source Separation (BSS) problems. ICA works by finding a transformation that maximizes the statistical independence of the components, often utilizing measures like non-Gaussianity. Unlike traditional methods such as Principal Component Analysis (PCA), which focuses on decorrelation and variance maximization, ICA extracts hidden factors that are statistically independent rather than merely uncorrelated. ICA has wide-ranging applications in fields such as neuroscience, audio processing, and finance. In EEG signal processing, ICA helps to isolate neural activity from artifacts like eye movements and muscle noise, enhancing the accuracy of brain signal interpretation. In audio processing, it is used to solve the "cocktail party problem," where multiple voices or sounds are separated from a mixed audio recording. Additionally, ICA finds applications in financial data analysis, where it helps to identify hidden factors influencing stock prices or market trends. Its ability to uncover independent sources from complex data makes it a powerful tool for diverse analytical challenges.

Objective: Separate mixed signals into their original independent sources.

Mathematical Model:

$X=AS$

Where:

X = Observed mixed signals

A = Mixing matrix

S = Source signals (independent components)

Focuses on statistical independence, unlike PCA which focuses on variance.Uses non-Gaussianity assumptions (e.g., kurtosis, negentropy) to separate sources. Unlike PCA, ICA does not require orthogonality of components.

Comparison FA, PCA and ICA

The key differences between Factor Analysis (FA), Principal Component Analysis (PCA), and Independent Component Analysis (ICA) in terms of their purpose, assumptions, outputs, and applications in Table 3.1. FA is used to identify latent factors that explain correlations among observed variables, making it popular in psychology and social sciences. PCA, on the other hand, focuses on dimensionality reduction by transforming data into uncorrelated principal components that capture the most variance, commonly used in data compression and visualization. ICA goes further by assuming statistical independence between components, making it useful for signal separation tasks like EEG analysis and audio processing. While FA models the covariance structure, PCA maximizes variance, and ICA extracts independent sources, making each method suitable for different analytical needs.

Table 3.1: Comparison between FA, PCA, and ICA.

Feature	Factor Analysis (FA)	Principal Component Analysis (PCA)	Independent Component Analysis (ICA)
Purpose	Find latent factors	Reduce dimensionality	Separate mixed signals
Assumptions	Latent variables explain correlations	Maximize variance	Sources are independent
Output	Factors (correlated)	Principal components (orthogonal)	Independent components
Method	Covariance structure analysis	Eigenvalue decomposition	Non-Gaussianity
Application	Psychology, social sciences	Data compression, visualization	Signal processing, finance

Latent Semantic Indexing (LSI)

Latent Semantic Indexing (LSI), also known as Latent Semantic Analysis (LSA), is a mathematical technique used in natural language processing (NLP) to analyze relationships between a set of documents and the terms they contain. It is based on the concept that words appearing in similar contexts tend to have similar meanings. LSI employs singular value decomposition (SVD) to reduce the dimensionality of a term-document matrix, allowing it to uncover hidden semantic structures and relationships that traditional keyword-based methods might miss. By capturing these latent patterns, LSI improves information retrieval, text classification, and topic modeling by identifying the underlying meaning of words rather than relying solely on exact keyword matches. One of the main advantages of LSI is its ability to address the problem of synonymy (different words with similar meanings) and polysemy (words with multiple meanings), making it particularly useful in search engines, document clustering, and automated summarization. For example, a search engine using LSI can retrieve relevant documents even if they do not contain the exact search terms but share a similar semantic context. However, LSI has limitations, such as high computational complexity and the need for a predefined number of latent topics. Despite these challenges, LSI remains a foundational approach in NLP and has inspired more advanced techniques like topic modeling with Latent Dirichlet Allocation (LDA) and word embeddings in deep learning.

LSI Works

Construct Term-Document Matrix – Rows represent words, columns represent documents.

Apply Singular Value Decomposition (SVD) – Decomposes the matrix into three matrices:

$$X = U\Sigma V^T$$

Where:

U represents word relationships.

Σ contains singular values (importance of components).

V represents document relationships.

Dimensionality Reduction: Keep only the top kk singular values to capture important semantics.

Key Features

- Identifies latent relationships between words and documents.
- Reduces noise in textual data.
- Addresses the problem of synonymy and polysemy.

Spectral Clustering

Spectral clustering is a powerful technique based on graph theory that clusters data points by leveraging eigenvalues of similarity matrices. Unlike traditional clustering methods such as K-means, which rely on distance-based metrics, spectral clustering transforms data into a new space where cluster structures become more evident. The process involves constructing a similarity graph, computing the graph Laplacian, and performing eigenvalue decomposition to find an optimal low-dimensional representation of the data. By applying clustering techniques, such as K-means, in this transformed space, spectral clustering can effectively detect complex and non-linearly separable clusters. It is particularly useful for problems involving irregularly shaped clusters or highly structured data. This approach is widely applied in areas like image segmentation, social network analysis, and bioinformatics, where relationships among data points play a crucial role. Its ability to capture global structures in data makes spectral clustering a valuable tool in machine learning and data science.

Spectral Clustering Works

Construct a Similarity Graph

Spectral clustering begins by representing the dataset as a similarity graph. Each data point is treated as a node, and edges between nodes represent the similarity between those points. The similarity can be determined using methods such as the Gaussian (RBF) kernel or k-nearest neighbors (k-NN). The weight of each edge reflects the degree of similarity between two points, with higher weights indicating stronger relationships. The goal of this step is to capture the structure of the dataset by encoding pairwise relationships. Depending on the problem, different types of graphs can be used, such as the fully connected graph, k-nearest neighbors' graph, or ε-neighborhood graph. This graphical representation helps reveal clusters based on connectivity rather than just distance, making spectral clustering particularly useful for non-convex and complex-shaped clusters. Once the similarity graph is constructed, the next step is to compute the Laplacian matrix, which encodes important structural properties of the graph.

Compute the Laplacian Matrix

The Laplacian matrix is a crucial mathematical representation of the similarity graph in spectral clustering. It is derived from the adjacency matrix (which contains edge weights) and the degree matrix (which contains the sum of edge weights for each node). The most commonly used Laplacian matrices include the unnormalized Laplacian, the normalized Laplacian, and the random walk Laplacian, each offering different advantages. The Laplacian matrix plays a vital role in capturing the connectivity structure of the graph, helping to distinguish clusters based on graph partitioning principles. Mathematically, the Laplacian matrix is computed as$L=D-A$, where D is the degree matrix and$A$ is the adjacency matrix. Normalization techniques, such as symmetric normalization, improve stability and performance. The eigenvalues and eigenvectors of the Laplacian matrix provide key insights into the graph structure, setting the stage for transforming the data into a new space for clustering.

Compute Eigenvectors

Once the Laplacian matrix is computed, its eigenvectors are used to transform the data into a lower-dimensional space where clustering becomes more effective. The eigenvectors of the Laplacian matrix provide a spectral decomposition of the graph, revealing hidden structures and cluster memberships. Typically, the smallest nonzero eigenvalues and their corresponding eigenvectors are selected to form a feature space. This transformation, known as spectral embedding, allows data points that belong to the same cluster to be mapped close to each other in the new space. The number of eigenvectors chosen corresponds to the desired number of clusters. These eigenvectors act as new feature representations of the original data, where the clustering structure is more pronounced. By reducing dimensionality while preserving cluster relationships, spectral embedding ensures that even non-linearly separable clusters can be identified. The next step involves applying a standard clustering algorithm, such as K-means, to the transformed data.

Apply K-means

After transforming the data using eigenvectors, a traditional clustering algorithm such as K-means is applied to identify clusters. The transformed data, now represented in a lower-dimensional space, exhibits clearer separability, making K-means an effective choice for final clustering. K-means operates by initializing cluster centroids and iteratively assigning points to the nearest centroid based on Euclidean distance. The centroids are updated until convergence is achieved, ensuring that data points within a cluster are more similar to each other than to points in other clusters. Since spectral clustering reduces the complexity of the original dataset and enhances the cluster structure, K-means can effectively group data points even in cases where direct application to the original space would fail. This final step yields the cluster assignments, completing the spectral clustering process. The resulting clusters often capture complex, non-convex structures that traditional clustering methods may struggle to identify.

When to Use Spectral Clustering

- When clusters have non-convex shapes.
- When the dataset has complex structures (e.g., "moons" or "circles").
- When traditional clustering methods fail to separate clusters effectively.

Markov Models

Markov models are mathematical frameworks used to represent systems that undergo transitions between different states based on certain probabilistic rules. The fundamental assumption behind Markov models is the Markov property, which states that the probability of transitioning to a future state depends only on the current state and not on the sequence of past states. This memoryless characteristic makes Markov models particularly useful in areas like finance, speech recognition, genetics, and artificial intelligence. These models are categorized into discrete-time and continuous-time versions, depending on whether transitions occur at fixed time intervals or continuously. A Markov model is typically represented using a state transition matrix, which outlines the probabilities of moving from one state to another. When probabilities remain constant over time, the model is said to be stationary. Applications of Markov models include predicting stock market trends, analyzing biological sequences, and natural language processing, where sequential patterns play a crucial role. The key concepts:

States

In a Markov process, a state represents a specific condition or status that the system can be in at any given moment. These states define the possible scenarios the system may transition between over time. For example, in a weather prediction model, states might be "sunny," "rainy," or "cloudy." In a board game, states could represent different positions of players on the board. The set of all possible states forms the state space, which can be finite or infinite. The behavior of the system is analyzed by examining how it moves from one state to another over time. States are crucial in defining the dynamics of the system, as they determine the probabilities associated with transitions. In a Markov chain, each state transition follows predefined probabilities, which help model various real-world processes like stock market fluctuations, disease spread, and queueing systems in customer service scenarios.

Transition Probabilities

Transition probabilities describe the likelihood of moving from one state to another in a stochastic system. In a Markov chain, each state has a set of probabilities associated with transitioning to other possible states. These probabilities are often represented in a transition matrix, where each row corresponds to a state and each column represents the probability of moving to another state. The sum of probabilities in each row must equal 1, ensuring that the system always moves to a new state. Transition probabilities can be deterministic (fixed rules) or stochastic (randomly assigned). They play a key role in predicting future states of the system. For example, in a weather model, if today's state is "rainy," the transition probability might indicate a 70% chance of remaining "rainy" and a 30% chance of transitioning to "sunny" the next day. These probabilities help in analyzing and forecasting sequential events in various domains.

Markov Property

The Markov Property is a fundamental principle stating that the future state of a system depends only on its present state and not on the sequence of past states. This property simplifies analysis by removing the need to track long histories, making computations more efficient.

Formally, ifS_t represents the system's state at time t, then the probability of the next stateS_{t+1} depends only onS_t:

$$P(S_{t+1}|S_t, S_{t-1}, ..., S_0) = P(S_{t+1}|S_t)$$

This memoryless property is useful in various applications, such as speech recognition, where the next phoneme depends only on the current one, or stock market analysis, where tomorrow's price is assumed to be influenced by today's price rather than a long historical trend. Systems that follow the Markov Property are easier to model and predict using Markov Chains, which serve as the basis for numerous stochastic and probabilistic models in science, engineering, and finance.

Types of Markov Models

Discrete-Time Markov Chains (DTMC)

Discrete-Time Markov Chains (DTMC) are stochastic models in which a system undergoes transitions between different states at fixed time intervals. The key characteristic of DTMCs is that the probability of transitioning from one state to another depends only on the current state and not on the sequence of states that preceded it, which is known as the Markov property. These models are represented by a state transition matrix, where each entry denotes the probability of moving from one state to another. DTMCs are widely used in various fields such as finance, queuing theory, genetics, and reliability analysis. They are particularly useful in modeling sequential decision-making problems, inventory control, and stochastic processes in natural and artificial systems. Common applications include predicting customer behavior, analyzing DNA sequences, and simulating the performance of computer networks. The mathematical foundation of DTMCs allows for efficient computation of long-term behaviors using steady-state probabilities and transient analysis.

Continuous-Time Markov Chains (CTMC)

Continuous-Time Markov Chains (CTMC) are an extension of discrete-time Markov chains, where state transitions occur at any arbitrary time rather than at fixed time steps. The system moves between states according to a set of continuous-time probabilities governed by an exponential distribution. These models are typically described using infinitesimal generators, which define the rate at which transitions between states occur. CTMCs are commonly used in applications requiring real-time modeling of systems, such as telecommunication networks, queuing systems, chemical reactions, and reliability engineering. Unlike DTMCs, where transitions are dictated by a predefined probability matrix, CTMCs rely on transition rates, making them suitable for dynamic and time-sensitive processes. These models help in studying complex systems where waiting times between state changes are of critical importance, such as predicting machine failures in industrial settings or analyzing population dynamics in ecological studies. Their mathematical formulation allows for solving differential equations to analyze system behavior.

Hidden Markov Models (HMMs)

Hidden Markov Models (HMMs) are a special type of Markov model where the system consists of hidden states that are not directly observable. Instead, each state generates observable outputs, and the sequence of observations provides indirect information about the underlying states. HMMs are characterized by three main components: a set of states, a transition probability matrix defining state changes, and an emission probability matrix that maps states to observations. These models are widely used in pattern recognition, speech processing, bioinformatics, and natural language processing. For example, in speech recognition, HMMs model spoken words as sequences of hidden phonetic states that produce observable sound waves. Similarly, in bioinformatics, they help analyze gene sequences by predicting hidden biological structures. HMMs use algorithms like the Viterbi algorithm for state estimation and the Baum-Welch algorithm for learning parameters. Their probabilistic framework allows for efficient handling of noisy or incomplete data.

Components of an HMM

Hidden States

Hidden states in a Hidden Markov Model (HMM) represent the underlying conditions of a system that are not directly observable. These states define the actual process driving the observed data, but their true values remain unknown. Instead, they can only be inferred based on observations. The number and nature of hidden states depend on the application of the HMM. For instance, in speech recognition, the hidden states could represent different phonemes spoken by a speaker, while in biological sequence analysis, they may correspond to different genetic patterns. Since these states cannot be measured directly, algorithms such as the Viterbi algorithm or Expectation-Maximization (EM) are used to estimate their most probable sequences. Understanding hidden states is crucial in modeling complex processes where direct measurement is either impossible or impractical. The accuracy of an HMM heavily depends on how well the hidden states represent the real-world system being analyzed.

Observations

Observations in an HMM refer to the visible outputs that are influenced by the hidden states. Since the true states of the system cannot be directly measured, observations serve as the only available data points for analysis. Each observation is generated based on a probability distribution linked to a hidden state. In practical applications, observations could be words in a speech recognition system, sensor readings in an IoT network, or even stock market fluctuations. The key challenge in HMMs is deciphering the hidden states from these observations. Statistical and machine learning techniques, such as the Forward-Backward algorithm, are commonly used to determine the likelihood of an observation sequence given a model. The quality of an HMM largely depends on how well the observations correlate with the hidden states, as inaccurate or noisy observations can make it difficult to infer the underlying process correctly.

Transition Probabilities

Transition probabilities in an HMM define the likelihood of moving from one hidden state to another. These probabilities are represented as a transition matrix, where each entry specifies the probability of transitioning from state $Si$to state Sj. The sum of probabilities in each row of this matrix must equal one, ensuring that the model follows a valid probability distribution. Transition probabilities capture the temporal dependencies between hidden states, making them a critical component in sequence modeling. For instance, in speech recognition, transition probabilities determine how likely one phoneme follows another. Similarly, in weather forecasting, they describe how probable it is for a sunny day to be followed by a rainy day. Training an HMM involves estimating these probabilities from historical data using algorithms like the Baum-Welch algorithm. Accurate transition probabilities are essential for making reliable predictions about future states in a given sequence.

Emission Probabilities

Emission probabilities in an HMM describe the likelihood of an observed output being generated by a particular hidden state. Each hidden state is associated with a probability distribution over possible observations, which forms the emission probability matrix. This matrix defines how observations are linked to the hidden states. In a speech recognition system, for example, a hidden state representing a specific phoneme may have different probabilities of producing various acoustic signals. In financial models, hidden states representing market trends may emit stock price fluctuations with certain probabilities. Estimating emission probabilities accurately is crucial for ensuring the HMM correctly associates observations with hidden states. These probabilities are typically learned from training data using statistical estimation methods like the Maximum Likelihood Estimation (MLE) or Expectation-Maximization (EM) algorithm. Poorly estimated emission probabilities can lead to incorrect inferences about hidden states, affecting the model's overall performance.

Initial Probabilities

Initial probabilities in an HMM define the likelihood of starting in each hidden state before any observations are made. These probabilities are represented as a vector where each entry indicates the probability of the system being in a specific state at time t=0. The sum of all initial probabilities must equal one, ensuring a valid probability distribution. Setting accurate initial probabilities is crucial because they influence the overall behavior of the HMM. In some cases, these probabilities are predefined based on domain knowledge, while in others, they are estimated from training data. For example, in weather forecasting, an initial probability distribution might favor certain weather conditions based on seasonal patterns. If initial probabilities are chosen incorrectly, they can skew the entire inference process, leading to suboptimal performance. Techniques like Maximum Likelihood Estimation (MLE) or Expectation-Maximization (EM) help refine these probabilities based on observed sequences.

Algorithms for HMMs

Forward Algorithm

The Forward Algorithm is a dynamic programming method used in Hidden Markov Models (HMMs) to compute the probability of an observed sequence given a model. It helps in determining how likely a particular sequence of observations is, considering different hidden state sequences. The algorithm proceeds recursively by computing probabilities for partial sequences and accumulating these values to calculate the total probability efficiently. This method significantly reduces the computational complexity compared to a brute-force approach that evaluates all possible state sequences. The algorithm involves three main steps:

- Initialization – Assign initial probabilities to each state based on given prior probabilities and the first observation.
- Recursion – Use the transition and emission probabilities to iteratively compute the likelihood of observing the sequence up to each time step.
- Termination – Sum up the probabilities of ending in any state to determine the overall probability of the given sequence.

This algorithm is crucial for applications like speech recognition, bioinformatics, and natural language processing.

Viterbi Algorithm

The Viterbi Algorithm is a dynamic programming approach used in HMMs to find the most probable sequence of hidden states that could have generated a given sequence of observations. Unlike the Forward Algorithm, which computes the total probability of an observation sequence, the Viterbi Algorithm focuses on identifying the single most likely path (also called the Viterbi path) through the state space. It works through three key steps:

- Initialization – Set initial probabilities based on the start probabilities and emission probabilities of the first observation.
- Recursion – Iteratively compute the maximum probability for each state at each time step using transition probabilities and previously computed values.
- Backtracking – Trace back through stored pointers to reconstruct the most probable sequence of hidden states.

This algorithm is widely used in fields like speech recognition, gene sequence analysis, and machine translation, where identifying the most probable underlying state sequence is critical.

Baum-Welch Algorithm

The Baum-Welch Algorithm is an expectation-maximization (EM) algorithm used in HMMs to estimate unknown parameters such as transition probabilities and emission probabilities. When working with an HMM without fully known parameters, the Baum-Welch Algorithm iteratively refines these parameters to maximize the likelihood of observed data. The process consists of two major steps:

- Expectation Step (E-Step) – Compute the expected values of state transition and emission counts using current parameter estimates. This is done using the Forward-Backward Algorithm to determine the probability distribution over hidden states given the observations.

- Maximization Step (M-Step) – Update transition and emission probabilities based on the expected counts computed in the E-step.

By iterating these steps, the algorithm converges to an optimal set of parameters that best explains the given observation sequence. It is extensively used in training HMMs for applications such as speech recognition, gene prediction, and handwriting analysis.

Algorithms for HMMs

Speech Recognition

Hidden Markov Models (HMMs) play a crucial role in speech recognition systems like Siri and Google Assistant. Speech is a sequential signal with temporal dependencies, making it ideal for HMM-based modeling. In these systems, HMMs analyze audio waveforms and convert them into text by recognizing phonemes (basic sound units). Each phoneme is represented as a hidden state, while the observed signal is the acoustic feature extracted from speech. HMMs model the probability transitions between phonemes, helping the system predict the most likely sequence of words spoken by the user. By integrating machine learning and deep learning techniques, modern voice assistants refine their predictions, improving accuracy. HMMs also help handle background noise, speaker variations, and different accents, making them a fundamental component of automatic speech recognition (ASR). Their ability to handle sequential data and probabilistic state transitions makes them highly effective in improving real-time voice-driven AI interactions.

Part-of-Speech Tagging in NLP

Hidden Markov Models (HMMs) are widely used in Natural Language Processing (NLP) for part-of-speech (POS) tagging, which assigns grammatical labels (e.g., noun, verb, adjective) to words in a sentence. Since language follows a sequential pattern, HMMs effectively model the probabilistic relationships between words and their respective tags. The hidden states in this model represent POS tags, while the observed variables are the words in a given text. Using a trained HMM, the most probable sequence of tags is determined based on a corpus of labeled text. For example, in the sentence “She runs fast,” HMMs help predict that "She" is a pronoun, "runs" is a verb, and "fast" is an adverb. POS tagging is essential for various NLP applications, including machine translation, sentiment analysis, and syntactic parsing. Though modern deep learning models like LSTMs and transformers outperform HMMs in complex NLP tasks, they remain a foundational technique in linguistic modeling.

Stock Market Prediction

Hidden Markov Models (HMMs) are applied in stock market prediction by modeling the hidden factors influencing stock prices. Financial markets are inherently stochastic and influenced by numerous unpredictable elements, including investor sentiment, economic trends, and geopolitical events. HMMs help identify underlying market states, such as bull (rising) or bear (falling) conditions, which are not directly observable but inferred from stock price movements. The observed states in the model include historical stock prices, trading volumes, and volatility measures. By estimating transition probabilities between different market phases, HMMs assist traders in making data-driven investment decisions. For example, if the model detects a high probability of transitioning from a stable to a volatile state, investors may adjust their strategies accordingly. While HMMs provide valuable insights, their effectiveness depends on high-quality data and external market influences. Advanced models, such as deep learning and reinforcement learning, are now integrated with HMMs for improved accuracy.

Bioinformatics

In bioinformatics, Hidden Markov Models (HMMs) are widely used for DNA sequence analysis, particularly in gene prediction and protein structure modeling. Since biological sequences exhibit inherent patterns and dependencies, HMMs are effective in identifying motifs, coding regions, and evolutionary relationships between genes. The hidden states in this context represent biological elements like exons (coding regions) and introns (non-coding regions), while the observed sequences are nucleotide bases (A, T, C, G). HMMs analyze the likelihood of certain sequences occurring within a genome, assisting researchers in identifying functional genes. For example, HMM-based tools like HMMER help in sequence alignment and detecting homologous proteins. Additionally, HMMs contribute to RNA structure prediction and evolutionary phylogenetics. Their ability to handle noisy biological data and infer hidden patterns makes them invaluable in genomic research. Although deep learning has enhanced bioinformatics, HMMs remain a fundamental approach for understanding complex biological sequences.

Summary

Unsupervised learning plays a crucial role in discovering patterns and structures in data without requiring labeled examples. Among its various techniques, clustering methods like K-means and the Expectation-Maximization (EM) algorithm are widely used for partitioning data into meaningful groups. The Mixture of Gaussians approach extends clustering by modeling data distributions probabilistically. Dimensionality reduction techniques such as Principal Component Analysis (PCA) and Independent Component Analysis (ICA) help uncover underlying structures, reduce computational complexity, and improve visualization. Factor analysis is another technique used to identify latent variables influencing observed data. Latent Semantic Indexing (LSI) is particularly useful in text analysis, helping extract meaningful concepts from large corpora. More advanced clustering methods like Spectral Clustering leverage graph-based approaches to identify complex structures in data. Probabilistic models such as Hidden Markov Models (HMMs) and Markov Models are powerful tools for modeling sequential data, with applications in speech recognition, bioinformatics, and financial forecasting. Overall, these unsupervised learning techniques provide essential frameworks for data exploration, knowledge discovery, and feature extraction. They have broad applications across various domains, including natural language processing, computer vision, and bioinformatics, making them indispensable for modern data science and artificial intelligence.

Exercise Questions

- What is the primary objective of clustering in unsupervised learning?
- How does the K-means algorithm determine the optimal cluster centers?
- What is the key difference between the Expectation-Maximization (EM) algorithm and K-means?
- How does the Mixture of Gaussians model differ from K-means clustering?
- What is the main purpose of Principal Component Analysis (PCA) in data processing?
- How does Independent Component Analysis (ICA) differ from PCA?
- What is Latent Semantic Indexing (LSI) used for in machine learning?
- What role does the adjacency matrix play in Spectral Clustering?
- What is the significance of Hidden Markov Models (HMMs) in sequence analysis?
- How does Factor Analysis help in reducing dimensionality in datasets?

4

REINFORCEMENT LEARNING AND OPTIMAL CONTROL

Reinforcement Learning (RL) and Optimal Control are two closely related fields in artificial intelligence and control systems, focusing on decision-making in dynamic environments. Reinforcement Learning is a machine learning paradigm where an agent learns to perform actions in an environment to maximize cumulative rewards. It is inspired by behavioral psychology, mimicking how humans and animals learn from interactions with their surroundings. Optimal Control, on the other hand, is a mathematical framework used in control theory to determine the best possible control strategy for a given system, minimizing a cost function over time. The core difference between RL and Optimal Control lies in their formulation and approach. While Optimal Control typically assumes complete knowledge of system dynamics and uses mathematical models to compute optimal strategies, RL often deals with uncertain or unknown environments and learns optimal policies through trial and error. RL employs techniques such as Markov Decision Processes (MDPs), dynamic programming, and function approximation to handle complex decision-making problems. Optimal Control relies on calculus of variations, Pontryagin's Maximum Principle, and Hamilton-Jacobi-Bellman equations to derive optimal solutions.

One of the major advantages of RL is its applicability in real-world scenarios where system dynamics are not explicitly known. It has been successfully applied in robotics, autonomous systems, game playing (such as AlphaGo and Deep Q-Networks in video games), healthcare, and finance. Optimal Control, on the other hand, has been widely used in engineering applications, including aerospace, electrical circuits, and economic modeling, where precise mathematical models can be constructed. The intersection of both fields has led to the development of Approximate Dynamic Programming (ADP) and Model-Based RL, which leverage insights from both disciplines to tackle complex optimization problems. The fundamental components of RL include the agent, environment, states, actions, rewards, and policy. The agent interacts with the environment, observes states, takes actions, and receives rewards as feedback. The goal is to learn an optimal policy that maximizes long-term rewards. Different RL algorithms, such as Q-learning, Policy Gradient Methods, and Actor-Critic Methods, have been developed to efficiently train agents for various tasks. Optimal Control problems, on the other hand, often involve Bellman's Principle of Optimality, which states that an optimal policy must be optimal for every subproblem of the decision process. One of the main challenges in RL is the trade-off between exploration and exploitation. The agent must explore new actions to discover better strategies while also exploiting known strategies to maximize rewards. Similarly, in Optimal Control, challenges arise in handling high-dimensional state spaces, real-time computations, and constraints on control inputs. Advances in deep learning have significantly boosted RL's capabilities, leading to Deep Reinforcement Learning (DRL), which integrates deep neural networks for function approximation, making it feasible to solve highly complex control problems. As research progresses, RL and Optimal Control continue to converge, with hybrid approaches emerging in domains such as robotics, self-driving cars, and energy management. The integration of model-based techniques in RL and learning-based approaches in Optimal Control is leading to more robust and efficient decision-making frameworks. The future of these fields lies in developing scalable, data-efficient, and safe learning algorithms that can operate in diverse and uncertain environments, paving the way for intelligent autonomous systems.

Reinforcement Learning and Control

Reinforcement Learning (RL) and Control Theory are closely related fields focusing on decision-making and system control. In RL, an agent learns by interacting with an environment, taking actions, and receiving feedback in the form of rewards or penalties. The aim is to discover an optimal policy that maximizes cumulative rewards over time, often using algorithms such as Q-learning, Deep Q-Networks, or Policy Gradient methods. In Control Theory, the focus is on designing controllers to regulate dynamic systems to achieve desired outcomes, often under uncertainty or disturbances. Both fields are concerned with optimizing behavior, but RL is more data-driven, relying on learning from experience, while control theory often involves analytical models and feedback mechanisms. These techniques have vast applications, including robotics, autonomous vehicles, and economics, where systems must adapt and respond to changing conditions in real-time, ensuring efficient decision-making and system stability. The key concepts in:

Agent

An agent is the core entity in reinforcement learning (RL) responsible for making decisions within an environment. It interacts with the environment by taking actions based on its observations and receives rewards as feedback for its choices. The agent's goal is to learn an optimal strategy that maximizes long-term rewards. This learning process can be based on trial and error, where the agent continuously refines its decision-making process over time. The agent can be a software program, a robotic system, or even a financial trading model, depending on the application. In RL, the agent improves its behavior by adjusting its policy—a set of rules that determine how actions are chosen in various states. The quality of an agent's decision-making depends on how well it balances exploration (trying new actions) and exploitation (choosing the best-known action). Ultimately, an intelligent agent learns to navigate complex environments efficiently to achieve a defined objective.

Environment

The environment in reinforcement learning (RL) refers to the external system or world with which the agent interacts. It provides the context in which the agent operates, presenting different states and responding to the agent's actions with new states and rewards. The environment defines the rules, constraints, and dynamics that shape the agent's learning process. It can be anything from a simulated game world to a real-world setting like a robotic workspace or financial market. The agent perceives the environment through observations and must learn how to navigate it effectively. The environment's complexity significantly impacts the difficulty of the learning task—deterministic environments are more predictable, while stochastic environments introduce uncertainty. In RL, the environment plays a crucial role in defining the reward function, which guides the agent's behavior. Understanding the environment is essential for designing effective RL models, as different environments require different approaches to training and optimization.

State (s)

A state in reinforcement learning (RL) represents the current situation or configuration of the environment at a given moment. It provides the agent with the necessary information to decide which action to take next. The state can be fully observable, meaning the agent has complete knowledge of the environment, or partially observable, where only limited information is available. In many RL applications, states are represented as numerical vectors or complex structures like images in deep learning-based RL models. The way states are defined significantly impacts the agent's learning process—poorly defined states may lead to suboptimal learning, while well-structured states can speed up convergence to an optimal policy. The agent's goal is to learn a mapping from states to actions that maximize cumulative rewards over time. Accurately modeling states is crucial, as it determines how well an agent understands and interacts with its environment.

Action (a)

An action in reinforcement learning (RL) is a decision or move the agent makes in response to its current state. Actions directly influence the environment, leading to changes in state and affecting the rewards received. The set of all possible actions an agent can take is known as the action space, which can be discrete (a limited number of choices, like moving left or right) or continuous (a range of possible values, like adjusting speed). Selecting the right actions is critical for achieving the agent's goal of maximizing long-term rewards. The agent learns an optimal policy that dictates which action to take in each state through trial and error. The effectiveness of an action depends on the specific task and environment—some actions may yield immediate rewards, while others contribute to delayed but greater rewards. Over time, the agent refines its action-selection strategy to improve performance and decision-making.

Reward (r)

A reward in reinforcement learning (RL) is a scalar value received by the agent after taking an action in a given state. It serves as feedback indicating how good or bad the action was in achieving the overall objective. Rewards can be positive (encouraging beneficial actions) or negative (discouraging poor choices). The agent's primary goal is to maximize cumulative rewards over time, which drives its learning process. The reward function, defined by the environment, determines how rewards are assigned. A well-designed reward function ensures the agent learns desirable behaviors efficiently, while poorly defined rewards can lead to unintended or suboptimal strategies. Rewards can be immediate or delayed—some environments require long-term planning, where short-term sacrifices lead to higher long-term rewards. Through repeated interactions, the agent adjusts its actions to maximize the expected reward, gradually improving its decision-making and policy effectiveness in achieving the task's objective.

Policy (π)

A policy in reinforcement learning (RL) is a mapping from states to actions that defines the agent's strategy for decision-making. It determines which action the agent takes in a given state based on its learned experiences. Policies can be deterministic (always choosing the same action in a given state) or stochastic (assigning probabilities to different actions). The goal of RL is to learn an optimal policy that maximizes long-term rewards. Policies are continuously updated as the agent gains more experience, either through direct updates in policy-based methods or by deriving them from value functions in value-based methods. The effectiveness of a policy depends on how well it balances exploration (trying new actions) and exploitation (choosing the best-known action). In practical applications, policies can be represented as lookup tables, neural networks, or mathematical functions, making them adaptable to various problem domains, from robotics to game playing.

Value Function (V)

A value function in reinforcement learning (RL) estimates the expected cumulative reward an agent can obtain from a given state while following a specific policy. It helps the agent evaluate which states are desirable based on future rewards rather than just immediate rewards. The value function is crucial for learning an optimal policy, as it guides decision-making by prioritizing states that lead to higher long-term rewards. There are two main types of value functions: the state-value function (V) and the action-value function (Q). The state-value function (V) measures the expected return from a state, assuming the agent follows a particular policy thereafter. It is updated iteratively using algorithms like dynamic programming or temporal difference learning. A well-learned value function helps the agent generalize its knowledge across different situations, improving its efficiency in navigating complex environments. The accuracy of the value function directly impacts the performance of an RL model.

Table 4.1: Comparing Exploration vs. Exploitation in the context of reinforcement learning.

Feature	Exploration	Exploitation
Definition	Trying new actions to discover potentially better strategies.	Selecting actions that have yielded the highest rewards so far.
Objective	Gather new knowledge about the environment.	Maximize immediate rewards based on known information.
Risk	Higher risk due to uncertainty.	Lower risk but may lead to suboptimal long-term results.
Learning Impact	Helps find the global optimum by avoiding local optima.	Can lead to faster convergence but may get stuck in local optima.
Time Horizon	Beneficial in the early stages of learning.	More useful in the later stages when enough data is collected.
Strategy Examples	Epsilon-greedy (choosing a random action with probability ε), Upper Confidence Bound (UCB), Thompson Sampling.	Greedy policy (always choosing the best-known action).
Real-World Applications	Drug discovery, robotics (learning new movement strategies), A/B testing.	Automated trading, chess engines, recommendation systems (optimizing known preferences).

Q-Function (Q)

A Q-function in reinforcement learning (RL) estimates the expected cumulative reward for taking a specific action in a given state and then following a policy. Unlike the value function, which only evaluates states, the Q-function evaluates state-action pairs, making it a crucial component of action selection. The Q-function is denoted as Q(s, a), where it provides a numerical estimate of the long-term benefit of choosing action a in state s. This function is fundamental to Q-learning, a popular RL algorithm that iteratively updates Q-values based on observed rewards. The agent uses the Q-function to select actions by choosing the one with the highest Q-value in a given state. Neural networks can approximate Q-functions in deep RL, enabling agents to handle complex environments. The effectiveness of an RL agent depends significantly on how well it learns the Q-function, as it directly influences decision-making and policy optimization.

Exploration vs. Exploitation

Exploration vs. exploitation is a fundamental trade-off in reinforcement learning (RL) that defines how an agent balances trying new actions (exploration) versus choosing the best-known action (exploitation) in Table 4.1. Exploration involves selecting actions that may not have been tried before, allowing the agent to discover potentially better strategies. Exploitation, on the other hand, involves selecting the action that currently appears to yield the highest reward based on past experience. Striking the right balance between these two is crucial for effective learning too much exploration can slow down convergence, while excessive exploitation may cause the agent to settle on suboptimal strategies. Various strategies, such as epsilon-greedy methods, Upper Confidence Bound (UCB), and Thompson sampling, help manage this balance. In real-world applications, this trade-off is critical in domains like robotics, gaming, and financial decision-making, where optimal performance depends on both learning new strategies and refining existing ones based on accumulated knowledge.

RL Algorithms

Model-Free vs. Model-Based Reinforcement Learning

Reinforcement Learning (RL) algorithms are categorized into Model-Free and Model-Based approaches in Table 4.2. Model-Free RL does not rely on a model of the environment, meaning the agent learns optimal behavior by interacting directly with the environment without predicting future states. Algorithms like Q-learning and SARSA belong to this category, where the agent updates its policy based solely on experience. These methods are often simpler to implement but require extensive exploration to learn effectively. On the other hand, Model-Based RL assumes that the agent has a model of the environment, enabling it to predict future states and rewards before taking an action. This allows for more efficient learning, as the agent can plan its actions based on estimated transitions. Model-based methods are particularly useful in real-world applications where trial-and-error learning is costly or impractical. However, their performance depends on the accuracy of the learned model, making them challenging to implement in complex environments.

Value-Based Methods in Reinforcement Learning

Value-based reinforcement learning methods focus on learning a value function, which estimates the long-term reward an agent can achieve from a given state. The agent uses this function to determine the optimal policy indirectly. The most well-known value-based methods include Q-learning and Deep Q-Networks

(DQN).Q-learning is an off-policy algorithm that learns an action-value function (Q-function) mapping states and actions to expected rewards. The agent updates the Q-values iteratively using the Bellman equation. A key advantage of Q-learning is that it converges to an optimal policy even if actions are chosen sub optimally during training.

Deep Q-Networks (DQN) extend Q-learning by using deep neural networks to approximate the Q-function. This is especially useful in environments with large or continuous state spaces, such as video games. However, DQN requires techniques like experience replay and target networks to stabilize training and prevent divergence.

Table 4.2: Comparative Model-Free vs. Model-Based Reinforcement Learning.

Aspect	Model-Free Reinforcement Learning	Model-Based Reinforcement Learning
Environment Model	No model of the environment is used	Requires or learns a model of the environment
Learning Approach	Learns directly from interactions and rewards	Learns by simulating/ predicting future states and rewards
Examples of Algorithms	Q-learning, SARSA, Policy Gradient	Dyna-Q, Model Predictive Control, MuZero
Exploration Needs	High – relies heavily on trial-and-error	Lower – can plan actions, reducing the need for exploration
Sample Efficiency	Less efficient – needs more data	More efficient – learns faster with fewer interactions
Implementation Complexity	Simpler to implement	More complex due to model learning and planning
Planning Capability	No planning – reactive only	Supports planning using the model
Performance Dependence	Depends on exploration strategy	Depends on the accuracy of the model
Best Suited For	Simulated or low-cost environments	Real-world or high-cost environments
Challenges	Slow learning, high data requirements	Model inaccuracies can lead to suboptimal decisions

Policy-Based Methods in Reinforcement Learning

Unlike value-based methods, policy-based reinforcement learning focuses on learning a policy directly rather than estimating value functions. A policy defines the probability distribution over actions given a state. These methods are particularly useful in environments with continuous action spaces where value-based approaches struggle. One of the most fundamental policy-based algorithms is REINFORCE, a Monte Carlo policy gradient method. It updates the policy parameters in the direction of higher expected rewards, using gradient ascent. By optimizing the policy directly, REINFORCE can handle stochastic policies and continuous action spaces effectively. However, it suffers from high variance, which can slow down learning.

Policy-based methods offer advantages such as better convergence properties and stability in high-dimensional action spaces. They are commonly used in robotics and complex decision-making tasks. Despite their strengths, they often require techniques like baseline subtraction to reduce variance and improve learning efficiency.

Actor-Critic Methods in Reinforcement Learning

Actor-Critic methods combine the best of both value-based and policy-based approaches by maintaining two components: an actor and a critic. The actor is responsible for selecting actions based on a learned policy, while the critic evaluates the chosen actions by estimating the value function. This architecture helps reduce the variance of policy gradient methods while improving learning efficiency. One popular actor-critic algorithm is A3C (Asynchronous Advantage Actor-Critic), which updates multiple agents asynchronously to enhance learning stability. Another widely used method is PPO (Proximal Policy Optimization), which improves training efficiency by ensuring smoother policy updates through clipped objective functions. Actor-critic methods are highly effective in continuous action spaces and complex environments where pure value-based or policy-based approaches struggle. They are extensively used in robotics, autonomous systems, and game playing, where adaptive and stable learning is crucial. Despite their advantages, these methods require careful tuning of hyperparameters and balancing between actor and critic updates.

Deep Reinforcement Learning (DRL)

Deep Reinforcement Learning (DRL) is the combination of deep learning and reinforcement learning, where deep neural networks are used to approximate value functions, policies, or models of the environment. This enables RL to handle high-dimensional state spaces, such as raw pixel inputs in video games or sensor data in robotics. A breakthrough in DRL was Deep Q-Networks (DQN), which applied deep learning to Q-learning, allowing agents to learn directly from visual inputs. Techniques like experience replay (storing and reusing past experiences) and target networks (stabilizing Q-value updates) were introduced to improve learning efficiency. Other DRL algorithms, such as Actor-Critic models (A3C, PPO) and Policy Gradient methods, leverage deep neural networks to optimize learning in complex environments. DRL has achieved significant success in tasks like robotic control, autonomous driving, and playing games like Go and Dota 2. However, it requires extensive computational resources and fine-tuning to achieve optimal performance.

Control Theory

Control Theory is a branch of engineering and mathematics that deals with the behavior of dynamical systems. It involves designing control systems that will cause a system to behave in a desired way. Key concepts in control theory:

- **System:** Any physical or abstract process that can be modeled and controlled (e.g., robotic arms, temperature regulation).
- **Control Input (u):** The input signal used to control the system, such as forces or torques in mechanical systems.
- **State (x):** The configuration of the system that is described by a set of variables.
- **Output (y):** The measurable response of the system.
- **Control Objective:** The goal is typically to drive the system's output to a desired value or set of values while satisfying certain performance criteria.

Control Strategies

Proportional-Integral-Derivative (PID) Control: A widely-used control strategy where the control action is a weighted sum of the proportional, integral, and derivative terms of the error signal.

- **Proportional:** Reacts to the current error.
- **Integral:** Reacts to the accumulation of past errors.
- **Derivative:** Reacts to the rate of change of the error.

State-Space Control

State-space control is a mathematical framework used to describe and control dynamic systems using state variables. Instead of using input-output relationships like classical control methods, it represents the system's internal state using differential or difference equations. The system's evolution over time is determined by a set of first-order equations, where control inputs directly influence the state. This approach is particularly useful for complex, nonlinear, and high-dimensional systems, where traditional methods become cumbersome. State-space representation is widely used in modern control theory because it allows for systematic design, analysis, and optimization of controllers. It provides a structured way to handle multiple-input and multiple-output (MIMO) systems efficiently. Furthermore, techniques like state feedback, pole placement, and observer design (such as the Kalman filter) are used to enhance control performance. Applications include robotics, aerospace systems, and automated industrial processes where precise state estimation and control are essential for achieving stability and optimal performance.

Optimal Control

Optimal control focuses on determining the best possible control inputs to achieve a specific goal while minimizing a given cost function. This cost function can represent factors like energy consumption, tracking error, or time taken to reach a desired state. The central idea is to optimize the system's performance over a given time horizon by adjusting control variables. One of the most common formulations of optimal control is the Linear Quadratic Regulator (LQR), which minimizes a quadratic cost function consisting of state deviations and control effort. LQR ensures a trade-off between performance and control effort, making it widely used in engineering applications. Other methods like the Pontryagin's Maximum Principle and Hamilton-Jacobi-Bellman equations are used for solving more complex optimal control problems. Applications range from autonomous vehicles and robotics to industrial automation and aerospace systems, where efficient and precise control is crucial for performance and cost-effectiveness.

Model Predictive Control (MPC)

Model Predictive Control (MPC) is an advanced control strategy that predicts the future behavior of a system and optimizes control inputs accordingly. It works by solving an optimization problem over a finite prediction horizon, using a model of the system to anticipate its response to different control actions. MPC is particularly effective for handling constraints on control inputs and state variables, making it suitable for complex and multi-variable control systems. Unlike traditional controllers that react to changes, MPC proactively adjusts control inputs by continuously updating predictions based on real-time data. This makes it highly effective in applications where safety, efficiency, and adaptability are critical, such as industrial process control, autonomous vehicles, and energy systems. Despite its advantages, MPC requires significant computational resources, which can be a limitation for real-time applications with high-speed dynamics. However, advancements in computing power and algorithms have made MPC increasingly viable for various engineering fields.

Robust Control

Robust control is designed to maintain stability and performance in the presence of uncertainties, disturbances, and model inaccuracies. Traditional control methods assume a perfectly known system model, but real-world systems often have unpredictable variations due to external disturbances or modeling errors. Robust control techniques aim to ensure reliable operation even under these uncertainties. Common approaches include H-infinity control, which optimizes the worst-case performance, and sliding mode control, which forces the system to follow a desired trajectory despite uncertainties. Robust control is widely used in aerospace, automotive, and industrial automation, where external disturbances and modeling inaccuracies are common. It ensures that the system remains stable and performs as expected despite unknown variations. Although robust control can be more complex to design compared to classical control methods, its ability to handle uncertainty makes it a crucial tool in engineering applications where reliability and safety are paramount.

Connection Between Reinforcement Learning and Control Theory

Dynamic Programming (DP)

Both reinforcement learning (RL) and control theory are deeply rooted in the principles of dynamic programming (DP). In control theory, optimal control problems often rely on solving the Bellman equation, which is central to DP. The Bellman equation helps in breaking down complex decision-making problems into smaller, manageable subproblems, ensuring computational efficiency. Similarly, in RL, the Bellman equation is used to estimate value functions that guide an agent's decision-making process. Methods such as value iteration and policy iteration in RL are analogous to dynamic programming techniques in control theory. While control theory typically deals with known system models, RL extends these principles to situations where the system model is unknown or partially known. This connection highlights the fundamental overlap between both fields in terms of sequential decision-making and optimization, where dynamic programming serves as the backbone for computing optimal policies and value functions efficiently.

Model Predictive Control (MPC) and RL

Model predictive control (MPC) and reinforcement learning (RL) share a fundamental connection in how they predict and optimize actions based on future outcomes. MPC is a control strategy where a model of the system is used to predict future states and determine an optimal control input at each step. Similarly, in model-based RL, an agent learns a model of the environment to predict future states and rewards, helping it makes informed decisions. The key similarity between MPC and model-based RL is the use of a forward model to plan and optimize actions over a horizon. However, RL can operate without an explicit system model (model-free RL), whereas MPC requires a known or learned model. Additionally, while MPC typically works with deterministic control inputs, RL handles stochastic environments, making it more flexible. This shared predictive approach underscores how RL can benefit from MPC strategies, particularly in applications requiring real-time decision-making.

Optimality

Optimal control in control theory and reinforcement learning (RL) shares the common objective of determining the best possible policy or strategy for decision-making. In control theory, techniques such as Linear Quadratic Regulator (LQR) and Model Predictive Control (MPC) are used to compute an optimal control law that minimizes a cost function. Similarly, in RL, the agent learns an optimal policy by maximizing the cumulative reward over time. Both fields employ optimization techniques like dynamic programming, gradient-based methods, and function approximation to improve decision-making. The difference lies in their application: control theory usually assumes a known system model, while RL can work with unknown or partially known environments. Additionally, RL algorithms like Q-learning and policy gradient methods iteratively refine the policy through trial and error, whereas control theory typically relies on analytical solutions. Despite these differences, both disciplines aim to achieve optimal performance in dynamic, complex systems.

Adaptive Control

Adaptive control and reinforcement learning (RL) both involve continuous adjustment of policies based on real-time feedback. In adaptive control, the controller dynamically updates its parameters to maintain system performance despite uncertainties or changes in the environment. Similarly, in RL, an agent continuously refines its policy based on the rewards received from interactions with the environment. This adaptive nature makes RL particularly effective in situations where system dynamics are unknown or non-stationary. Methods like Q-learning and actor-critic models can be viewed as adaptive control techniques, as they adjust their decision-making strategies based on learned experiences. Additionally, in adaptive control, parameter estimation techniques like recursive least squares are used to update system models, akin to how RL employs function approximators like neural networks. This parallel between adaptive control and RL showcases how both fields leverage feedback loops to improve decision-making, making RL a powerful tool for adaptive decision-making in complex environments.

Markov Decision Process (MDP)

An MDP is a mathematical model used to describe decision-making in situations where the outcome is partially random and partially under the control of an agent. It provides a framework for modeling environments where the state of the system evolves over time due to both the actions of an agent and random effects. MDPs are used to formalize decision problems in both reinforcement learning (RL) and control theory.

Components of an MDP:

An MDP is formally defined by the tuple:

- States (S): A set of possible states that the system can be in. States represent all the possible configurations of the system at any point in time.
- Actions (A): A set of actions that the agent can take. At each state, the agent chooses an action to transition to another state.
- Transition function (P): This describes the probability of transitioning from one state to another after taking an action. It's typically represented as P(s′|s,a), which is the probability of moving from state s to state s′ when action a is taken.
- Reward function (R): This gives a numerical reward for each transition. It is a function R(s,a,s′) that provides the immediate reward received when action a is taken in state sss, resulting in a new state s′.
- Discount factor (γ): A number between 0 and 1 that models the agent's preference for immediate rewards over future rewards. A value close to 1 means the agent values future rewards nearly as much as immediate rewards. A value closer to 0 means the agent prefers immediate rewards over long-term ones.
- Policy (π): A policy is a strategy that the agent uses to decide which action to take in each state. A policy can be deterministic (a fixed action for each state) or stochastic (a probability distribution over actions for each state).
- Value function (V): The value function V(s) gives the expected sum of rewards that an agent can accumulate starting from states, following a specific policy π. The value of a state depends on both the immediate rewards and the future rewards.
- Q-function (Q): The Q-function Q(s,a) is similar to the value function but provides the expected sum of rewards starting from state s, taking action a, and then following policy π. It essentially measures the "quality" of a state-action pair.

Key Concepts in MDPs:

Bellman Equations: The Bellman equation is a recursive relationship that defines the value function in terms of immediate rewards and the values of successor states. For the value function, the Bellman equation is given by:

$$V(s) = \mathbb{E}[R(s, a, s') + \gamma V(s')]$$

For the Q-function:

$$Q(s, a) = \mathbb{E}[R(s, a, s') + \gamma \sum_{s'} P(s'|s, a) Q(s', \pi(s'))]$$

Optimal Policy: An optimal policy $\pi*$ maximizes the expected cumulative reward for the agent over time. This can be found by solving the Bellman optimality equation:

$$V^*(s) = \max_a \mathbb{E}[R(s,a,s') + \gamma V^*(s')]$$

Similarly, for Q-values:

$$Q^*(s,a) = \mathbb{E}[R(s,a,s') + \gamma \max_{a'} Q^*(s',a')]$$

MDPs form the core of many reinforcement learning and control systems, providing a structured way to model decision-making under uncertainty. The powerful methods and algorithms developed from MDP theory allow for the design of intelligent agents capable of making optimal decisions in a wide range of domains.

Value Iteration and Policy Iteration

Value Iteration and Policy Iteration are two key algorithms for solving Markov Decision Processes (MDPs), which are central to reinforcement learning (RL). Both algorithms aim to compute an optimal policy that maximizes the expected cumulative reward in an environment. Value Iteration works by iteratively updating the value of each state. Initially, arbitrary values are assigned to all states, and then the value for each state is updated based on the expected rewards from possible actions, considering the values of successor states. This process continues until the values converge to the optimal state values, from which the optimal policy can be derived. Policy Iteration alternates between two steps: policy evaluation and policy improvement. In policy evaluation, the value of each state is calculated under the current policy, and in policy improvement, the policy is updated by choosing the action that maximizes the expected reward based on the current state values. This process repeats until the policy converges to the optimal one.

Value Iteration

Value Iteration is a dynamic programming algorithm used to solve Markov Decision Processes (MDPs) by iteratively updating the value function until it converges to the optimal solution. It operates by repeatedly applying the Bellman optimality equation, which helps estimate the maximum expected reward for each state. At each iteration, the algorithm updates the value of a state based on the expected returns from possible actions, considering the transition probabilities and rewards. This process continues until the values stabilize, meaning further updates result in negligible changes. The advantage of Value Iteration is its ability to efficiently find the optimal policy by refining value estimates without explicitly storing policies at each step. Once the value function converges, an optimal policy can be extracted by choosing actions that maximize expected rewards in each state. Compared to Policy Iteration, which involves explicit policy evaluation and improvement steps, Value Iteration tends to converge faster in many scenarios as it directly refines state values. This makes it a preferred approach for solving MDPs in reinforcement learning and decision-making problems.

Algorithm Steps

- Initialize the value function arbitrarily:

$$V(s) = 0, \quad \forall s \in S$$

- Bellman Update Rule: For each state s, update V(s) using:

$$V(s) = \max_{a \in A} \sum_{s'} P(s'|s,a)[R(s,a,s') + \gamma V(s')]$$

- Repeat step 2 until the values converge (i.e., the maximum change in V(s) is below a small threshold ϵ.

Extract Optimal Policy

$$\pi^*(s) = \arg\max_{a \in A} \sum_{s'} P(s'|s,a)[R(s,a,s') + \gamma V(s')]$$

Policy Iteration

Policy Iteration explicitly maintains and improves a policy π until convergence.

Algorithm Steps

- Initialize an arbitrary policy π(s).
- Policy Evaluation (Compute $V^\pi(s)$):

Solve the system of equations:

$$V^\pi(s) = \sum_{s'} P(s'|s,\pi(s))[R(s,\pi(s),s') + \gamma V^\pi(s')]$$

This can be done iteratively using:

$$V^\pi(s) \leftarrow \sum_{s'} P(s'|s,\pi(s))[R(s,\pi(s),s') + \gamma V^\pi(s')]$$

Policy Improvement:

Update the policy using:

$$\pi(s) = \arg\max_{a \in A} \sum_{s'} P(s'|s,a)[R(s,a,s') + \gamma V^\pi(s')]$$

Repeat steps 2 and 3 until the policy converges.

Comparison: Value Iteration vs. Policy Iteration

Value Iteration and Policy Iteration are two fundamental algorithms for solving Markov Decision Processes (MDPs). Value Iteration updates the value function iteratively using the Bellman optimality equation until convergence and then extracts the optimal policy, making it computationally efficient but sometimes slow to converge due to repeated updates. Policy Iteration, on the other hand, explicitly maintains a policy, alternating between policy evaluation (computing the value of a given policy) and policy improvement (updating the policy based on computed values), leading to faster convergence in fewer iterations in Table 4.3. While Value Iteration is easier to implement and works well for small to medium-sized problems, Policy Iteration is more stable and efficient for larger MDPs due to fewer iterations required for convergence.

Table 4.3: Comparison: Value Iteration vs. Policy Iteration.

Feature	Value Iteration	Policy Iteration
Approach	Iteratively updates value function	Iteratively updates policy
Computational Efficiency	Faster for small problems	Faster for large problems
Convergence Speed	Can take many iterations	Converges in fewer iterations
Stability	Less stable due to max operation	More stable due to explicit policy evaluation
Memory Usage	Requires storage for value function	Requires storage for both policy and value function

Example Calculation

Consider an MDP with three states S= $\{s_1, s_2, s_3\}$, two actions A= $\{a_1, a_2\}$, and the following transition probabilities and rewards in Table 4.4:

Table 4.4: Three states S transition probabilities.

State	Action	Next State	Probability	Reward
s_1	a_1	s_2	0.8	5
s_1	a_1	s_3	0.2	2
s_2	a_2	s_3	1.0	10

Using Value Iteration:

- Initialize $V(s_1) = V(s_2) = V(s_3) = 0V$.
- Apply Bellman updates iteratively.
- Extract the optimal policy.

Using Policy Iteration:

- Start with a random policy.
- Evaluate Vπ(s).
- Improve the policy iteratively.

Linear quadratic regulation (LQR)

Linear Quadratic Regulation (LQR) is an optimal control technique used to regulate dynamic systems efficiently while minimizing a predefined cost function. It is widely applied in engineering, robotics, and economics to ensure system stability and performance. LQR works by determining an optimal control input that minimizes a quadratic cost function, which typically balances system state deviations and control effort. The method is based on solving the Riccati equation to derive a feedback gain matrix that ensures optimal system behavior. In automatic control systems, LQR plays a crucial role in stabilizing dynamic systems such as robotic arms, autonomous vehicles, and power grids. By continuously adjusting control inputs based on real-time system states, LQR ensures smooth operation while minimizing energy consumption and unwanted fluctuations. Its ability to handle multi-variable systems with constraints makes it a preferred choice for designing controllers in aerospace, industrial automation, and economic policy optimization.

Problem Formulation

LQR aims to control a linear time-invariant (LTI) system given by:

$$\dot{x}(t) = Ax(t) + Bu(t)$$

where:

x(t) is the system state vector,

u(t) is the control input vector,

A is the system matrix,

B is the control matrix.

The goal of LQR is to design a control law:

$$u(t) = -Kx(t)$$

such that it minimizes a quadratic cost function:

$$J = \int_0^\infty \left(x^T Q x + u^T R u\right) dt$$

Where:

Q is a positive semi-definite matrix that penalizes large states,

R is a positive definite matrix that penalizes large control efforts,

The trade-off between state deviation and control effort is determined by Q and R.

Solution Approach

LQR uses the Riccati equation to determine the optimal gain matrix K. The steps are:

Solve the Algebraic Riccati Equation (ARE):

$$A^T P + PA - PBR^{-1}B^T P + Q = 0$$

P is the solution of this equation.

P is a symmetric positive semi-definite matrix.

Compute the Optimal Gain Matrix K:

$$K = R^{-1}B^T P$$

Apply the Optimal Control Law:

$$u(t) = -Kx(t)$$

This feedback control law ensures that the system remains stable.

Properties of LQR

Optimality

Linear Quadratic Regulator (LQR) is fundamentally characterized by its optimality in control systems design. It systematically derives the most efficient control law by minimizing a predefined quadratic cost function, typically balancing system performance against control effort. This quadratic function is composed of state deviations weighted by the matrixQ and control actions weighted by the matrix R. The resultant optimal solution is unique and explicitly determined by solving the Algebraic Riccati Equation (ARE), ensuring mathematical rigor and computational efficiency. Unlike heuristic or trial-and-error methods, the LQR's optimality provides a clear and structured framework for controller synthesis. This optimal control law guarantees minimal cumulative cost in transitioning the system from an initial state to the desired equilibrium, simultaneously satisfying performance and efficiency criteria. Due to this explicit optimality, LQR has been extensively utilized across various engineering fields, from aerospace systems and robotics to automotive control and economic modeling.

Robustness

Robustness is another pivotal attribute of the Linear Quadratic Regulator (LQR). This quality implies that LQR-based controllers inherently demonstrate strong resistance to external disturbances and parameter variations, provided the underlying system is fully controllable. When faced with unforeseen disturbances or modeling uncertainties, an LQR controller ensures the system's stability and satisfactory performance within acceptable bounds. Such robustness arises from the stability margins embedded within the controller's design, typically ensuring that minor variations in system parameters do not significantly degrade the closed-loop system's stability or performance. Although LQR does not explicitly incorporate robustness criteria as seen in robust control methods like $H\infty$, it naturally accommodates uncertainties within a certain range. This robustness makes LQR highly valuable in practical implementations where exact models are often unavailable or subject to change. Consequently, LQR controllers have found widespread application in real-world scenarios, including industrial automation, flight stabilization, and power system regulation.

Trade-off Between Energy and Performance

The Linear Quadratic Regulator (LQR) provides designers with a flexible framework to balance energy consumption against dynamic performance through its cost matrices Q and R. Specifically, the matrix Q assigns weights to state variables, emphasizing the importance of reducing deviations from desired trajectories, thereby improving the system's responsiveness and speed. Conversely, matrix R regulates the weight placed on control inputs, thus directly managing the energy or effort expended by actuators. Adjusting these weighting matrices creates a customizable trade-off, enabling engineers to finely tune the controller according to specific performance or energy constraints. For instance, higher emphasis on performance (larger Q) yields faster responses but demands increased control energy, while prioritizing energy efficiency (larger R) leads to gentler actuator actions and slower dynamics. This adjustable nature of LQR has made it particularly attractive in fields where resource conservation is critical, such as aerospace, automotive engineering, renewable energy systems, and robotics.

Discrete-Time LQR

For discrete-time systems:

$$x_{k+1} = Ax_k + Bu_k$$

The cost function is:

$$J = \sum_{k=0}^{\infty}(x_k^T Q x_k + u_k^T R u_k)$$

The solution follows a similar approach using the Discrete Riccati Equation:

$$P = A^T PA - A^T PB(B^T PB + R)^{-1} B^T PA + Q$$

and the control gain is:

$$K = (B^T PB + R)^{-1} B^T PA$$

Applications of LQR

Robotics

In robotics, Linear Quadratic Regulator (LQR) is widely used to control robotic arms and mobile robots. LQR allows for optimal trajectory planning, ensuring smooth, precise movements by minimizing energy consumption and avoiding undesirable oscillations. For robotic arms, LQR is utilized to compute control signals that ensure each joint moves with minimal error and time delay, effectively handling tasks like assembly or surgery. In mobile robotics, LQR assists in path planning and navigation, ensuring robots move efficiently while avoiding obstacles. This optimal control technique is especially useful in complex environments where precise coordination between multiple joints or wheels is crucial for task success. The LQR method provides robustness, as it can maintain system stability even in uncertain conditions or when faced with disturbances. Overall, LQR enhances the performance and adaptability of both robotic arms and mobile robots in a range of applications.

Aerospace

LQR plays a vital role in aerospace applications, particularly in the design of autopilot systems for aircraft. These systems are designed to maintain stable flight by continuously adjusting control inputs such as pitch, roll, and yaw. LQR ensures that the aircraft follows a desired flight path while minimizing fuel consumption, travel time, and control effort. By optimizing the control signals, LQR helps aircraft stay on course, even in the presence of turbulence or other environmental disturbances. Additionally, LQR can be used to design systems that automatically respond to emergency conditions, such as turbulence or system failures, providing a safe and efficient means of keeping the aircraft under control. The ability of LQR to handle both stability and performance makes it ideal for autopilot systems, ensuring aircraft can fly autonomously with high precision, thus improving safety and efficiency in modern aviation.

Automotive

In the automotive industry, LQR is integral to the development of advanced driver-assistance systems such as adaptive cruise control (ACC) and lane-keeping assistance (LKA). In ACC, LQR optimizes the throttle and braking inputs to maintain a safe and comfortable distance from the vehicle ahead, adjusting the speed based on real-time traffic conditions. This helps reduce the driver's workload and improves safety by preventing rear-end collisions. For LKA, LQR ensures the vehicle stays centered within the lane, making necessary adjustments to the steering input to correct small deviations. By continuously adjusting the vehicle's trajectory with minimal delay and energy consumption, LQR enhances the smoothness and reliability of these systems. Furthermore, the use of LQR in automotive applications can reduce wear and tear on mechanical components by optimizing control actions, thus improving the overall efficiency and longevity of the vehicle while providing a safer driving experience.

Power Systems

LQR is used in power systems to optimize the control of voltage and frequency regulation, critical for maintaining a stable and efficient electrical grid. In power generation, LQR helps control the outputs of various generators to match the load demands while maintaining the correct voltage and frequency levels. This ensures that electrical power is distributed consistently without causing overloading or system instability. By minimizing deviations from the set points for voltage and frequency, LQR helps prevent disruptions, such as power outages or equipment damage. It can also optimize the operation of power plants by reducing fuel consumption and increasing system efficiency. LQR-based controllers are especially useful in systems where renewable energy sources, such as solar or wind, are integrated, as these can fluctuate. The ability of LQR to adapt to changes in load and generation while maintaining optimal system performance makes it a vital tool for modern power systems.

Economics

In economics, Linear Quadratic Regulator (LQR) is applied to model and solve optimal investment and resource allocation problems. It enables economists and financial analysts to determine the best strategies for allocating resources, such as capital, labor, or time, in order to maximize returns or minimize costs. Using LQR, decision-makers can develop dynamic models that account for changes over time, such as fluctuating market conditions, investment returns, or economic growth rates. The LQR approach helps in optimizing long-term strategies by balancing risk and return in a manner that minimizes the overall cost or loss to the system. For example, in investment portfolio management, LQR can determine the best allocation of assets to maximize returns while minimizing the risk of financial loss. Similarly, in resource allocation, LQR ensures the most efficient use of resources to achieve desired economic outcomes while minimizing waste and inefficiency.

Linear Quadratic Gaussian (LQG)

Linear Quadratic Gaussian (LQG) control is a fundamental approach in optimal control theory that integrates Linear-Quadratic Regulator (LQR) and Kalman Filtering to manage systems influenced by process and measurement noise. LQG control is widely applied in aerospace, robotics, and industrial systems due to its robustness in handling uncertainties. It is designed for linear systems subject to Gaussian noise, optimizing control performance while accounting for disturbances and sensor errors. The LQG controller comprises two key components: the Linear-Quadratic Regulator (LQR), which provides an optimal state feedback control law by minimizing a quadratic cost function, and the Kalman Filter, which estimates the system's state in the presence of noisy measurements. This combination allows LQG to generate optimal control inputs, even when the system's state is not fully observable. The result is a reliable control solution that ensures efficiency and stability in systems where noise and uncertainty are prevalent.

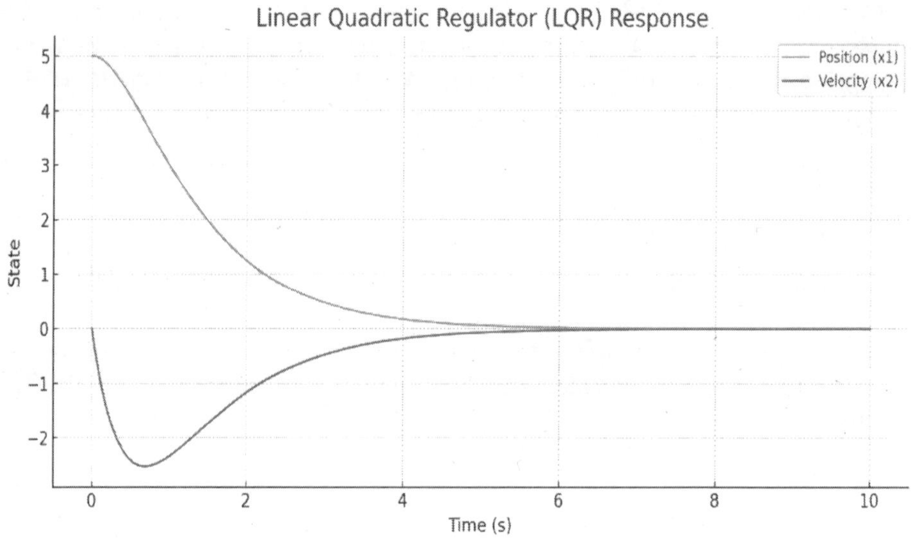

Figure 4.1: Response of Linear Quadratic Regulator (LQR).

Linear Quadratic Regulator (LQR)

TheLQR is a control technique that determines the optimal control policy for a system assuming perfect state information in Figure 4.1. It is widely used in systems that can be described by linear dynamics, where the goal is to minimize a quadratic cost function that typically includes terms for system performance and control effort. LQR calculates control inputs based on the current state of the system, ensuring that the system reaches the desired state while minimizing control energy and maintaining stability. One key advantage of LQR is its ability to balance trade-offs between performance (e.g., how quickly the system reaches the target state) and energy consumption (e.g., control effort required). The method assumes that the system's state is fully observable and accurate, meaning it doesn't account for any measurement noise or uncertainties, thus requiring a reliable state estimation source for optimal results.

Kalman Filter

The Kalman Filter is an optimal estimation algorithm used to estimate the state of a dynamic system based on noisy or incomplete measurements. Unlike LQR, which requires perfect state information, the Kalman Filter is designed for scenarios where measurements are subject to noise and uncertainties. It operates in a two-step process: prediction and correction. In the prediction step, the filter uses the system's model to predict the next state and uncertainty. In the correction step, it adjusts this prediction by incorporating noisy measurements, blending the predicted state with the actual data based on their respective uncertainties. This results in an optimal estimate of the system's true state. The Kalman Filter is widely used in various fields such as aerospace, robotics, and navigation systems, where accurate state estimation is critical, even in the presence of unreliable measurements. Its ability to work with real-time data makes it a powerful tool for dynamic system analysis. Thus, LQG control is ideal for situations where full state information is not available due to measurement noise.

Mathematical Formulation

Consider a continuous-time linear system:

$$\dot{x}(t) = Ax(t) + Bu(t) + w(t), \quad w(t) \sim \mathcal{N}(0, Q)$$

$$y(t) = Cx(t) + v(t), \quad v(t) \sim \mathcal{N}(0, R)$$

where:

x(t) is the state vector.

u(t) is the control input.

y(t) is the measured output.

w(t) is process noise (zero-mean Gaussian with covariance Q).

v(t) is measurement noise (zero-mean Gaussian with covariance R).

The goal of LQG control is to design a controlleru(t) that minimizes the quadratic cost function:

$$J = \mathbb{E}\left[\int_0^\infty \left(x^T Q x + u^T R u\right) dt\right]$$

where Q and Rare weight matrices that penalize state deviations and control efforts.

Components of LQG Control

Linear Quadratic Regulator (LQR)

LQR solves the optimal control problem assuming full state feedback. The optimal control law is:

$$u(t) = -Kx(t)$$

K is the feedback gain matrix obtained from the Riccati equation:

$$A^T P + PA - PBR^{-1}B^T P + Q = 0$$

$$K = R^{-1}B^T P$$

Here,

P is the solution to the algebraic Riccati equation (ARE).LQR provides the best deterministic control if all states are available.

Kalman Filter (State Estimation)

Since full state feedback is not always available, a Kalman Filter is used to estimate the state x^(t) from noisy measurements:

$$\dot{\hat{x}}(t) = A\hat{x}(t) + Bu(t) + L(y - C\hat{x})$$

Where

L is the Kalman gain, determined by solving the Kalman filter Riccati equation:

$$AP + PA^T - PC^T R^{-1}CP + Q = 0$$

$$L = PC^T R^{-1}$$

The Kalman filter provides an optimal estimate x^(t), minimizing the mean-square estimation error.

Optimality

LQG control is optimal in the mean-square sense, specifically for systems that are linear and subject to Gaussian noise. In these systems, the goal is to minimize the expected value of a cost function, typically represented as the sum of squared errors between the system's actual and desired states. The LQG controller achieves this optimality by combining two key components: LQR and Kalman filtering. The LQR optimizes the control inputs, while the Kalman filter estimates the system's state in the presence of measurement noise. By solving this combined system, LQG ensures that the system's performance is optimal by minimizing the variance of the estimation error and the control effort. This makes LQG particularly suitable for scenarios where systems operate under noisy conditions, like in communication systems, aerospace, and robotics, providing both high accuracy and efficient control.

Separation Principle

The separation principle is a key property of LQG control that allows the design of the LQR and the Kalman filter to be performed independently. This principle simplifies the control design process by decoupling the control law from the state estimation process. In practice, the LQR controller is designed first to minimize the cost function, typically related to state error and control effort. Simultaneously, the Kalman filter is designed to optimally estimate the state of the system in the presence of noise, using the system's measurements. Because these two components can be designed independently, it reduces the complexity of the design process, making LQG a flexible and efficient approach to optimal control. The separation principle also ensures that each component can be tailored for its specific purposestate estimation for the Kalman filter and control optimization for the LQRwhile maintaining overall system performance.

Robustness to Noise

LQG (Linear Quadratic Gaussian) control is designed to handle stochastic disturbances, such as Gaussian noise in the system dynamics and measurements. This makes LQG particularly effective in environments where random fluctuations are present, ensuring that the system remains stable and performs optimally in the presence of noise. By using the Kalman filter to estimate the system's state and the LQR to compute the optimal control actions, LQG effectively reduces the impact of noise on system performance. However, LQG is not inherently robust to model uncertainties, such as mismatched dynamics or unmodeled disturbances. If the actual system behavior deviates significantly from the assumed model, the performance of the LQG controller may degrade. Unlike some robust control methods, LQG does not automatically compensate for uncertainties in the model, making it sensitive to inaccuracies in the system's dynamics or external disturbances that are not accounted for during the design phase.

Q-Learning

Q-learning is a popular model-free reinforcement learning (RL) algorithm used to determine the optimal action-selection policy for an agent interacting with an environment. Unlike other RL methods, Q-learning doesn't require a model of the environment, which means it can be applied to situations where the agent does not have knowledge of the system dynamics or transition probabilities. The core concept of Q-learning is learning the Q-value, which represents the expected future rewards of taking a particular action in a given state and following the optimal policy thereafter. The Q-value is updated iteratively using the Bellman equation, where the agent adjusts its Q-values based on feedback from the environment. Over time, Q-learning converges to the optimal policy, allowing the agent to make decisions that maximize long-term rewards. This approach makes Q-learning well-suited for problems where the environment is dynamic or not entirely known in advance.The key idea behind Q-learning is to iteratively update the Q-values using the Bellman equation:

$$Q(s,a) \leftarrow Q(s,a) + \alpha[r + \gamma \max_{a'} Q(s',a') - Q(s,a)]$$

where:

s is the current state,

a is the action taken,

r is the reward,

s′ is the next state,

α is the learning rate, and

γ is the discount factor.

Applications of Q-Learning

Q-learning has a wide range of applications in various fields due to its model-free nature and ability to find optimal policies in complex environments. In gaming, Q-learning is often used for training AI agents to play games like chess, Go, or video games by teaching them how to maximize their scores through optimal decision-making. In robotics, Q-learning helps robots learn to perform tasks such as navigation, object manipulation, and coordination without requiring pre-programmed strategies. In finance, Q-learning can be applied to develop trading strategies that adapt to market changes by learning from past actions. Q-learning is also used in healthcare for personalized treatment planning, where the agent learns the best interventions based on patient data and outcomes. Additionally, Q-learning finds applications in autonomous vehicles, natural language processing, and network management, demonstrating its versatility in solving complex decision-making problems across diverse domains.

Value Function Approximation

Value function approximation is a technique used in reinforcement learning and dynamic programming to estimate the value of states or state-action pairs, particularly when the state space is too large to store exact values for every state. In many real-world problems, the state space can be vast, continuous, or even infinite, making it infeasible to explicitly store values for each state. Instead of maintaining a large table of values, value function approximation employs a mathematical function, such as a linear or nonlinear model, to generalize and approximate the value for unseen states based on a subset of the state space. By utilizing this approach, an agent can effectively handle large or continuous environments, learning optimal policies even with limited computational resources. This method allows for more scalable reinforcement learning algorithms that can be applied to a wide range of real-world applications, such as robotics, gaming, and autonomous systems.

Linear approximation is one common method, where the value function is approximated as a weighted sum of features:

$$V(s) = \theta^T \phi(s)$$

where θ is the weight vector and ϕ(s) represents a feature vector derived from state s.

In action-value approximation, the same approach is applied to Q-values, where Q(s,a)is approximated instead.

Benefits of Value Function Approximation

Value function approximation offers significant benefits, especially in problems involving large or continuous state spaces. One of the primary advantages is the ability to generalize from limited data. Rather than relying on exact values for every state, approximation functions allow the system to make reasonable predictions about the values of unseen states based on known examples. This can dramatically reduce memory requirements and improve computational efficiency, making it possible to solve problems that would otherwise be infeasible. Additionally, value function approximation supports the application of reinforcement learning techniques in complex environments, such as robotics, where the state space is dynamic and large. This method also facilitates continuous learning and adaptation, allowing systems to improve over time as they encounter new states. Overall, value function approximation enhances the scalability and flexibility of reinforcement learning algorithms, enabling their use in a wide range of real-world tasks.

Challenges of Value Function Approximation

While value function approximation offers many benefits, it also comes with several challenges. One of the key issues is the potential for approximation error, which can lead to suboptimal policies if the approximation function does not adequately capture the true value function. This problem becomes more pronounced as the complexity of the state space increases. Furthermore, the choice of the approximation model (linear or nonlinear) can significantly impact the performance of the agent. Overfitting is another concern, particularly when using nonlinear function approximators like neural networks, as the model may memorize training data rather than generalizing to new, unseen states. Additionally, the approximation process requires careful selection of features and parameters, which can be time-consuming and difficult to optimize. Finally, convergence issues can arise when using approximation methods in reinforcement learning, especially in highly dynamic or uncertain environments, complicating the learning process.

Applications of Value Function Approximation

Value function approximation is widely used in various fields, particularly in reinforcement learning, robotics, and artificial intelligence. One of the most notable applications is in autonomous vehicles, where the state space involves continuous variables such as speed, position, and environmental factors. By using value function approximation, autonomous vehicles can make real-time decisions without explicitly needing to store values for every possible state. Another key application is in robotics, where value function approximation allows robots to learn optimal policies for tasks such as navigation, manipulation, and exploration in complex environments. In game-playing AI, such as in chess or Go, value function approximation helps the agent evaluate board states and predict the outcomes of various moves. Moreover, in finance, value function approximation is used to model optimal decision-making strategies, such as portfolio management or stock trading, where the state space can involve numerous continuous factors.

Policy Search: Direct Optimization of Policies

Policy search methods focus on directly optimizing the policy itself, which defines the mapping from states to actions. Unlike traditional value-based methods such as Q-learning, which estimate the value of actions in each state and derive a policy from them, policy search optimizes the policy parameters directly to maximize performance. This approach is particularly useful in environments where value-based methods may not be applicable, such as continuous action spaces or environments with high-dimensional state-action spaces. In policy search, a policy is typically parameterized by a function, and the goal is to find the set of parameters that yields the best overall performance. This direct optimization eliminates the need for discretizing action spaces, making it more effective in scenarios where discrete action choices are impractical. Popular techniques for policy search include gradient-based methods and evolutionary algorithms, both of which help refine the policy to improve decision-making and system performance in real-time applications.

Policy Search in Continuous Action Spaces

Policy search methods excel in continuous action spaces, where traditional value-based techniques like Q-learning struggle. In continuous action spaces, the number of possible actions is infinite or very large, making it impractical to compute and store value functions for each action. Instead, policy search directly optimizes the policy, which is a mapping from states to real-valued actions. This approach works well in environments such as robotics or control systems, where actions like velocity or torque require precise continuous adjustments. Policy search allows for a direct parameterization of the policy, such as a neural network or a linear function, and uses optimization algorithms to adjust these parameters for improved performance. The advantage of policy search in continuous spaces is its ability to explore the full range of possible actions, making it possible to find optimal or near-optimal solutions even in highly complex environments where value-based methods fail to perform efficiently. Some common policy search methods include:

Gradient-based Methods (e.g., Policy Gradient)

Gradient-based methods, such as Policy Gradient, are a class of techniques used in reinforcement learning to optimize policies by directly adjusting their parameters based on the gradients of the expected return with respect to those parameters. The central idea behind Policy Gradient methods is to parameterize the policy as a neural network and use gradient ascent to update the policy towards actions that maximize cumulative rewards. Policy Gradient methods work by calculating the gradient of the expected reward with respect to the policy parameters and then adjusting these parameters in the direction that increases the expected reward. This approach allows for more direct learning of complex policies, especially in environments with high-dimensional action spaces. The main advantage of gradient-based methods is their ability to learn continuous and stochastic policies, which are essential for many real-world applications, such as robotic control or game-playing agents.

Evolutionary Strategies and Other Optimization-based Methods

Evolutionary strategies (ES) and other optimization-based methods are used in reinforcement learning to optimize policies through population-based search techniques inspired by natural selection. In evolutionary strategies, a population of candidate solutions (policies) is generated, and the best-performing policies are selected based on their fitness, which is typically determined by their performance in the environment. These selected policies undergo mutation and recombination to generate new candidate solutions, and the process is repeated over multiple generations. This method is advantageous in complex optimization problems where traditional gradient-based methods might struggle, particularly when the reward function is noisy or non-differentiable. ES is known for its ability to handle large, high-dimensional search spaces and its robustness to local minima. Other optimization-based methods, such as genetic algorithms or simulated annealing, also rely on similar principles of searching through a population of possible solutions, iteratively refining them to improve performance and discover optimal policies.

REINFORCE (Monte Carlo Policy Gradient)

REINFORCE is a policy gradient algorithm used in reinforcement learning (RL) to optimize the decision-making policy of an agent. The goal of REINFORCE is to learn a policy that maximizes the expected cumulative reward over time. In this algorithm, the policy is typically parameterized by a neural network, which maps the states of the environment to actions that the agent can take. REINFORCE uses Monte Carlo methods to update the policy. This means it evaluates the agent's performance after completing an entire episode, observing the total accumulated rewards. The policy gradient is then updated using the gradients of the log probability of the actions taken, weighted by the observed returns. This process helps improve the policy over time by making actions with higher rewards more likely. The REINFORCE algorithm, despite its simplicity, is effective in solving complex reinforcement learning problems by directly optimizing the policy through trial and error.The REINFORCE update rule is:

$$\theta \leftarrow \theta + \alpha \nabla_\theta \log \pi_\theta(s,a) G_t$$

where:

$\pi_\theta(s,a)$ is the policy probability of taking action a in state s,

G_t is the return following time step t,

α is the learning rate, and

∇_θ is the gradient of the policy.

Policy Parameterization and Updates

In REINFORCE, the policy is usually parameterized by a neural network that takes the current state of the environment as input and outputs a probability distribution over possible action. The neural network is trained using the policy gradient method, which involves updating the parameters of the network in the direction of the gradient of the expected cumulative reward. Unlike value-based methods, which focus on estimating the value of states or actions, REINFORCE directly optimizes the policy itself. After each episode, the total reward obtained by the agent is computed, and the policy is updated based on the rewards associated with the actions taken. The gradients are calculated using the log probability of the actions chosen, and these gradients are scaled by the observed returns to adjust the policy parameters. This iterative process allows REINFORCE to improve the policy by reinforcing successful actions that lead to higher rewards, facilitating the agent's ability to learn optimal behavior.

Monte Carlo Methods in REINFORCE

Monte Carlo methods play a crucial role in the REINFORCE algorithm, as they are used to estimate the expected cumulative rewards for a given policy. In REINFORCE, an episode is executed from start to finish, and once the episode is complete, the total accumulated reward is computed. This total reward, or return, is then used to update the policy. Unlike other RL methods that rely on bootstrapping (estimating values from previous estimates), Monte Carlo methods require waiting until the end of the episode to observe the full return. This makes the REINFORCE algorithm simpler but can be less sample-efficient. The key advantage of Monte Carlo methods in REINFORCE is that they provide an unbiased estimate of the return, as they directly use the observed rewards without any approximation. However, the variance in the rewards can cause high variability in the gradient updates, which is why variance reduction techniques are often employed to improve stability.

Challenges in REINFORCE

While REINFORCE is conceptually simple and effective, it faces several challenges, particularly related to high variance in the gradient estimates. Since REINFORCE uses Monte Carlo methods, the total reward for an episode can vary significantly, leading to large fluctuations in the gradient updates. These fluctuations can slow down the learning process and make it difficult for the algorithm to converge to an optimal policy. Additionally, REINFORCE does not use value estimation techniques, which can make it less sample-efficient compared to other reinforcement learning methods, such as Q-learning or actor-critic algorithms. The high variance problem is often mitigated by employing techniques like baseline subtraction, which reduces the variance of the returns. Furthermore, REINFORCE requires a large number of episodes to learn effectively, which can make it computationally expensive. Despite these challenges, REINFORCE remains a valuable tool in reinforcement learning for problems where policy-based learning is appropriate.

Applications of REINFORCE

REINFORCE, as a policy gradient method, is particularly useful in applications where the environment is complex and a direct mapping from states to actions is required. It has been successfully applied in various domains such as robotics, game playing, and autonomous driving. In robotics, REINFORCE can be used to teach an agent how to perform tasks like object manipulation or navigation by learning from trial and error. In game playing, REINFORCE has been applied to train agents to play games like Go, chess, and video games, where learning an optimal policy directly from raw experiences is essential. REINFORCE is also used in autonomous driving, where an agent must learn to navigate through dynamic and uncertain environments. Although the algorithm can be sample-inefficient, its ability to directly optimize the policy makes it particularly powerful in settings where the reward structure is sparse or difficult to model using value-based methods.

Partially Observable Markov Decision Processes (POMDPs)

Partially Observable Markov Decision Processes (POMDPs) are an extension of traditional Markov Decision Processes (MDPs) that introduce the element of uncertainty by allowing the agent to receive only partial observations of the environment's true state. In a POMDP, the agent doesn't have direct access to the full state of the system but instead must rely on a limited, possibly noisy, observation. This incomplete information makes decision-making more complex as the agent needs to infer the hidden aspects of the environment based on past actions, current observations, and a belief about the state.The decision-making process in a POMDP is guided by the concept of belief states, which represent a probability distribution over all possible states based on the agent's observations and actions. Since the agent cannot observe the state directly, it maintains and updates this belief over time, making the decision-making process inherently more challenging compared to MDPs. The agent must determine the optimal action by balancing exploration (gathering more information) and exploitation (maximizing rewards based on the current belief). This introduces additional computational complexity in planning and solving POMDPs, as finding optimal policies often requires sophisticated techniques like dynamic programming, approximation methods, or reinforcement learning algorithms. A POMDP is defined by the tuple:

$(S,A,T,R,\Omega,O,\gamma)$

Where:

S: A set of states representing the possible situations of the environment.

A: A set of actions that the agent can take.

T(s′|s,a): Transition function that defines the probability of reaching state s′ from state s when taking action a.

R(s,a): Reward function that specifies the immediate reward received for taking action aaa in state s.

Ω: A set of possible observations that the agent can receive.

O(o|s′,a): Observation function that defines the probability of receiving observation o given the new state s′ after taking action a.

γ: Discount factor ($0 \leq \gamma \leq 1$), which determines the importance of future rewards.

Example: Robot Navigation in a POMDP

Consider a robot that needs to navigate a warehouse while avoiding obstacles. The robot does not have perfect sensors and might not always detect obstacles correctly.

- States (S): Robot's position in the warehouse.
- Actions (A): Move forward, turn left, turn right, stop.
- Transition Function (T): Probability of reaching a new position based on the action taken.
- Observations (Ω): Sensor readings (e.g., detecting an obstacle).
- Observation Function (O): Probability of receiving an observation given the true position.
- Rewards (R): Positive rewards for reaching goals, negative for collisions.

The robot maintains a belief state about its position and updates it as it moves and gathers new observations.

Summary

Reinforcement learning (RL) and control theory provide powerful frameworks for decision-making in dynamic environments. Markov Decision Processes (MDPs) form the foundation of RL by modeling sequential decision problems using states, actions, rewards, and transition probabilities. The Bellman equations help define optimal policies through recursive relationships, leading to efficient solution techniques like value iteration and policy iteration.For continuous control, Linear Quadratic Regulation (LQR) and its extension, Linear Quadratic Gaussian (LQG), offer optimal strategies by minimizing quadratic cost functions under linear dynamics. Q-learning, a model-free approach, allows agents to learn optimal policies from experience by estimating action values. However, due to the high-dimensional nature of real-world problems, value function approximation is often necessary to generalize learning.Policy search methods directly optimize policies, overcoming challenges of value-based approaches. Reinforce, a Monte Carlo policy gradient method, updates policies based on sampled trajectories. Partially Observable Markov Decision Processes (POMDPs) extend MDPs to situations where state information is uncertain, requiring belief-state representations for optimal control. Together, these techniques contribute to advancements in artificial intelligence, robotics, and automated decision-making. By combining theoretical foundations with practical algorithms, reinforcement learning continues to evolve, enabling intelligent systems to adapt and optimize in complex, uncertain environments.

Exercise Questions

- What is a Markov Decision Process (MDP) and what are its key components?
- How does the Bellman equation represent the relationship between a state's value and its successor states?
- What are the primary differences between value iteration and policy iteration when solving MDPs?
- How is Linear Quadratic Regulation (LQR) applied in control systems for optimal performance?
- What distinguishes Linear Quadratic Gaussian (LQG) control from LQR?
- How does Q-learning update its action-value function through interactions with the environment?
- What role does value function approximation play in handling large or continuous state spaces?
- How does policy search differ from value-based methods in the context of reinforcement learning?
- What is the core mechanism of the REINFORCE algorithm in policy gradient methods?
- How do Partially Observable Markov Decision Processes (POMDPs) extend the framework of standard MDPs?

5

NEURAL NETWORKS AND DEEP LEARNING

Neural Networks and Deep Learning are subfields of artificial intelligence (AI) and machine learning (ML) that have revolutionized the way we approach complex problem-solving tasks. Neural Networks are computational models inspired by the structure and functioning of the human brain. They are designed to recognize patterns in data through a network of interconnected nodes or "neurons" that mimic biological neurons. These models consist of layers of neurons, including an input layer, hidden layers, and an output layer, allowing them to learn from data by adjusting weights during the training process. Deep Learning, a subset of machine learning, focuses on utilizing deep neural networks with many layers, hence the term "deep." The primary advantage of deep networks lies in their ability to automatically learn hierarchical features from raw data, without the need for manual feature extraction. This makes them particularly powerful for tasks involving large amounts of unstructured data, such as image recognition, speech processing, and natural language understanding.

The architecture of neural networks has evolved significantly over time. Early neural network models, such as the perceptron, were relatively simple, but they laid the groundwork for more sophisticated models. Today, deep learning architectures like Convolutional Neural Networks (CNNs) and Recurrent Neural Networks (RNNs) are widely used in applications ranging from computer vision to natural language processing (NLP). These networks can capture intricate patterns in data, enabling breakthroughs in areas such as autonomous vehicles, healthcare diagnostics, and AI-driven content creation. Training neural networks is a computationally intensive process that requires vast amounts of data and high-performance hardware, such as Graphics Processing Units (GPUs). During the training phase, neural networks adjust their internal parameters (weights and biases) through an optimization process, often using techniques like backpropagation. The goal is to minimize the error between the model's predictions and the actual outcomes, allowing the network to improve its accuracy over time. One of the key breakthroughs in deep learning has been the development of techniques that mitigate challenges like overfitting, vanishing gradients, and computational inefficiencies. Innovations such as dropout regularization, batch normalization, and the use of activation functions like ReLU (Rectified Linear Unit) have greatly enhanced the performance and scalability of deep neural networks. These techniques allow deep learning models to generalize better and improve their ability to handle real-world data. Despite their remarkable successes, deep learning models still face challenges, including the need for large datasets, the interpretability of models, and the potential for biased outcomes due to the data they are trained on. Nonetheless, the rapid advancement of deep learning continues to unlock new possibilities across various domains. As technology progresses, neural networks and deep learning are expected to play an increasingly central role in shaping the future of AI and its applications in society.

Introduction to Neural Networks

Neural networks are computational models inspired by the human brain, designed to recognize patterns and solve problems in areas such as image recognition, language processing, and decision-making. At their core, neural networks consist of layers of interconnected nodes, or "neurons," that process data through weighted connections. Each neuron takes in input, applies a mathematical function, and passes the output to the next layer. This structure allows neural networks to learn from data by adjusting the weights of connections during training to minimize errors in predictions. The basic structure of a neural network includes three types of layers: the input layer, the hidden layers, and the output layer. The input layer receives raw data, such as an image or text. Hidden layers, located between the input and output layers, perform complex transformations and learn patterns in the data. Finally, the output layer provides the network's prediction or decision. These layers work together, with data flowing from the input to the output, and the network adjusting itself through backpropagation and optimization techniques like gradient descent. Neural networks can be classified into different types based on their architecture and function. For example, feedforward neural networks are the simplest form, where data flows in one direction, while recurrent neural networks (RNNs) are designed for sequential data, allowing for feedback loops. Convolutional neural networks (CNNs) are specialized for image processing tasks, utilizing layers that focus on spatial hierarchies in images. Through training with large datasets, neural networks can perform complex tasks such as natural language processing, medical diagnosis, and even autonomous driving, revolutionizing numerous industries.

Structure of a Neural Network

A neural network typically consists of three layers:

- Input Layer: Receives initial data (features or attributes).
- Hidden Layers: Intermediate layers that transform the inputs. Can have multiple hidden layers (deep neural networks).

- Output Layer: Provides the final prediction or decision.

Each neuron in a layer connects to neurons in adjacent layers, forming a highly interconnected structure.

Basic Components

Artificial Neuron (Perceptron)

An artificial neuron performs a weighted sum of inputs and applies an activation function:

$$y = f\left(\sum_{i=1}^{n} w_i x_i + b\right)$$

xi: Inputs.

wi: Weights (learnable parameters).

b: Bias term (offset).

f: Activation function.

y: Output of the neuron.

Activation Functions

Activation functions introduce non-linearity, enabling neural networks to learn complex patterns. Common activation functions include:

Sigmoid

$$\sigma(x) = \frac{1}{1 + e^{-x}}$$

ReLU (Rectified Linear Unit)

$$\mathrm{ReLU}(x) = \max(0, x)$$

Tanh:

$$\tanh(x) = \frac{e^x - e^{-x}}{e^x + e^{-x}}$$

Softmax (used in output layers for multi-class classification):

$$\mathrm{Softmax}(x_i) = \frac{e^{x_i}}{\sum_j e^{x_j}}$$

Types of Neural Networks

Feedforward Neural Networks (FFNN)

Feedforward Neural Networks (FFNN) are one of the most basic types of neural networks, where information flows in one direction: from the input layer, through hidden layers, and finally to the output layer. FFNNs are called "feedforward" because there is no feedback or cycles in the network. Each neuron in a layer is connected to all the neurons in the next layer, making them fully connected networks. These networks are primarily used for tasks where the relationship between input and output is relatively simple, such as classification and regression problems. FFNNs are popular due to their simplicity and ease of implementation. However, they are limited in capturing temporal dependencies or spatial hierarchies in data. Their primary function is to map input features directly to output predictions, making them suitable for many basic machine learning tasks, but not as effective for more complex, sequential, or image-based tasks that require advanced architectures.

Convolutional Neural Networks (CNN)

Convolutional Neural Networks (CNN) are specialized neural networks primarily designed for processing grid-like data, such as images. CNNs use convolutional layers, which apply a set of filters (or kernels) to the input data to automatically learn spatial hierarchies of features. These filters are able to detect patterns like edges, textures, and shapes at various levels, allowing CNNs to capture complex features in images with minimal preprocessing. In addition to convolutional layers, CNNs typically include pooling layers, which reduce the spatial dimensions of the data, making the network more computationally efficient. CNNs are widely used in computer vision tasks like image classification, object detection, and segmentation. Their architecture allows them to outperform traditional machine learning models when dealing with image data due to their ability to automatically learn relevant features without the need for manual feature extraction. CNNs have become foundational in applications such as facial recognition and autonomous driving.

Recurrent Neural Networks (RNN)

Recurrent Neural Networks (RNN) are designed for sequential data and can capture temporal dependencies in time-series data. Unlike feedforward networks, RNNs have loops that allow information to be passed from one step of the network to the next, making them particularly effective for tasks such as natural language processing (NLP), speech recognition, and time-series forecasting. In an RNN, each output is influenced by both the current input and the previous hidden state, enabling it to maintain a memory of past inputs. This makes RNNs suitable for tasks that require context or understanding of sequences, such as generating text or predicting the next value in a sequence. However, standard RNNs have limitations in capturing long-term dependencies due to problems like vanishing or exploding gradients. Despite this, they remain a foundational architecture for sequential data processing, and more advanced versions like LSTMs and GRUs were developed to address these limitations.

Long Short-Term Memory (LSTM)

Long Short-Term Memory (LSTM) networks are a special type of Recurrent Neural Network (RNN) designed to overcome the limitations of standard RNNs in handling long-term dependencies. LSTMs address the vanishing gradient problem, which can occur in traditional RNNs when trying to learn from long sequences. They use a unique architecture that includes memory cells, which store information for long periods, and gates (input, output, and forget gates) that control the flow of information. These gates decide which information should be remembered or forgotten at each time step. LSTMs are particularly effective in tasks that involve long-range dependencies, such as language modeling, machine translation, and speech recognition. Their ability to capture temporal dynamics over long periods makes them suitable for applications like text generation, video analysis, and time-series prediction. LSTMs have significantly advanced the field of sequential data modeling and are widely used in many deep learning applications.

Gated Recurrent Units (GRU)

Gated Recurrent Units (GRU) are a variant of Recurrent Neural Networks (RNNs) that were introduced to address some of the shortcomings of traditional RNNs and Long Short-Term Memory (LSTM) networks. GRUs simplify the LSTM architecture by combining the forget and input gates into a single update gate, making them computationally more efficient. Despite this simplification, GRUs still maintain the ability to capture long-term dependencies in sequential data. The GRU architecture consists of two primary gates: the update gate and the reset gate. The update gate controls how much of the past information should be carried forward, while the reset gate determines how much of the past hidden state should be ignored. GRUs are especially effective in tasks that require learning from sequential data, such as language modeling, machine translation, and speech recognition, but they tend to train faster and with fewer parameters than LSTMs while maintaining similar performance.

Generative Adversarial Networks (GAN)

Generative Adversarial Networks (GANs) are a class of neural networks designed to generate new data that is similar to a given dataset. GANs consist of two components: a generator and a discriminator. The generator creates fake data, while the discriminator evaluates whether the data is real or fake. The two networks are trained together in a competitive process, where the generator tries to produce increasingly realistic data to fool the discriminator, and the discriminator tries to become better at distinguishing real from fake data. This adversarial process results in the generator learning to produce high-quality, realistic data, such as images, text, or audio. GANs have been groundbreaking in applications like image generation, deepfake creation, and data augmentation. They have also been used in art, fashion, and even drug discovery. The adversarial nature of GANs makes them powerful tools for generative tasks, but they require careful tuning to avoid issues like mode collapse, where the generator produces limited variations of data.

Neural Networks Learn

Learning involves adjusting weights and biases to minimize errors. The standard process is:

Forward Propagation

Forward propagation is the first step in the learning process of neural networks. It involves the flow of input data through the network, layer by layer, to produce an output. Initially, the input is fed into the network, where each neuron in a layer performs a weighted sum of the inputs, and a bias is added. The result is then passed through an activation function, such as ReLU or Sigmoid, to introduce non-linearity. This transformed output is then passed on to the next layer. This process continues until the final layer of the network, where the final output is generated. The output is typically compared to the actual target value to calculate the error or loss. Forward propagation enables the network to make predictions, and the learned parameters—weights and biasesare adjusted based on the error computed in the subsequent steps to improve performance.

Error Calculation

Error calculation is an essential step in the learning process of neural networks, where the difference between the predicted output and the actual target is computed. The purpose is to measure how well the network's predictions match the true values. Commonly, the loss function is used to quantify this error, with popular options being Mean Squared Error (MSE) for regression tasks and Cross-Entropy Loss for classification tasks. The error gives an indication of how far off the network's predictions are from the actual targets. A smaller error means better performance, while a larger error suggests the network's predictions need improvement. After the error is calculated, it serves as a basis for adjusting the network's parameters (weights and biases). This calculated error is crucial in guiding the backpropagation step, which iteratively reduces the error and allows the neural network to improve its predictions as learning progresses.

Backpropagation

Backpropagation is the process by which a neural network learns by updating its weights and biases to reduce the error calculated during forward propagation.

After the error is computed, backpropagation helps minimize this error by adjusting the weights in the network in the direction that reduces the loss. This is done by calculating the gradient of the loss function with respect to each weight using the chain rule of calculus. These gradients are then used to update the weights and biases in the network. Essentially, backpropagation works by propagating the error backward through the network from the output layer to the input layer. This iterative process ensures that the network learns the optimal parameters that minimize error. The success of backpropagation in training neural networks is due to its ability to fine-tune weights and biases with each pass, ultimately improving the model's performance and enabling it to generalize to new data.

Gradient Descent Optimization

Gradient Descent is an optimization algorithm used to minimize the error in a neural network. It works by iteratively adjusting the weights and biases in the network in the direction that reduces the loss function. At each iteration, the algorithm calculates the gradient of the loss function, which indicates the direction of the steepest ascent, and moves in the opposite direction to find the minimum loss. The step size, or learning rate, controls how large each update to the weights is. Gradient descent helps the neural network learn by iteratively making small adjustments to the parameters, improving the network's predictions over time. The process continues until the network converges to a minimum loss or a predetermined stopping criterion is reached. Variants of gradient descent, such as Stochastic Gradient Descent (SGD), Adam, and RMSProp, are commonly used to improve performance, especially in large-scale models, by adapting the learning rate and improving convergence speed.

Popular variants include:

Stochastic Gradient Descent (SGD)

Stochastic Gradient Descent (SGD) is a variant of gradient descent used to optimize neural networks. Unlike standard gradient descent, which uses the entire dataset to compute the gradient of the loss function, SGD updates the model parameters based on a single randomly selected data point or a small batch of data points at each iteration. This introduces more noise into the learning process but can lead to faster convergence, especially when dealing with large datasets. The noisy updates help escape local minima, potentially leading to better global solutions. However, the trade-off is that the updates may be less stable, requiring careful tuning of the learning rate. Despite this, SGD is widely used in deep learning because of its efficiency in handling large-scale data and its ability to learn faster compared to batch gradient descent. In practice, SGD can be improved with techniques like momentum or learning rate schedules.

Adam Optimizer

Adam (Adaptive Moment Estimation) is an advanced optimization algorithm that combines the benefits of both SGD and momentum-based methods. It computes adaptive learning rates for each parameter by using both the first and second moments of the gradients (mean and variance). This helps the optimizer adjust the learning rate dynamically for each parameter, allowing for more efficient training. Adam's primary advantage is that it adapts the learning rate based on the past gradients and their second moments, leading to faster convergence, especially for complex models. It also reduces the sensitivity to the choice of learning rate and is more robust to noisy data or sparse gradients. Adam is commonly used in training deep neural networks and is favored for its efficiency in handling large datasets and its ability to perform well across a wide range of tasks without requiring significant tuning of hyperparameters.

RMSProp

RMSProp (Root Mean Square Propagation) is another popular optimization algorithm used to train neural networks. It addresses some limitations of traditional gradient descent, such as slow convergence and sensitivity to the choice of learning rate. RMSProp adapts the learning rate for each parameter based on the moving average of the squared gradients. This allows the algorithm to adjust the learning rate for each parameter individually, helping prevent oscillations in the learning process. The algorithm performs well on problems involving non-stationary objectives, such as training on noisy or sparse data. It is particularly effective in online learning scenarios or when training deep neural networks with large datasets. By normalizing the gradient updates, RMSProp ensures stable and efficient learning, making it a valuable tool in many deep learning tasks, especially when training on problems that require the network to generalize well without overfitting.

Applications of Neural Networks

Image and Video Recognition

Neural networks, particularly Convolutional Neural Networks (CNNs), are extensively used in image and video recognition tasks. These networks excel at automatically identifying patterns and features within images and videos, making them ideal for applications like facial recognition, object detection, and image classification. CNNs are designed to mimic the human visual system by processing data through layers that detect edges, textures, and more complex features as the image passes through the network. In video recognition, neural networks can analyze frames sequentially to understand motion patterns, enabling real-time applications such as surveillance, autonomous vehicles, and video content indexing. Additionally, neural networks have been successful in medical imaging, where they can identify anomalies such as tumors in X-rays or

MRI scans. Their ability to learn and adapt from vast amounts of visual data has led to breakthroughs in fields like security, healthcare, and entertainment, where image and video processing is essential.

Natural Language Processing (NLP)

Neural networks play a crucial role in Natural Language Processing (NLP), enabling machines to understand, interpret, and generate human language. Deep learning models, such as Recurrent Neural Networks (RNNs) and Transformers, are especially effective in handling tasks like language translation, sentiment analysis, text generation, and speech recognition. RNNs and their variants, like Long Short-Term Memory (LSTM) networks, excel at sequential data, making them well-suited for processing text, where word order and context are essential. More recently, transformer models like GPT and BERT have revolutionized NLP by offering state-of-the-art performance in tasks such as question answering, summarization, and dialogue generation. These neural networks are trained on large corpora of text data, enabling them to generate coherent and contextually accurate outputs. NLP applications powered by neural networks are widely used in chatbots, virtual assistants, search engines, and translation services, making communication with machines more intuitive and effective.

Forecasting and Time Series

Neural networks are widely used in forecasting and time series analysis, where predicting future values based on past data is essential. Recurrent Neural Networks (RNNs) and their enhanced versions, such as Long Short-Term Memory (LSTM) networks, are particularly effective for handling sequential data and capturing temporal dependencies in time series. These models are used in various applications, including stock market prediction, weather forecasting, energy consumption forecasting, and demand planning in supply chains. Neural networks can learn complex patterns in the data, making them more accurate in predicting future trends compared to traditional methods. Additionally, they can adapt to changes in data over time, improving the model's robustness and accuracy. The ability of neural networks to process large datasets and learn from them makes them a powerful tool in fields that rely on accurate forecasting, enabling businesses and governments to make informed decisions based on future predictions.

Anomaly Detection

Neural networks are highly effective for anomaly detection, which involves identifying unusual patterns or outliers in data that deviate from expected behavior. This is critical in various fields such as cybersecurity, fraud detection, industrial monitoring, and healthcare. Neural networks, including Autoencoders and Generative Adversarial Networks (GANs), can be trained to understand the normal behavior of a system and flag instances that deviate significantly from this norm. For example, in fraud detection, neural networks can analyze transaction data and recognize suspicious patterns that might indicate fraudulent activity. In cybersecurity, they can detect network intrusions or unusual activity that could signal a security breach. In manufacturing, neural networks can monitor equipment behavior to identify early signs of failure, allowing for preventative maintenance. By learning from large datasets and continuously improving, neural networks can enhance the accuracy and efficiency of anomaly detection systems, reducing the risk of undetected problems in critical systems.

Perceptron and Multi-layer Perceptron (MLP)

A Perceptron, introduced by Frank Rosenblatt in 1957, is the simplest form of an artificial neural network. It consists of a single layer of artificial neurons, where each neuron receives input signals, applies weights, and computes a weighted sum. This sum is passed through an activation function to produce an output, typically for binary classification tasks, such as distinguishing between two classes. The Perceptron can be trained using the Perceptron learning rule, adjusting weights to minimize classification errors. A Multi-layer Perceptron (MLP) extends the Perceptron by adding multiple layers of neurons, allowing it to solve more complex tasks. In an MLP, the input layer is followed by one or more hidden layers, and an output layer. Each neuron in one layer is connected to neurons in the next layer. This architecture enables MLPs to model non-linear relationships, making them capable of solving a wide range of problems, including multi-class classification and regression tasks. It can perform binary classification tasks (e.g., classifying inputs into two classes).

Structure:

A perceptron consists of:

- **Input Nodes:** Represent the input features.
- **Weights (w):** Numerical parameters associated with each input.
- **Bias (b):** Threshold term to shift the decision boundary.

Activation function: Usually a step function, providing a binary output.

Mathematical Representation:

A perceptron calculates a weighted sum of inputs:

$$y = f\left(\sum_{i=1}^{n} w_i x_i + b\right)$$

Where:

x_i is the ith input.

w_i is the weight of thei^{th} input.

b is the bias term.

f(x) is the activation function, typically a step function:

$$f(x) = \begin{cases} 1 & x \geq 0 \\ 0 & x < 0 \end{cases}$$

Multi-layer Perceptron (MLP)

To overcome limitations of single-layer perceptrons, Multi-layer Perceptrons (MLP) were developed. MLP is a feedforward artificial neural network with multiple layers (input, hidden, and output layers). They can model complex, nonlinear relationships.

Structure:

An MLP typically has:

- **Input Layer:** Receives input features.
- **Hidden Layers:** Intermediate computational layers with neurons/nodes.
- **Output Layer:** Outputs predictions or classifications.

Neurons are fully connected: each neuron in one layer is connected to all neurons in the subsequent layer.

Mathematical Representation:

For a single hidden-layer MLP:

$$y = f_{out}\left(\sum_{j} w_j \cdot f_{hid}\left(\sum_{i} w_{ji}x_i + b_j\right) + b_{out}\right)$$

f_{hid} andf_{out} are activation functions in hidden and output layers respectively.

Typical activation functions:

Hidden layers: Sigmoid, Tanh, ReLU (Rectified Linear Unit).

Output layer: Sigmoid (binary classification), Softmax (multi-class), or Linear (regression).

Training an MLP (Backpropagation)

MLPs learn through backpropagation, an iterative gradient-based optimization method.Steps in backpropagation:

- **Forward propagation:** Compute outputs for given inputs.
- **Compute loss/error:** The difference between predicted and actual output.
- **Backward propagation:** Errors are propagated backward from output to input layers to compute gradients.

- **Weight update:** Gradients update weights and biases, usually via an optimization algorithm (e.g., Gradient Descent).

Example weight update rule (gradient descent):

$$w_{new} = w_{old} - \eta \frac{\partial E}{\partial w}$$

Where:

E is the error function (like mean squared error or cross-entropy loss).

Both perceptrons and multi-layer perceptrons have significantly influenced modern AI, with MLP serving as a foundation for deep learning advancements.

Backpropagation Algorithm

The backpropagation algorithm is a key technique in training artificial neural networks. It operates through a supervised learning process where the network learns from its mistakes by adjusting its internal weights to minimize the output error. Backpropagation works by calculating the gradient of the error function with respect to each weight in the network using the chain rule of calculus. During training, an input is passed through the network, producing an output, which is then compared to the expected target output. The difference between the actual and expected output (the error) is propagated back through the network, layer by layer. As the error moves backward, the algorithm adjusts the weights in the network in small increments, using gradient descent or other optimization methods. This iterative process allows the network to gradually improve its performance, making backpropagation a fundamental algorithm for neural network learning, particularly in deep learning applications.

Setup

A feedforward neural network is a type of artificial neural network in which information moves in one direction: from input to output. The network is structured in layers, typically consisting of an input layer, one or more hidden layers, and an output layer. The input layer receives data that represents the features of a problem, such as images, text, or other types of information. This data is then passed to the hidden layers, where the network performs computations, often involving activation functions to introduce non-linearity. The output layer generates the network's predictions or classifications. Each neuron in a layer is connected to neurons in the subsequent layer via weighted connections. These weights are crucial as they determine the influence of each neuron's output on the next layer's input. During training, the weights are adjusted based on the error between the predicted and actual outputs to improve the network's performance. Backpropagation is typically used in a feedforward neural network, where:

Backpropagation is a fundamental algorithm used to train neural networks, particularly in a feedforward network. The process starts by performing a forward pass, where inputs are passed through the network, layer by layer, producing an output. This output is then compared to the actual target values, and the error is computed. The core idea behind backpropagation is to minimize this error by adjusting the weights of the network. In a backward pass, the error is propagated back through the network from the output layer to the input layer. During this process, the partial derivatives of the error with respect to each weight are calculated using the chain rule of calculus. These derivatives guide how the weights should be updated to reduce the error. The weights are typically adjusted using gradient descent or its variants, making backpropagation an essential component in the supervised learning process of feedforward neural networks.

Forward Pass (Propagation)

In the forward pass, input data is passed through the network:

- The inputs are fed into the input layer.
- Each neuron in the hidden layers computes its output by applying a weighted sum of the inputs and passing the result through an activation function (like sigmoid, ReLU, etc.).
- The output layer computes the final output of the network.

Error Calculation

Once the output is computed, the error is calculated by comparing the predicted outputy^ with the actual target output y using a loss function. Common loss functions include:

- Mean Squared Error (MSE): $L = \frac{1}{2}(y - \hat{y})^2$
- Cross-Entropy Loss: Often used in classification tasks.

The loss function computes how far the network's output is from the desired output.

Backpropagation (Backward Pass)

Backpropagation refers to the process of propagating the error backward through the network to update the weights. This is done in two main steps:

Compute Gradient of the Loss Function

In machine learning, particularly in neural networks, the first step in optimizing the model's performance is to compute the gradient of the loss function with respect to each weight in the network. The gradient, often denoted as ∇L, measures the rate of change of the loss function as the weights change. Essentially, it tells us how much a particular weight contributed to the error or loss in the model's predictions. This gradient is calculated using the chain rule of calculus, where the partial derivative of the loss function with respect to each weight is computed layer by layer, starting from the output layer back to the input layer. This process is known as backpropagation. Once the gradients are computed, they can be used to adjust the weights in the opposite direction of the gradient to minimize the loss and improve the accuracy of the model. Using the chain rule of calculus, the backpropagation algorithm computes the gradient for each layer:

Output Layer: The gradient of the loss function with respect to the output layer weights is computed first. For each output neuron, the gradient of the loss function with respect to its input is calculated as:

$$\frac{\partial L}{\partial z_k} = (\hat{y}_k - y_k) \cdot f'(z_k)$$

Where $f'(z_k)$ is the derivative of the activation function with respect to the input to the neuron z_k.

Hidden Layers: The gradients for the hidden layers are computed using the chain rule:

$$\frac{\partial L}{\partial z_j} = \sum_k \frac{\partial L}{\partial z_k} \cdot \frac{\partial z_k}{\partial a_j} \cdot f'(z_j)$$

where z_k refers to the output of neurons in the next layer, and$f'(z_j)$ is the derivative of the activation function at layer j.

Weight Update

After computing the gradients, the weights are updated using an optimization technique like gradient descent. The update rule is:

$$w_{ij} \leftarrow w_{ij} - \eta \cdot \frac{\partial L}{\partial w_{ij}}$$

Where:

wij is the weight between neurons i and j,

η is the learning rate (a small positive value),

$\frac{\partial L}{\partial w_{ij}}$= is the gradient of the loss with respect to the weight.

Repeat

The training process in neural networks involves iteratively adjusting the model's weights to minimize the loss function. This process is repeated for each training example in the dataset, ensuring the model learns from the provided data. At each step, the weights are updated based on the gradient of the loss function with respect to the model's parameters. Over multiple iterations, also known as epochs, the network gradually converges to optimal weight values that allow it to make accurate predictions. Each training example contributes to this gradual learning process, enabling the model to improve its performance incrementally. The process of repeating the weight adjustment helps the neural network refine its parameters by continuously reducing the prediction error. As the network's weights converge over time, the model becomes increasingly accurate, ultimately resulting in a trained model capable of making reliable predictions on unseen data.

Gradient Descent Variants

There are different variations of gradient descent used in backpropagation:

Batch Gradient Descent

Batch Gradient Descent (BGD) is a variation of gradient descent where the weights of a model are updated after calculating the gradient of the cost function with respect to all the training data. In this method, the model computes the error for the entire dataset and adjusts the weights accordingly. The process is repeated for multiple iterations until convergence. This approach ensures that the model sees the full dataset in each update, leading to a more stable and smooth optimization process. However, BGD can be computationally expensive for large datasets, as it requires processing the entire dataset in each step. Despite its high computational cost, it tends to provide more accurate and reliable results, especially when the dataset is small. Batch Gradient Descent is often preferred when the dataset size is manageable and the goal is to achieve precise convergence toward the minimum of the cost function.

Stochastic Gradient Descent (SGD)

Stochastic Gradient Descent (SGD) is a variant of gradient descent where the weights of the model are updated after processing each individual training example. This method contrasts with Batch Gradient Descent, which computes the gradient over the entire dataset. By updating weights after each example, SGD can provide faster convergence and can escape local minima more effectively. However, this also introduces high variance in the updates, leading to a noisier optimization process. While this randomness can prevent the algorithm from settling in local minima, it may also cause the convergence to oscillate around the optimal value, making it slower to reach the minimum. Despite this, SGD is preferred in scenarios where computational efficiency is important, especially when dealing with large datasets, as it can significantly reduce memory usage and computational load per iteration, making it well-suited for real-time or online learning systems.

Mini-batch Gradient Descent

Mini-batch Gradient Descent is a hybrid approach that combines the advantages of both Batch Gradient Descent and Stochastic Gradient Descent (SGD). In this method, the model updates its weights after processing a small subset (mini-batch) of the training data instead of the entire dataset or just a single example. Typically, mini-batches range from 32 to 512 examples, allowing for a balance between computational efficiency and the benefits of gradient descent's convergence properties. This approach reduces the computational burden compared to full-batch updates, while also maintaining the ability to explore the solution space more effectively than stochastic updates. The mini-batch approach leads to faster convergence than batch processing and more stable updates than pure SGD, as it benefits from the reduced variance of updates. Mini-batch Gradient Descent is commonly used in deep learning models, where the datasets are large, and optimization speed is crucial without sacrificing convergence quality.

Activation Functions (ReLU, Sigmoid, Tanh)

Activation functions introduce non-linearities in neural networks, enabling the network to learn complex patterns and relationships in data. Here's an in-depth explanation of the three most common activation functions:

Rectified Linear Unit (ReLU)

ReLU is the most widely-used activation function, particularly in hidden layers. Mathematical function:

$$f(x) = \max(0, x)$$

Range:From 0 to ∞

Sigmoid Function

The sigmoid function is traditionally used in binary classification problems. Mathematical function:

$$\sigma(x) = \frac{1}{1 + e^{-x}}$$

Range: From 0 to 1

Hyperbolic Tangent (Tanh)

The tanh activation function resembles sigmoid but is symmetric around zero, making it zero-centered. Mathematical function:

$$\tanh(x) = \frac{e^{x} - e^{-x}}{e^{x} + e^{-x}}$$

Range: From −1 to 1

Each activation function has unique strengths and weaknesses. Choosing the right activation function depends on the problem type, network architecture, and computational resources available.

Deep Learning Basics

Deep learning is a subset of machine learning that uses neural networks with many layers to model complex patterns in data. At the core of deep learning are architectures like Convolutional Neural Networks (CNNs) and Recurrent Neural Networks (RNNs). CNNs are primarily used for image recognition and computer vision tasks. They leverage convolutional layers to automatically learn spatial hierarchies in data, allowing the model to identify patterns such as edges, textures, and shapes without manual feature extraction. CNNs excel in tasks like object detection, facial recognition, and image classification. RNNs, on the other hand, are designed for sequence-based data, such as time-series or natural language processing tasks. They have loops within their architecture, enabling the model to maintain a memory of previous inputs, making them ideal for tasks like speech recognition, language translation, and forecasting. Both CNNs and RNNs require large amounts of data and computational power for training, but they can achieve remarkable accuracy in complex tasks:

Convolutional Neural Networks (CNNs)

Convolutional Neural Networks (CNNs) are a class of deep learning models that excel in analyzing visual data, such as images and videos. Their primary strength lies in their ability to automatically detect patterns and hierarchies in spatial data, making them highly effective for tasks like image recognition, object detection, and facial recognition. CNNs operate by applying convolutional filters to input images, which extract features such as edges, textures, and shapes. These features are then passed through pooling layers, which reduce the dimensionality of the data, and fully connected layers that help make predictions. CNNs can also be applied to text classification tasks, where they treat text as a sequence of words or characters, capturing local patterns in word sequences. By using shared weights for the convolutional filters, CNNs can efficiently process large datasets, making them powerful tools for both visual and text-based tasks in machine learning.The core components are:

- Convolution Layer: Applies filters (kernels) across the input image, extracting meaningful features (edges, textures, patterns).
- Pooling Layer: Reduces spatial size and controls overfitting by summarizing information in local regions (commonly Max Pooling).
- Fully Connected Layer: Combines extracted features into final output categories.

Recurrent Neural Networks (RNNs):

Recurrent Neural Networks (RNNs) are a specialized class of neural networks designed to handle sequential data such as text, speech, and time series. Unlike traditional feedforward neural networks, RNNs have a unique architecture where the output of each layer is dependent on both the current input and the previous hidden state, effectively giving the network a form of memory. This allows RNNs to capture temporal dependencies and context from earlier inputs in a sequence. RNNs are particularly useful in tasks like language modeling, machine translation, speech recognition, and time series forecasting. They process data step by step, maintaining information about previous steps, which helps predict future events based on past patterns. However, traditional RNNs face challenges with long-range dependencies due to the vanishing gradient problem, leading to the development of more advanced models like Long Short-Term Memory (LSTM) and Gated Recurrent Unit (GRU) networks, which mitigate these issues for more effective learning. The Core Components are:

- Recurrent Layer:Maintains hidden states that pass information through sequential steps, allowing context awareness.
- Activation Functions (tanh, ReLU):Non-linearities that manage signal propagation across sequential steps.

Applications of Deep Learning

Image Recognition

Deep learning has significantly advanced the field of image recognition, enabling machines to accurately identify and classify objects within images. By utilizing convolutional neural networks (CNNs), deep learning algorithms can learn hierarchical features from raw pixel data, making them highly effective for image classification tasks. In image recognition, deep learning models are trained on large datasets with labeled images, which enables them to detect objects like animals, vehicles, faces, and even medical conditions in X-rays or MRI scans. This has practical applications in areas such as autonomous vehicles, where image recognition is essential for detecting obstacles, pedestrians, and traffic signs. In healthcare, it aids in diagnosing diseases through medical imaging. Deep learning's ability to automatically extract features and learn complex patterns from data has revolutionized industries, improving accuracy and efficiency in visual recognition tasks, while also expanding possibilities in fields like security, retail, and entertainment.

Natural Language Processing (NLP)

Deep learning plays a crucial role in natural language processing (NLP), which focuses on enabling machines to understand, interpret, and generate human language. Through techniques like recurrent neural networks (RNNs) and transformer models, deep learning algorithms can perform tasks such as language translation, sentiment analysis, text summarization, and speech-to-text conversion. These models are trained on vast amounts of text data, allowing them to learn semantic and syntactic relationships between words, sentences, and contexts. In applications like chatbots, virtual assistants, and customer service automation, NLP models enable machines to understand user input and generate relevant responses. Moreover, deep learning has improved machine translation systems, such as Google Translate, making cross-language communication smoother and more accurate. In sentiment analysis, NLP models help businesses understand customer opinions and feedback. Overall, deep learning has dramatically enhanced the performance of NLP systems, making them more intuitive and context-aware.

Speech Processing

Deep learning has transformed speech processing, enabling more accurate and natural interaction between humans and machines. Through the use of models like deep neural networks (DNNs) and long short-term memory (LSTM) networks, speech recognition systems can now transcribe spoken words into text with high accuracy. This is especially valuable in applications like virtual assistants (e.g., Siri, Alexa), automated transcription services, and voice-controlled devices. Deep learning also powers speaker identification, emotion detection, and speech synthesis (text to speech), enabling machines to not only recognize speech but also understand the speaker's identity and emotional state. Furthermore, deep learning algorithms can handle noisy environments and various accents, making speech recognition more versatile and accessible worldwide. In medical fields, speech processing has been applied in diagnostics, where it can analyze speech patterns to detect conditions such as Parkinson's disease or Alzheimer's. Overall, deep learning has enhanced speech processing technology, improving user experience and broadening its applications.

Summary

Neural Networks and Deep Learning represent revolutionary technologies transforming various fields, from healthcare to finance, by enabling complex data processing and insightful decision-making. Their ability to mimic human cognitive functions has led to remarkable advancements in image and speech recognition, natural language processing, and autonomous systems. Despite these successes, challenges remain, including issues of interpretability, computational complexity, and ethical concerns around data privacy and algorithmic biases. Ongoing research continues to enhance efficiency, transparency, and applicability of deep learning models, promising broader adoption and further innovations. As we move forward, a collaborative approach involving researchers, industry experts, and policymakers will be critical in addressing these challenges, ensuring responsible AI development. Ultimately, neural networks and deep learning hold immense potential for positive societal impact, provided they are designed and deployed thoughtfully, ethically, and sustainably, fostering advancements beneficial to humanity.

Exercise Questions

- What is a neural network?
- Define deep learning.
- Name three applications of neural networks.
- What is backpropagation?
- How does a convolutional neural network differ from a regular neural network?
- What is supervised learning in neural networks?
- Mention one limitation of deep learning.
- What role does activation function play in neural networks?
- What is the significance of the hidden layer in neural networks?
- What ethical issues are associated with deep learning?

6

APPLICATIONS OF MACHINE LEARNING

Machine learning (ML) has evolved from a niche field of computer science to a transformative technology with wide-reaching applications across various industries. At its core, machine learning allows systems to learn from data, improving their performance over time without explicit programming. This adaptability makes ML a powerful tool in solving complex problems, enabling innovations that were once thought to be impossible. From healthcare to finance, retail to entertainment, machine learning is shaping the future of many sectors by offering new ways to process, analyze, and predict data-driven outcomes. One of the most prominent applications of machine learning is in the field of healthcare. Machine learning algorithms are used to predict diseases, assist in diagnostics, and personalize treatment plans. By analyzing vast amounts of medical data, such as patient history and diagnostic images, machine learning models can detect patterns that may be missed by human practitioners. For example, ML is used in radiology to identify signs of tumors in X-rays and MRIs, and in genomics to predict genetic predispositions to diseases. This allows for more accurate, faster diagnoses and the development of customized treatment strategies, improving patient outcomes. In the finance sector, machine learning plays a crucial role in enhancing decision-making processes and improving customer experiences. Banks and financial institutions use ML for fraud detection, risk assessment, and predictive analytics. Machine learning algorithms can analyze transactional data in real time, identifying unusual patterns that might indicate fraudulent activities. Additionally, ML models help in algorithmic trading by predicting stock price movements based on historical data, giving traders an edge in decision-making. These applications have revolutionized the way financial institutions operate, making them more efficient and secure. Retail and e-commerce industries also benefit immensely from machine learning, particularly in customer behavior analysis, inventory management, and personalized marketing. ML algorithms analyze customer data to predict purchasing patterns, enabling businesses to offer personalized recommendations and promotions. E-commerce platforms use recommendation engines to suggest products to users based on their browsing history, purchase behavior, and preferences. Furthermore, ML helps optimize inventory by forecasting demand, ensuring that products are stocked in optimal quantities and reducing wastage.

The field of autonomous vehicles has seen significant advancements due to machine learning. Self-driving cars rely on ML models to interpret sensor data, make real-time decisions, and navigate roads safely. By processing information from cameras, radar, and lidar sensors, ML algorithms enable vehicles to understand their surroundings and adapt to changing conditions. This technology is paving the way for safer and more efficient transportation, reducing accidents and potentially transforming the entire landscape of mobility. Finally, natural language processing (NLP) is one of the most exciting applications of machine learning, enabling machines to understand and interact with human language. Virtual assistants like Siri, Alexa, and Google Assistant leverage NLP to process voice commands and provide intelligent responses. Machine learning is also used in sentiment analysis, where algorithms analyze social media posts, reviews, and customer feedback to gauge public opinion about products or services. This application of ML is essential in various sectors, including customer service, marketing, and social media monitoring, providing businesses with valuable insights into consumer preferences.

Machine Learning in Healthcare (Disease Prediction, Medical Imaging)

Machine Learning (ML) involves training algorithms to detect patterns and relationships in data, enabling predictive analytics, automation, and intelligent decision-making. In healthcare, ML assists medical professionals by enhancing accuracy, early disease detection, personalized treatments, and efficient medical workflows.

Disease Prediction Using ML

Disease prediction leverages ML algorithms to analyze patient data and identify risks, forecast disease onset, and support preventive care strategies.

Types of Data Used for Disease Prediction

Electronic Health Records (EHR)

Electronic Health Records (EHR) are an essential type of data used in disease prediction. EHRs contain comprehensive patient information, such as medical histories, clinical notes, and lab test results, which are crucial for understanding a patient's health status over time. Medical histories provide insights into past illnesses, surgeries, and treatments, while clinical notes from healthcare providers document symptoms, diagnoses, and treatment plans. Lab test results, including blood work and imaging reports, help identify abnormalities that could signal the onset of diseases. By analyzing this data, machine learning models can predict potential health risks, early signs of chronic conditions, and the likelihood of disease progression. EHR data allows for personalized healthcare, enabling clinicians to make informed decisions, offer tailored treatments, and improve disease outcomes. The integration of EHR data in predictive models enhances the accuracy and timeliness of disease diagnosis and prevention strategies.

Genomic Data

Genomic data is increasingly used in disease prediction, as it provides valuable insights into a person's genetic makeup and its role in health and disease. This data includes genetic profiles, DNA sequences, and biomarkers, which can reveal predispositions to various diseases such as cancer, cardiovascular conditions, and genetic disorders. Genetic profiles offer information about specific genes that may be linked to diseases, while DNA sequencing provides detailed information on genetic variations that could contribute to disease risk. Biomarkers, which are measurable indicators of disease or infection, can be identified through genomic data and help track the progression of diseases or response to treatment. By incorporating genomic data into predictive models, healthcare providers can forecast an individual's risk for developing certain diseases and implement early interventions or personalized therapies. This type of data is crucial for precision medicine, allowing for targeted treatments based on a patient's unique genetic makeup.

Wearable Device Data

Wearable device data plays a crucial role in disease prediction by continuously monitoring key health metrics such as heart rate, blood pressure, glucose levels, and physical activity. These devices, such as smartwatches and fitness trackers, collect real-time data that offers insights into an individual's health status, enabling early detection of potential health issues. Heart rate and blood pressure readings can reveal abnormal patterns indicative of cardiovascular conditions, while glucose level monitoring is critical for detecting and managing diabetes. Activity monitoring helps track physical exercise and sedentary behavior, which are important factors in assessing the risk of lifestyle-related diseases like obesity and hypertension. By integrating wearable device data into predictive models, healthcare professionals can monitor trends over time, identify emerging health risks, and intervene promptly. This data enables proactive management of chronic conditions, improves disease prevention efforts, and enhances the overall health and well-being of individuals.

Social and Behavioral Data

Social and behavioral data is a significant contributor to disease prediction, as it provides context for understanding the broader factors influencing an individual's health. This data includes lifestyle choices, diet, physical activity, and social determinants such as socioeconomic status, education, and access to healthcare. Lifestyle factors like smoking, alcohol consumption, and sleep patterns can contribute to the risk of various diseases, including heart disease, diabetes, and respiratory conditions. Dietary habits, such as the consumption of processed foods or a lack of nutrients, can significantly impact an individual's risk for obesity, cancer, and metabolic disorders. Social determinants, like living in an underserved area or facing financial instability, can also exacerbate health disparities and increase the likelihood of chronic conditions. Incorporating this type of data into predictive models allows healthcare professionals to understand the environmental and behavioral factors affecting a patient's health, enabling more effective and holistic disease prevention and management strategies.

Common ML Techniques in Disease Prediction

Classification Algorithms

Classification algorithms are widely used in disease prediction models to categorize patients into different groups based on various health parameters. These algorithms help in diagnosing diseases by predicting a patient's condition as one of several categories, such as "disease present" or "disease absent." Common classification algorithms include Logistic Regression, Decision Trees, Random Forests, and Support Vector Machines (SVM). For example, in predicting diseases like diabetes, a classification algorithm might analyze factors such as age, BMI, glucose levels, and family history to classify patients as either at risk or not at risk for the disease. These models are trained using labeled data, where the outcomes are known, and they learn patterns that can be applied to new, unseen data. The ability to classify patients accurately helps in early diagnosis, personalized treatment planning, and ultimately improving patient outcomes by detecting diseases at an early stage when they are most treatable.

Ensemble Methods

Ensemble methods combine multiple machine learning models to improve prediction accuracy by leveraging the strengths of different algorithms. In disease prediction, ensemble techniques like Random Forests, Gradient Boosting Machines (GBM), and AdaBoost are used to enhance the performance of classification models. By aggregating the predictions from multiple models, ensemble methods can reduce overfitting, improve generalization, and increase the robustness of disease prediction systems. For example, in predicting cancer, an ensemble model might combine decision trees or support vector machines to yield a more accurate diagnosis by minimizing errors. These methods work by creating a variety of models trained on the same dataset but with different approaches or data subsets. The final prediction is made based on a majority vote or weighted averaging of all individual model predictions, ensuring that the overall model benefits from higher accuracy and reliability, which is crucial for medical decision-making.

Deep Learning Models

Deep learning models, particularly neural networks, have gained significant traction in disease prediction due to their ability to automatically learn complex patterns from large, unstructured datasets like medical images, electronic health records, and genomic data. Convolutional Neural Networks (CNNs), Recurrent Neural Networks (RNNs), and other deep learning architectures are particularly useful for predicting diseases such as cancer, Alzheimer's, and cardiovascular conditions. These models can detect subtle relationships between variables that traditional methods might overlook. For example, CNNs are used in medical imaging to identify tumor patterns in X-rays, MRIs, or CT scans. RNNs, on the other hand, excel at analyzing sequential data, such as patient health history over time. Deep learning models excel in handling large datasets and can offer high predictive accuracy, making them a powerful tool for early disease detection. Their ability to improve with more data makes them a critical component of advanced healthcare analytics and diagnostics.

Use Cases and Examples:

Machine Learning (ML) significantly enhances medical imaging across various healthcare applications in Table 6.1. For instance, Convolutional Neural Networks (CNNs) and U-Net models applied to mammography, CT, and MRI scans achieve high accuracy in tumor detection and segmentation for breast, lung, and brain cancers. Similarly, chest diseases like COVID-19 and pneumonia are rapidly and accurately classified using CNN architectures such as ResNet and DenseNet on X-rays and CT images. Additionally, CNNs combined with transfer learning in MRI and CT scans allow early detection and precise segmentation of brain strokes and lesions. Finally, CNN-based analysis of fundus images provides accurate, scalable screening and diagnosis for retinal diseases like diabetic retinopathy.

Table 6.1: use cases and example of medical image.

Application	Imaging Type	ML Method	Result
Cancer Detection (Breast, Lung, Brain)	Mammography, CT, MRI	CNN, U-Net	Tumor detection and segmentation with high accuracy
Chest Disease Classification (COVID-19, pneumonia)	Chest X-ray, CT	CNN (ResNet, DenseNet)	Rapid, accurate disease identification
Brain Stroke & Lesion Detection	MRI, CT	CNN, transfer learning	Early lesion detection, precise segmentation
Retinal Disease (Diabetic Retinopathy)	Fundus images	CNN	Accurate, scalable screening and diagnosis

Workflow for ML-based Medical Imaging

Image Acquisition

The first step in a workflow for ML-based medical imaging is image acquisition, which involves collecting high-quality medical images for analysis. This typically includes modalities such as X-rays, CT scans, MRIs, and ultrasounds. High-quality images are crucial because the accuracy of machine learning models heavily depends on the quality and resolution of the input data. Images should be obtained with standardized protocols to ensure uniformity across datasets and minimize artifacts that may affect analysis. Advanced imaging techniques, such as contrast enhancement or specific scanning parameters, may also be used to improve the visibility of key features relevant to medical diagnoses. Proper image acquisition is fundamental as it sets the foundation for subsequent steps in the ML pipeline, ensuring that models are trained on reliable and relevant data. This phase might also involve ensuring that the collected images have proper labeling and metadata for effective model training.

Data Preprocessing & Augmentation

Data preprocessing and augmentation play a critical role in improving the performance of ML models in medical imaging. Preprocessing involves tasks such as image normalization, where pixel values are standardized to a common scale, and noise reduction, where unwanted distortions are minimized. These steps help enhance the clarity of important features in the medical images, making it easier for machine learning models to detect patterns accurately. Augmentation techniques, such as rotating, flipping, or cropping images, are applied to artificially increase the size and diversity of the training dataset. This helps prevent overfitting by exposing the model to various orientations, scales, and perspectives of the medical conditions. Additionally, augmentation can simulate different imaging conditions that may be encountered in real-world clinical scenarios. Combined, these preprocessing and augmentation techniques help ensure that the model generalizes well to unseen data, ultimately improving its ability to accurately diagnose medical conditions.

Model Training & Validation

Model training and validation are central to the development of ML-based medical imaging systems. Convolutional Neural Networks (CNNs) are commonly used for their ability to automatically learn spatial hierarchies in images. During model training, labeled imaging data (images with corresponding ground truth diagnoses) are fed into the CNN. The model adjusts its internal parameters (weights) based on the loss function to minimize the difference between predicted and actual outcomes. Validation is performed using a separate set of images not used during training to assess the model's ability to generalize. This helps ensure that the model does not overfit to the training data and performs well on new, unseen images. Regularization techniques such as dropout or batch normalization may be used to improve model performance. Additionally, hyperparameters like learning rate and batch size are tuned to optimize the training process, ensuring the model converges effectively for high accuracy in medical diagnoses.

Performance Evaluation

Once the model is trained, performance evaluation is essential to measure its effectiveness in medical imaging tasks. Key evaluation metrics include accuracy, sensitivity, specificity, and the AUC-ROC curve. Accuracy measures the proportion of correct predictions, while sensitivity (true positive rate) indicates how well the model identifies relevant conditions, such as tumors or diseases. Specificity (true negative rate) assesses how well the model avoids false positives, ensuring it doesn't misidentify healthy tissues as diseased. The AUC-ROC curve plots the model's true positive rate against the false positive rate at various thresholds, providing a comprehensive view of the model's diagnostic ability across different decision boundaries. These metrics allow clinicians and researchers to assess not only the overall accuracy but also the model's ability to minimize false negatives and false positives, which is crucial for making reliable medical diagnoses. Proper evaluation ensures the model's robustness and readiness for clinical deployment.

Clinical Integration & Real-time Analysis

The final step in the ML-based medical imaging workflow is clinical integration and real-time analysis. After the model has been trained and evaluated, it is deployed into imaging equipment or diagnostic software for practical clinical usage. This integration allows clinicians to use the model as a decision support tool, helping them analyze medical images quickly and accurately. The model can be embedded into imaging devices such as MRI machines, CT scanners, or X-ray systems, where it processes images in real time, providing immediate feedback to healthcare professionals. In some cases, it can assist in detecting abnormalities or suggesting possible diagnoses based on the analysis of the images. Clinical integration must meet strict regulatory standards, ensuring the model operates reliably and safely within healthcare environments. Real-time analysis also requires that the system is efficient, providing results without significant delay, which is critical for urgent medical decision-making in fields like radiology and pathology.

Machine Learning in Finance (Fraud Detection, Stock Market Prediction)

Financial institutions worldwide suffer significant financial losses due to fraudulent activities like identity theft, credit card fraud, insurance fraud, money laundering, and cyberattacks. Machine learning provides an intelligent, proactive approach to identifying and mitigating fraud.

Machine Learning Detects Fraud

Machine learning (ML) has become a powerful tool in detecting fraudulent activities across various industries, particularly in finance. By analyzing vast amounts of transaction data, machine learning algorithms can uncover hidden patterns that indicate fraudulent behavior, even when those patterns are subtle or previously unknown. Unlike traditional methods that rely on predefined rules, ML continuously improves by learning from historical data, enabling it to adapt to emerging fraud tactics. The ability to process large datasets in real-time allows these systems to flag suspicious transactions quickly, reducing the potential damage from fraudulent activities. The use of algorithms such as decision trees, neural networks, and ensemble methods enables more accurate and dynamic detection models that go beyond simple rule-based approaches, making ML an essential part of modern fraud prevention strategies.

Typical Approach

Data Collection

The first step in applying machine learning for fraud detection is data collection. A wide range of data points are gathered, including historical transaction records, user account details, and behavioral data like transaction frequency, spending patterns, and login times. Geolocation data, such as the IP address or GPS coordinates, and device fingerprints (e.g., browser or device identifiers) are also important, as they can help identify unusual activity or anomalies. Additional data, such as the user's typical transaction amounts and locations, can further enrich the model's ability to detect fraud. Collecting comprehensive data helps build a more accurate profile of normal user behavior, allowing the machine learning model to identify deviations that may indicate fraudulent actions. This data forms the foundation for training the model and detecting subtle fraud patterns that could go unnoticed using traditional methods.

Data Preprocessing

Data preprocessing is a critical step in fraud detection, where raw data is cleaned, normalized, and transformed into meaningful features that can be used by machine learning algorithms. Cleaning involves removing inconsistencies, such as missing values or duplicates, to ensure the data is accurate. Normalization ensures that all features are on a similar scale, which is essential for algorithms that rely on distance or gradient-based methods. Feature engineering involves creating new features or selecting the most relevant ones, such as calculating transaction frequency, determining account age, or identifying geographic inconsistencies in a user's activity. By transforming raw data into a more structured and meaningful form, preprocessing improves the model's ability to learn from the data and detect fraudulent patterns with higher accuracy, making it an essential part of the fraud detection pipeline.

Supervised Models

In fraud detection, supervised machine learning models are commonly used, where the model is trained on labeled data that includes both fraudulent and non-fraudulent transactions. Some popular supervised models include logistic regression, random forests, XGBoost, and support vector machines (SVM). Logistic regression is often used for binary classification tasks, such as predicting whether a transaction is fraudulent or not. Random forests and XGBoost are ensemble methods that build multiple decision trees to improve prediction accuracy and robustness. SVMs work well in high-dimensional spaces and are particularly effective when the data has clear margins of separation. These models learn to predict fraud by identifying patterns in the data that distinguish legitimate transactions from fraudulent ones. Once trained, they can be used to classify new transactions, allowing for real-time fraud detection and prevention.

Unsupervised Models

Unsupervised machine learning models are used in fraud detection when labeled data is unavailable or insufficient. These models focus on identifying patterns in data without the need for predefined labels, allowing them to detect anomalous behavior that may indicate fraud. Clustering algorithms like K-Means group similar transactions together, making it easier to spot outliers or anomalies that deviate from typical patterns. Isolation Forest is another unsupervised model that isolates anomalies by randomly selecting features and partitioning the data, making it effective for identifying rare fraudulent activities. Autoencoders, a type of neural network, are used for anomaly detection by learning a compressed representation of the input data, reconstructing it, and identifying discrepancies. Unsupervised models are valuable in fraud detection because they can uncover novel fraud patterns that have not yet been labeled or discovered, providing an adaptive approach to evolving fraud techniques.

Model Evaluation

Once a machine learning model is trained for fraud detection, its performance needs to be evaluated to ensure it is both accurate and reliable. Key evaluation metrics include precision, recall, F1-score, ROC-AUC, and confusion matrix analysis. Precision measures how many of the flagged fraudulent transactions were actually fraudulent, while recall measures how many fraudulent transactions were successfully detected. The F1-score is the harmonic mean of precision and recall, providing a balance between the two. ROC-AUC (Receiver Operating Characteristic - Area Under Curve) is used to assess the trade-off between the true positive rate and false positive rate across different thresholds. The confusion matrix further breaks down the model's performance into categories like true positives, true negatives, false positives, and false negatives, helping to identify areas of improvement. Regular evaluation ensures the model continues to perform optimally and adapt to changing fraud patterns.

Model Deployment

After training and evaluating the machine learning model, it is deployed for real-time transaction monitoring and fraud detection. The model is integrated into the transaction processing system, where it can score each new transaction for its likelihood of being fraudulent. High-risk transactions can trigger alerts or automatic actions, such as blocking the transaction, requiring additional authentication, or flagging it for review. The deployment involves continuous monitoring to ensure the model remains effective and accurate over time. Regular updates and retraining may be necessary as new fraud patterns emerge. By deploying the model in real-time, financial institutions and businesses can detect and prevent fraudulent activities as they occur, minimizing potential damage and improving overall security. Effective deployment of the model also involves setting thresholds and fine-tuning parameters to balance fraud detection and user experience.

Challenges in Stock Prediction with ML

Market Volatility

One of the biggest challenges in stock prediction using machine learning (ML) is the inherent volatility of financial markets. Stock prices are often influenced by unpredictable global events, such as natural disasters, political upheavals, or shifts in economic policies. These events create sudden, significant changes in market conditions that are difficult for models to anticipate. ML algorithms are designed to find patterns and trends in historical data, but such disruptive events do not always follow the patterns established in the past. This leads to unpredictable outcomes that undermine the accuracy of predictions. Furthermore, even if the model incorporates global events as features, it may struggle to process them in real-time or account for their impact effectively. As a result, while ML models can be highly effective in stable market conditions, they are much less reliable during periods of high volatility, making predictions less accurate and more uncertain.

Overfitting

Overfitting is a significant challenge in stock prediction with machine learning. It occurs when a model becomes too complex, capturing not only the true underlying patterns in the data but also the noise or random fluctuations. As a result, the model performs well on training data but poorly on unseen data, leading to unreliable predictions. Financial markets are inherently noisy and contain many unpredictable elements, such as market sentiment and sudden events. If an ML model is too complex, it might interpret these random fluctuations as meaningful patterns, thereby overfitting the data. This is particularly problematic in stock prediction, where the goal is to generalize well to new, unseen data. Techniques like regularization and cross-validation are often used to mitigate overfitting, but it remains a challenging issue due to the complex and dynamic nature of financial markets. Ensuring that the model captures only relevant trends is crucial for reliable stock predictions.

Data Quality

Another major challenge in stock prediction with machine learning is the quality of data. Financial data often suffers from issues like noise, incompleteness, and outdated information, which can severely impact the accuracy of predictions. Noisy data refers to random fluctuations that do not reflect real trends, and machine learning models can easily misinterpret these as valuable signals. Incomplete data is also common in financial markets, where missing information about stocks, economic indicators, or market sentiment can lead to skewed predictions. Additionally, outdated data can cause models to rely on trends that no longer hold in current market conditions. Since ML models are highly dependent on the data used to train them, any inaccuracies or gaps in the data can result in poor predictions. Addressing these issues requires high-quality, up-to-date, and complete datasets, which can be difficult to obtain, further complicating the task of making reliable stock predictions.

Model Interpretability

Model interpretability is another significant challenge when using machine learning for stock prediction. Many ML models, particularly deep learning and ensemble methods, operate as "black boxes," making it difficult to understand how they arrive at their predictions. This lack of transparency creates a barrier for investors, regulators, and stakeholders who need to trust the model's decisions. In financial markets, understanding the rationale behind predictions is critical for decision-making and regulatory compliance. For example, if a model predicts a significant price movement, investors want to know why the model made that prediction to assess its reliability. Similarly, regulators need to ensure that the models used are fair, unbiased, and compliant with legal standards. The complexity of modern ML models often complicates these explanations, and the inability to interpret predictions may reduce confidence in the model, limiting its adoption in the financial industry. This challenge highlights the need for more interpretable and explainable AI techniques in finance.

Machine Learning in Robotics (Autonomous Systems, Reinforcement Learning in Robotics)

Machine Learning (ML) enables robots to perform complex tasks autonomously by improving performance through experience. Robotics involves perception, control, navigation, and interaction tasks, and ML provides tools to enhance each of these domains. Common ML techniques used in robotics include:

Supervised Learning: Image/Object Recognition, Motion Prediction

Supervised learning is a machine learning technique that relies on labeled datasets to train models to make predictions or classifications. In image and object recognition, supervised learning algorithms are trained with labeled images that contain specific objects, enabling the system to identify and categorize new, unseen images. Convolutional neural networks (CNNs) are commonly used for this task, learning features such as edges, textures, and patterns to recognize objects in an image. Similarly, in motion prediction, supervised learning algorithms can be trained on historical data of object movements, such as human motion or vehicle trajectories, to predict future positions or behaviors. This is useful in areas like robotics, autonomous driving, and sports analytics. By providing labeled examples, supervised learning ensures the model can generalize well to new, unseen data, improving accuracy and performance in real-world applications. Overall, supervised learning is essential for tasks requiring high precision and clear output categories.

Unsupervised Learning: Anomaly Detection, Clustering Sensor Data

Unsupervised learning is a machine learning technique where models are trained on unlabeled data to uncover patterns or structures without prior knowledge of the output. In anomaly detection, unsupervised learning helps identify unusual or unexpected behavior within datasets, making it valuable in applications like fraud detection, network security, or predictive maintenance. By identifying data points that deviate significantly from normal behavior, unsupervised algorithms can flag potential issues before they escalate. In clustering sensor data, unsupervised learning groups similar data points together, revealing underlying structures or patterns. This is particularly useful in applications like environmental monitoring, where sensor data from different sources (temperature, humidity, etc.) is clustered to identify trends or outliers. Clustering algorithms such as k-means or DBSCAN can segment sensor data into meaningful categories without the need for labeled examples. Unsupervised learning is particularly beneficial when labels are unavailable or impractical to obtain, offering powerful insights from raw data.

Reinforcement Learning: Decision-Making, Control, Skill Acquisition

Reinforcement learning (RL) is a type of machine learning where an agent learns to make decisions by interacting with an environment and receiving feedback in the form of rewards or penalties. In decision-making, RL is used to optimize actions in complex, dynamic environments. For example, an RL agent might be trained to play a video game, where it learns to make moves that maximize its score by trial and error. In control systems, RL is used to optimize the behavior of systems such as robots or autonomous vehicles, where the agent must continuously make decisions to achieve goals like path following, obstacle avoidance, or efficient energy usage. In skill acquisition, RL is vital for learning complex tasks, like learning to walk, manipulate objects, or play sports, by rewarding the agent for improving its performance over time. Reinforcement learning is ideal for problems where the optimal solution is not known in advance but must be discovered through interaction with the environment.

Autonomous Robotics Systems

Autonomous robotics systems operate independently without human intervention, performing complex tasks by sensing their environment, making decisions, planning, and executing actions. The key components:

Perception

Perception in robotics refers to the use of various sensors to understand and interpret the environment in which a robot operates. Cameras, Lidar, radar, and Inertial Measurement Units (IMUs) play crucial roles in this process. Cameras capture visual data, allowing robots to recognize objects, detect colors, and identify surroundings. Lidar and radar sensors provide depth and distance information, enabling the robot to map its environment in 3D and detect obstacles even in low-light conditions. IMUs help measure the robot's acceleration, orientation, and angular velocity, providing critical feedback on the robot's motion and stability. The integration of these sensors allows robots to build a comprehensive understanding of their environment, recognize objects, and navigate complex spaces. This perception capability is essential for autonomous vehicles, drones, and robots operating in dynamic and unstructured environments, as it allows for safe interaction with the surroundings.

Localization and Mapping (SLAM)

Localization and mapping, often implemented through Simultaneous Localization and Mapping (SLAM), is a key task for autonomous robots. SLAM allows a robot to determine its position within an environment while simultaneously creating a map of the surrounding space. This is critical in scenarios where the robot does not have prior knowledge of its surroundings, such as in unknown or changing environments. By using data from sensors like Lidar, cameras, and IMUs, SLAM algorithms continuously update the robot's position and the map of its environment in real-time. This enables the robot to track its movement and avoid obstacles while building an accurate representation of the space. SLAM is used in applications like autonomous vehicles, indoor navigation systems, and robotic vacuum cleaners, where accurate positioning and real-time mapping are essential for safe and efficient operation. The combination of localization and mapping ensures that robots can navigate autonomously and adapt to dynamic environments.

Motion Planning and Navigation

Motion planning and navigation involve determining a robot's path to reach a destination while avoiding obstacles and optimizing movement. The process begins with creating a map or model of the environment, which is then used to plan the most efficient and safe route. The robot must consider factors like obstacles, terrain, and space constraints when calculating its path. Advanced algorithms, such as A* or RRT (Rapidly-exploring Random Trees), allow robots to determine paths while avoiding collisions. Additionally, motion planning often includes optimization tasks that minimize energy consumption, time, or other operational constraints. Path optimization ensures that the robot reaches its goal in the most efficient manner possible. This is crucial in scenarios like autonomous vehicles navigating through traffic, drones flying through obstacles, or industrial robots performing precise operations in confined spaces. Effective motion planning and navigation are vital for the robot's autonomy, efficiency, and safety in real-world environments.

Control Systems

Control systems in robotics are responsible for adjusting the robot's actuators and joints to perform desired physical actions. These systems use control algorithms to process input commands and generate control signals that drive the robot's motors or actuators. For example, in robotic arms, control systems adjust the position and speed of the arm's joints, ensuring precise movements required for tasks like assembly, painting, or surgery. In mobile robots, control systems regulate wheel speeds and steering to achieve desired motion. The control system must respond to changes in the robot's environment, such as external forces or unexpected obstacles, ensuring continuous stability and performance. Techniques like PID (Proportional-Integral-Derivative) control and model-based control are commonly used to achieve smooth and responsive actions. Control systems are essential for executing complex tasks with high accuracy and reliability, and their development is key to advancing robotics in applications ranging from manufacturing to healthcare.

ML Applications in Autonomous Robotics

Computer Vision (CNNs, Vision Transformers)

In autonomous robotics, computer vision plays a crucial role in enabling robots to perceive and understand their surroundings. Convolutional Neural Networks (CNNs) have been widely used for tasks such as object detection, image classification, and segmentation due to their ability to automatically learn hierarchical features from visual data. CNNs can process large amounts of image data efficiently, making them ideal for real-time applications in autonomous robots. Vision Transformers (ViTs) are an emerging alternative to CNNs, leveraging transformer architecture to capture long-range dependencies in visual data, which helps in improving accuracy in tasks like object recognition and scene interpretation. ViTs offer a more flexible approach, particularly for complex visual tasks involving high-resolution or long-range dependencies. Together, CNNs and ViTs empower robots to understand the world visually, enabling them to navigate, detect obstacles, recognize objects, and perform tasks autonomously in environments ranging from industrial settings to homes.

Sensor Fusion (Bayesian Methods, Deep Learning)

Sensor fusion is essential in autonomous robotics, combining data from multiple sensors to generate a more accurate and comprehensive understanding of the environment. Bayesian methods are widely used for sensor fusion, providing a probabilistic framework for combining sensor data, especially when dealing with uncertainty or noisy inputs. By estimating the likelihood of various states or sensor readings, Bayesian approaches improve the robot's ability to make informed decisions. Deep learning techniques also play a significant role in sensor fusion, allowing robots to integrate data from various sources, such as cameras, LiDAR, and IMUs, to create a unified, high-dimensional representation of the environment. Deep learning models can automatically learn complex relationships between sensor modalities, improving robustness in dynamic or unpredictable environments. Sensor fusion, powered by Bayesian methods and deep learning, enables autonomous robots to navigate, map, and interact with their surroundings with greater precision, efficiency, and adaptability in real-time.

Path Planning and Navigation (Deep RL, Graph Neural Networks)

Path planning and navigation are key components of autonomous robotics, allowing robots to move efficiently and safely in their environment. Deep Reinforcement Learning (Deep RL) is commonly used for path planning, where the robot learns optimal navigation strategies by interacting with the environment and receiving feedback in the form of rewards or penalties. Deep RL enables robots to adapt to dynamic environments, learning not only how to reach a destination but also how to handle obstacles and unexpected changes. Graph Neural Networks (GNNs) have also emerged as an effective tool for navigation, particularly in complex, structured environments like urban streets or warehouses. GNNs model spatial relationships between nodes (e.g., intersections, rooms) and edges (paths, roads), enabling robots to efficiently plan routes and navigate through these networks. Together, Deep RL and GNNs enable autonomous robots to make intelligent, real-time navigation decisions, optimizing path planning and ensuring safe, efficient movement in a variety of settings.

Reinforcement Learning (RL) in Robotics

RL involves training agents (robots) to make decisions through trial-and-error interactions with the environment, maximizing cumulative rewards. The Basic Components of RL:

- **Agent (Robot):** The decision-maker.
- **Environment:** External world interacting with the robot.
- **State (s):** Representation of environment conditions.
- **Action (a):** Decisions/actions the robot performs.
- **Reward (r):** Numerical feedback from the environment to guide learning.
- **Policy (π):** Strategy mapping states to actions.

RL Algorithms Popular in Robotics

Q-Learning / Deep Q-Networks (DQN)

Q-Learning and Deep Q-Networks (DQN) are popular reinforcement learning (RL) algorithms in robotics, particularly for tasks with a discrete action space. These algorithms are used in decision-making tasks where the robot selects from a set of predefined actions, such as grasping objects or navigating through a simple maze. Q-Learning helps the robot learn a policy that maximizes long-term rewards by iteratively updating action-value estimates. DQN, an extension of Q-Learning, leverages deep neural networks to approximate Q-values, making it suitable for more complex, high-dimensional tasks that are difficult for traditional Q-Learning methods to handle. In grasping tasks, for example, the robot learns the optimal sequence of actions to successfully grasp an object. DQN's ability to handle large state spaces allows robots to generalize across various environments, making it highly effective for real-world applications where decisions must be made quickly and with limited prior knowledge.

Policy Gradient Methods (REINFORCE, PPO, A3C)

Policy gradient methods such as REINFORCE, Proximal Policy Optimization (PPO), and Asynchronous Advantage Actor-Critic (A3C) are widely used for continuous control tasks in robotics. These methods are particularly effective when dealing with problems where the robot's actions are continuous, such as robot arm manipulation or humanoid robot balancing. Policy gradient algorithms optimize the policy directly by adjusting the parameters of a neural network that represents the policy function. REINFORCE is one of the simplest policy gradient methods, but PPO and A3C improve its efficiency and stability by using techniques like advantage estimation and asynchronous updates. These algorithms are well-suited for complex tasks that involve precise control and fine-tuning of actions, such as adjusting the torque in robot arms for manipulation tasks or maintaining balance in humanoid robots. Policy gradient methods allow for the handling of complex, high-dimensional state and action spaces, making them essential for real-world robotic applications.

Actor-Critic Methods (DDPG, SAC)

Actor-Critic methods, such as Deep Deterministic Policy Gradient (DDPG) and

Soft Actor-Critic (SAC), are key reinforcement learning techniques used in robotics to balance exploration and exploitation while ensuring stable control. These methods combine the advantages of both value-based and policy-based approaches, which makes them highly effective in environments requiring continuous control and high precision. DDPG is well-suited for tasks where the action space is continuous, such as controlling robotic arms, and SAC improves upon DDPG by incorporating entropy regularization to promote exploration, enhancing the stability of the learning process. The actor component of these methods generates actions based on the current policy, while the critic evaluates the quality of actions taken by estimating value functions. By balancing exploration (trying new actions) and exploitation (refining known actions), these methods ensure that robots can effectively learn stable control policies for complex, dynamic tasks, making them invaluable in real-world robotics applications like autonomous vehicles and robotic manipulation.

Applications of RL in Robotics

Robot Manipulation

Reinforcement Learning (RL) has revolutionized robot manipulation, allowing robots to autonomously learn how to perform complex tasks such as picking, placing, and assembling objects. In robot manipulation, RL enables robots to optimize their actions by exploring and interacting with their environment. For instance, a robot can learn to manipulate objects by receiving rewards for successfully completing tasks like grasping or stacking objects, and penalizing unsuccessful attempts. Over time, RL algorithms enable robots to fine-tune their motor skills and adapt to varying object shapes, textures, or environmental conditions. RL allows robots to handle real-world unpredictability by continually improving through trial and error. This approach is particularly useful in environments where explicit programming of every possible movement is impractical, such as in warehouses, factories, or surgical procedures. The application of RL in robot manipulation significantly enhances automation efficiency, improving precision and reliability in industrial and service-based robotic systems.

Autonomous Vehicles

Reinforcement Learning (RL) plays a significant role in the development of autonomous vehicles by enabling them to learn and make decisions in dynamic and complex environments. In this context, RL is used to optimize vehicle control systems for tasks such as path planning, obstacle avoidance, and traffic management. Through RL algorithms, autonomous vehicles can learn to navigate urban roads, adjust their speed based on traffic flow, and make decisions in real-time, all while ensuring safety. The system rewards the vehicle for making safe and efficient driving decisions and penalizes unsafe behaviors. Over time, RL allows the vehicle to improve its decision-making, adapt to new scenarios, and learn from experience, such as handling unexpected obstacles or adapting to adverse weather conditions. By continuously improving through feedback, RL enables autonomous vehicles to make better driving decisions, contributing to safer and more efficient transportation systems in the future.

Legged Robots and Humanoids

Reinforcement Learning (RL) has enabled significant advancements in the control and movement of legged robots and humanoids. These robots are tasked with navigating complex terrains, maintaining balance, and performing human-like movements. With RL, legged robots and humanoids learn to adapt to various environments by interacting with the surroundings and adjusting their movements based on feedback. For example, RL allows humanoid robots to improve their walking or running capabilities by adjusting their gait and posture to maintain stability on uneven surfaces or when carrying loads. Similarly, RL helps legged robots navigate rough terrains by continuously improving their balance and coordination, learning how to recover from falls or missteps. This ability to learn and refine movements makes RL especially valuable in applications like search and rescue, where robots must operate in challenging environments, or assistive robotics, where humanoids support people with disabilities. RL's ability to improve robot autonomy is critical in these complex scenarios.

Drone Navigation

In the field of drone navigation, Reinforcement Learning (RL) is used to train drones to navigate through complex environments autonomously. RL enables drones to learn optimal flight paths and control actions by receiving rewards for successful navigation and penalties for collisions or unsafe behavior. With RL, drones can autonomously adjust their flight trajectories to avoid obstacles, adjust altitude, and optimize energy consumption, all while handling dynamic and unpredictable conditions like wind or changes in terrain. Drones can learn to explore new environments, map areas, or deliver packages with high precision. RL also allows drones to improve their behaviors over time by adapting to new obstacles or environmental changes, making them more efficient and reliable. In applications like search and rescue, surveillance, or delivery services, RL-powered drones enhance autonomous decision-making, providing more effective and adaptable solutions in real-world scenarios. RL allows drones to continually learn from their environment, improving performance with every flight.

Machine Learning in E-commerce (Recommendation Systems, Customer Segmentation)

Recommendation Systems use machine learning (ML) algorithms to predict and recommend products or services to customers based on historical data, user behavior, preferences, and patterns.

Types of Recommendation Systems

Collaborative Filtering (CF)

Collaborative Filtering (CF) is one of the most widely used techniques for building recommendation systems. It works by analyzing user interactions and preferences to recommend items based on the behavior of other users. There are two main types of collaborative filtering: user-based and item-based. In user-based collaborative filtering, the system identifies users who are similar to the target user and recommends items that these similar users have liked. In item-based collaborative filtering, the system recommends items that are similar to the ones the user has already interacted with. CF is particularly effective when there is a large amount of user-generated data, as it doesn't require detailed information about the items themselves. However, CF can struggle with issues such as the cold-start problem (when new users or items lack enough data) and sparsity (when there are not enough ratings to draw meaningful conclusions).

Content-Based Filtering

Content-Based Filtering is a recommendation system technique that makes suggestions based on the attributes or features of items, rather than relying on user interactions or behaviors. It analyzes the content of items—such as genre, keywords, or tags—and compares them with a user's past preferences or interactions. For example, if a user has watched several science fiction movies, the system will recommend more movies within that genre based on the similarity of content. This method requires a good understanding of item features and user profiles. Content-based filtering can be highly accurate, especially in domains where items have clearly defined attributes, such as books, movies, or products. However, it has limitations, such as a tendency to recommend only items similar to those a user has already interacted with, leading to a lack of diversity in recommendations. This can create a so-called "filter bubble," where users are exposed to a narrow set of content.

Hybrid Systems

Hybrid recommendation systems combine multiple recommendation techniques, such as collaborative filtering and content-based filtering, to overcome the limitations of each individual approach. By integrating these methods, hybrid systems can provide more accurate, diverse, and personalized recommendations. For example, a hybrid system might use collaborative filtering to recommend items based on user similarity, but also consider the content attributes of items to further refine the recommendations. This approach helps to mitigate common issues in recommendation systems, such as the cold-start problem (where new users or items lack data) and the "filter bubble" effect (where recommendations become too narrow). Hybrid systems can be implemented in several ways, such as combining the outputs of different models, weighting recommendations from multiple sources, or using one method to filter the results of another. The flexibility of hybrid systems makes them suitable for a wide range of applications, including e-commerce, media, and social networks, where the diversity and relevance of recommendations are crucial.

Customer Segmentation in E-commerce

Customer segmentation in e-commerce is a critical strategy that involves dividing customers into distinct groups based on common traits or behaviors to optimize marketing efforts. This practice enables businesses to create targeted campaigns, personalize product offerings, and improve overall customer engagement. By understanding the preferences, behaviors, and demographics of different customer segments, companies can increase the efficiency of their marketing strategies and provide a more personalized shopping experience. Customer segmentation also enhances product recommendations, promotional offers, and customer service by aligning these elements with the specific needs of each segment. Additionally, segmentation helps identify high-value customers, improve customer retention, and increase conversion rates. Overall, customer segmentation is essential for e-commerce businesses aiming to maximize their marketing ROI and deliver a tailored shopping experience that drives customer satisfaction and loyalty.

Types of customer segmentation

Demographic Segmentation

Demographic segmentation divides customers based on characteristics such as age, gender, income, education, occupation, and family size. This form of segmentation is one of the most commonly used in e-commerce as it provides easily measurable and widely available data. Understanding the demographic profile of customers helps businesses tailor their products, services, and marketing messages to specific groups. For example, a company selling luxury goods might target high-income individuals, while a toy store could focus on families with children. Demographic segmentation allows e-commerce businesses to create focused advertisements and promotions that appeal to specific age groups or income brackets, increasing the likelihood of engagement and purchase. It also assists in inventory management by aligning product offerings with the preferences of the target demographic. Ultimately, demographic segmentation is a powerful tool for improving customer targeting and driving higher sales in e-commerce.

Behavioral Segmentation

Behavioral segmentation is based on customers' behaviors, such as purchasing patterns, product usage, brand loyalty, and response to previous marketing campaigns. This segmentation method helps e-commerce businesses understand how and why customers make purchasing decisions, enabling them to create more targeted and effective marketing strategies. For example, customers who frequently purchase products on sale may be targeted with personalized discounts, while high-value, repeat customers may receive loyalty rewards. Behavioral segmentation also helps businesses analyze customers' buying journey and identify opportunities for improvement. E-commerce companies can use this data to optimize their website, refine their product recommendations, and design tailored promotions that resonate with specific customer behaviors. Additionally, businesses can segment customers based on how often they visit the website, their level of interaction with the brand, or how they respond to emails and ads. Ultimately, behavioral segmentation enhances customer satisfaction and boosts conversion rates by delivering relevant content and offers.

Psychographic Segmentation

Psychographic segmentation focuses on understanding customers based on their lifestyles, values, interests, personalities, and social status. Unlike demographic segmentation, which deals with quantifiable data, psychographic segmentation delves deeper into the psychological and emotional aspects of customer behavior. By analyzing customers' preferences, attitudes, and motivations, e-commerce businesses can tailor their marketing strategies to connect with consumers on a more personal level. For example, a company selling eco-friendly products might target customers who value sustainability and environmental responsibility, while a brand focused on fitness apparel might cater to health-conscious individuals. Psychographic segmentation allows e-commerce businesses to craft messages that resonate with customers' deeper desires and aspirations, creating stronger emotional connections. By addressing the specific needs and values of each segment, companies can improve customer engagement, increase brand loyalty, and ultimately drive more conversions.

Geographic Segmentation

Geographic segmentation divides customers based on their location, such as country, region, city, or even climate zone. This segmentation method is particularly useful for e-commerce businesses that want to customize their offerings based on geographic factors that may influence purchasing behavior. For example, an e-commerce company selling winter clothing may target customers in colder regions with tailored ads for seasonal items, while a brand selling beachwear might focus on customers in warmer climates. Geographic segmentation also allows businesses to adapt to local cultural preferences, language, and trends, ensuring that their marketing and product offerings are relevant to each area. Moreover, it helps with logistics and supply chain management by identifying regional demand patterns and optimizing inventory distribution. By using geographic segmentation, e-commerce businesses can improve their market penetration, increase sales in specific regions, and create more localized and effective marketing campaigns that resonate with regional customer needs and preferences.

Practical Applications and Examples

Amazon

Amazon utilizes a hybrid recommendation system that combines collaborative filtering and content-based approaches to suggest products to its customers. Collaborative filtering relies on user behavior, such as browsing history and previous purchases, to recommend items that others with similar preferences have bought. Content-based filtering, on the other hand, makes recommendations based on the features of the items, like their descriptions, categories, and customer reviews. Amazon segments customers using a variety of factors, including browsing patterns, purchase history, and demographics, enabling highly targeted marketing strategies. This segmentation allows Amazon to deliver personalized advertisements and promotions tailored to individual users, improving conversion rates. By leveraging machine learning algorithms and vast customer data, Amazon ensures that its recommendation engine adapts to evolving user preferences, providing a personalized shopping experience. This approach enhances customer satisfaction, boosts sales, and reinforces customer loyalty by making product discovery more relevant and efficient.

Netflix

Netflix employs collaborative filtering along with advanced clustering algorithms to enhance its content recommendation system. Collaborative filtering helps Netflix predict what users might like based on the viewing habits of other users with similar preferences. In addition, Netflix uses clustering algorithms to group users with similar tastes, refining content recommendations for each cluster. By analyzing the vast amount of data generated from user interactions, such as watched content, ratings, and search behavior, Netflix personalizes its suggestions to suit individual preferences. This allows Netflix to provide highly accurate recommendations, which improves user engagement and retention. The system continuously learns and adapts to changes in user behavior, ensuring that content recommendations remain fresh and relevant. Additionally, Netflix has successfully integrated this technology into its platform's user interface, making it easier for users to discover new shows and movies tailored to their tastes, ultimately driving customer satisfaction and reducing churn.

Spotify

Spotify uses machine learning-based clustering techniques and personalized recommendation algorithms to provide tailored playlist suggestions and music discovery features for its users. By analyzing listening habits, user interactions, and music preferences, Spotify clusters users with similar tastes and recommends content that aligns with their interests. The recommendation system is powered by complex algorithms that process factors like song genre, tempo, artist preferences, and even mood based on listening history. Machine learning helps

Spotify improve the accuracy of recommendations over time by continually refining its models based on user feedback and behavior. Personalized playlists such as "Discover Weekly" and "Release Radar" are examples of how Spotify uses these techniques to keep users engaged and encourage exploration of new artists and genres. Additionally, the integration of these algorithms with Spotify's user interface creates a seamless and enjoyable music discovery experience, increasing user satisfaction and encouraging longer listening sessions.

Flipkart/Myntra

Flipkart and Myntra, two of India's largest e-commerce platforms, use machine learning (ML) to enhance customer segmentation and provide personalized shopping experiences. By analyzing demographic data, browsing behavior, and purchase history, ML algorithms segment customers into distinct groups, allowing for more targeted product recommendations and personalized marketing efforts. For example, if a customer frequently buys athletic wear, Myntra might suggest new arrivals in the fitness category. Similarly, Flipkart can leverage customer behavior to optimize recommendations across categories like electronics, fashion, and home goods. The platforms also use ML to power dynamic pricing models, inventory management, and advertising campaigns. Personalized advertising is a key feature, as the platforms target customers with relevant ads based on their browsing history and demographic characteristics. This personalized approach increases customer engagement and boosts conversion rates, as shoppers are more likely to find products they are interested in, ultimately improving the overall shopping experience and driving sales.

Future Trends in ML-based E-commerce

Deep Learning (Neural Networks)

The future of ML-based e-commerce is heavily influenced by deep learning, particularly through neural collaborative filtering. This technique leverages neural networks to improve recommendation systems by identifying complex patterns in consumer behavior, such as preferences, buying history, and interactions with products. Neural networks enable highly personalized and dynamic recommendations that go beyond traditional collaborative filtering methods, which often rely on simpler statistical models. By incorporating deep learning into recommendation systems, e-commerce platforms can deliver more accurate and relevant product suggestions, leading to increased customer satisfaction and conversion rates. Deep neural networks can capture non-linear relationships in user data, improving the prediction of customer preferences even in cases with sparse or noisy data. As computing power grows and more sophisticated algorithms are developed, deep learning will continue to enhance the ability to offer personalized shopping experiences, shaping the future of e-commerce recommendations.

Real-Time Personalization

Real-time personalization is becoming a cornerstone of ML-based e-commerce, driven by the availability of streaming data. In the near future, e-commerce platforms will increasingly use real-time data streams, such as customer clicks, browsing patterns, and interactions with products, to make instantaneous recommendations. This capability allows e-commerce websites and apps to offer a truly dynamic shopping experience, where product suggestions are tailored to a customer's immediate interests and actions. For instance, if a user shows interest in a particular category or product, the system can instantly update recommendations to highlight similar or complementary items. Real-time personalization improves user engagement and conversion by offering highly relevant suggestions as they occur. This use of streaming data is key for creating adaptive systems that respond to changes in behavior in near real-time, allowing businesses to stay competitive in a fast-moving marketplace by providing a more responsive and customized shopping experience.

Explainable AI (XAI)

Explainable AI (XAI) is emerging as a critical trend in ML-based e-commerce to address the need for transparency and accountability in recommendation algorithms. As e-commerce platforms rely increasingly on AI-driven recommendations, it becomes essential for customers and businesses to understand how these recommendations are generated. XAI techniques help to make the decision-making process of machine learning models more transparent, allowing users to understand why certain products are being recommended. This transparency is important for building trust with customers, especially in sensitive areas such as data privacy and biased recommendations. Additionally, XAI can assist e-commerce businesses in refining their algorithms to ensure fairness, accuracy, and accountability in how recommendations are made. By ensuring that AI models are not "black boxes," businesses can improve customer satisfaction, reduce the risk of algorithmic bias, and comply with regulations regarding ethical AI usage, paving the way for a more responsible and trustworthy AI-driven e-commerce environment.

Multimodal Recommendations

The future of e-commerce is increasingly leaning towards multimodal recommendation systems, which integrate various types of data, such as images, text, and video, to provide richer and more accurate product suggestions. By combining these different data sources, ML models can better understand a customer's preferences and offer personalized recommendations based on a broader range of inputs. For example, images can help analyze visual preferences, while text can capture sentiment from product descriptions or reviews, and videos can reveal interests in how products are used. Multimodal recommendations allow for a more holistic understanding of a user's behavior and needs. This integration enhances the personalization of e-commerce experiences, as products can be recommended not only based on previous purchases or clicks but also by considering a customer's interaction with diverse types of media. As the technology advances, multimodal systems will provide more contextually relevant suggestions, improving user engagement and satisfaction across e-commerce platforms.

Ethical and Social Implications of Machine Learning

Machine learning (ML) significantly impacts society, presenting both ethical opportunities and challenges. Here are the primary ethical and social implications to consider:

Ethical Implications

Bias and Fairness

Machine Learning (ML) algorithms often mirror and amplify biases present in training data, which can lead to discriminatory outcomes based on factors such as race, gender, ethnicity, or socioeconomic status. These biases arise from historical data that may reflect existing societal prejudices. Addressing fairness in ML requires careful curation of data, ensuring diverse representation across different groups, and implementing checks to minimize bias. Additionally, transparent algorithms and fairness-aware training methods are crucial for mitigating harmful biases. It is vital to create models that provide equal treatment and opportunities for all groups, regardless of their demographic attributes. Without such precautions, ML systems can unintentionally perpetuate inequality, which is why fairness must be a priority in algorithm design and deployment, especially in sensitive domains like hiring, healthcare, and criminal justice.

Privacy Concerns

Machine learning models often require vast amounts of data, much of which may include sensitive personal information such as health records, financial details, and social behaviors. These data-driven models pose significant privacy risks, including unauthorized access to or use of personal information. Privacy concerns arise from potential data breaches, inadequate consent processes, and the misuse of data for unintended purposes. To mitigate these risks, strict privacy regulations, such as the General Data Protection Regulation (GDPR) in Europe, are necessary to ensure data is collected, processed, and stored responsibly. Moreover, implementing privacy-preserving technologies like differential privacy or federated learning can help safeguard user confidentiality while still enabling the benefits of ML. Organizations must prioritize protecting individuals' rights and provide transparency about how personal data is utilized within ML models.

Transparency and Explainability

Many machine learning algorithms, especially complex ones like deep neural networks, function as "black boxes," making it difficult to understand the reasoning behind their decisions. This lack of transparency can undermine trust in the system, particularly in critical areas such as healthcare, finance, and criminal justice, where decisions have significant consequences. The challenge lies in making these models interpretable while maintaining their performance. To address this, there is a growing emphasis on developing explainable AI (XAI) techniques, which aim to provide insights into how models make predictions. This transparency is essential for accountability, as it allows stakeholders to scrutinize and validate decisions. In high-stakes applications, explainability fosters trust, ensures compliance with regulations, and helps prevent the deployment of unfair or harmful algorithms. Ethical AI design must focus on balancing accuracy with clarity.

Accountability and Responsibility

The increasing deployment of machine learning systems raises questions about accountability, especially when these systems cause harm or produce inaccurate results. In many cases, pinpointing responsibility for an ML system's behavior is challenging due to the complexity of its design and operation. Who is liable when an autonomous system makes a faulty decision? Developers, organizations, and users must establish clear accountability frameworks to ensure ethical use. This includes creating ethical guidelines for algorithmic decision-making, with specific roles outlined for developers, implementers, and stakeholders. Additionally, it's important to ensure transparency in how ML models are tested, validated, and monitored over time to avoid unintended consequences. With proper accountability in place, there is greater assurance that systems will be deployed in a way that minimizes harm and promotes fairness, safety, and trust.

Manipulation and Autonomy

Machine learning algorithms are increasingly used in recommendation systems, targeted advertising, and social media platforms, which can influence user behavior and decision-making. While these technologies can provide personalized experiences, they also have the potential to manipulate users by exploiting psychological and emotional triggers. This manipulation may affect user autonomy, as individuals may be nudged toward choices that are not in their best interest, or influenced to act in ways that prioritize commercial objectives over personal well-being. It is essential to ensure that these algorithms are designed to respect user autonomy, with transparency about how recommendations are made and clear consent about data usage. Ethical guidelines must be established for persuasive technologies to prevent manipulation and safeguard individual freedom. Users should have control over their interactions with these systems, with the ability to opt-out or adjust their preferences.

Automation and Job Displacement

The rise of machine learning and automation has led to significant advancements in productivity, but it also presents challenges regarding job displacement. As ML systems automate tasks traditionally performed by humans, there is growing concern about the future of employment, especially for workers in industries vulnerable to automation. This displacement may exacerbate economic inequality and social instability, as individuals may struggle to find new roles that match their skill sets. To mitigate these effects, ethical responsibility lies in supporting retraining and reskilling programs for displaced workers. Additionally, policymakers must ensure that the benefits of automation are distributed equitably, promoting inclusive economic growth. This includes fostering the development of new industries and job opportunities that leverage emerging technologies. A balanced approach is necessary to ensure that ML-driven progress does not leave behind those most impacted by technological shifts.

Social Implications

Impact on Employment

While automation through machine learning (ML) can significantly enhance productivity and efficiency, it also poses a risk to employment, particularly for lower-skilled workers. The automation of routine tasks in industries such as manufacturing, retail, and logistics could lead to job displacement, exacerbating unemployment and widening economic disparities. Workers in these sectors, who may lack the skills for higher-level tasks, are most vulnerable to this shift. To mitigate these effects, societies must implement proactive measures such as retraining programs, reskilling initiatives, and lifelong learning opportunities. By investing in education and workforce development, economies can better prepare workers for new roles in emerging industries, ensuring a smoother transition in the face of technological advancements.

Digital Divide and Inequality

The widespread adoption of machine learning (ML) technologies risks deepening the digital divide, particularly between developed and developing nations, as well as between affluent and marginalized communities. Access to ML-driven innovations, such as smart technologies and data-driven solutions, is often limited by unequal access to resources like high-speed internet, modern infrastructure, and quality education. Rural areas and lower-income populations may face barriers to adopting these technologies, widening existing economic and social inequalities. To combat this, equitable access to digital education, technological infrastructure, and inclusive policies is essential. Governments and organizations must prioritize bridging this gap to ensure that ML's benefits are accessible to all, regardless of geographical location or socio-economic status.

Social Surveillance and Control

Machine learning technologies, such as facial recognition systems, predictive policing algorithms, and social credit scoring, have raised significant concerns regarding privacy, surveillance, and civil liberties. While these tools are often marketed as solutions for improving security or efficiency, they can lead to overreach in monitoring individuals, potentially infringing upon fundamental rights. ML-enabled surveillance systems can create environments of constant observation, eroding personal freedoms and fostering social control. To prevent misuse and abuse, robust oversight mechanisms, democratic accountability, and clear ethical guidelines must be established. This would ensure that the implementation of such technologies is transparent, responsible, and aligned with human rights principles.

Impact on Democracy and Governance

Machine learning-powered tools, such as deepfakes, algorithmically targeted misinformation, and automated social media bots, pose serious threats to democracy and governance. These technologies enable the spread of disinformation, which can sway public opinion, manipulate electoral processes, and polarize societies. As a result, the integrity of democratic institutions and informed decision-making is compromised. It is essential to establish ethical standards, regulatory frameworks, and oversight mechanisms to combat the proliferation of misinformation and safeguard democratic values. Governments, tech companies, and civil society must collaborate to ensure the responsible use of ML technologies and protect public trust in democratic processes.

Changes in Human Interaction and Relationships

Machine learning technologies, including chatbots, recommendation algorithms, and virtual assistants, are transforming how people communicate, interact, and form relationships. While these innovations enhance convenience, they also risk altering social dynamics by replacing face-to-face interactions with digital communication. As individuals increasingly turn to ML-driven platforms for support and information, concerns about social isolation, emotional detachment, and manipulation arise. These tools may also foster unhealthy dependencies on technology, potentially diminishing genuine human connections. To mitigate these risks, it is crucial to deploy ML technologies ethically, ensuring that they enhance, rather than replace, meaningful human interaction. Ethical guidelines should be established to balance convenience with the preservation of social and emotional well-being.

Environmental Impact

Training large-scale machine learning models requires vast computational resources, leading to substantial energy consumption and a corresponding environmental impact. The process of training these models involves running complex algorithms across massive datasets, often on powerful servers that consume significant amounts of electricity. This contributes to the growing carbon footprint of the tech industry, exacerbating climate change. As ML technologies continue to advance, there is a pressing need to prioritize sustainability in AI development. By adopting energy-efficient computing methods, leveraging renewable energy sources, and optimizing model designs to reduce resource consumption, the environmental impact of ML can be minimized. Sustainable practices should be integrated into the development lifecycle of machine learning to ensure that technological progress does not come at the expense of the planet.

Future Trends in AI and Machine Learning

Generative AI

Generative AI, including advanced models like GPT, DALL-E, and Midjourney, is rapidly transforming creative industries by automating content creation. These models can generate high-quality text, images, and even videos, enabling businesses to produce personalized content at scale. This efficiency reduces human labor and accelerates content generation, which is particularly useful in fields such as marketing, design, and entertainment. The evolution of generative AI also enables hyper-personalization, where content can be tailored specifically to individual preferences or needs, enhancing user experience. As these models improve, they will likely take on more complex creative tasks, such as generating innovative ideas or even developing new products. Moreover, generative AI will empower users to create and innovate without the need for specialized skills, democratizing creative processes and fostering a new wave of content creation across industries, education, and entertainment.

Explainable AI (XAI)

As AI systems become more embedded in critical decision-making processes, the demand for explainable AI (XAI) is growing. XAI focuses on making AI models transparent and interpretable, ensuring that users understand how decisions are made. This is crucial for gaining trust, especially in sectors like healthcare, finance, and law, where AI decisions directly affect people's lives. The increased focus on XAI will facilitate better compliance with regulations, as organizations will need to explain AI-driven decisions in clear, understandable terms. It will also help address ethical concerns, such as fairness and accountability, by making AI models more transparent and auditable. As AI becomes more autonomous, XAI will become essential for ensuring ethical responsibility and minimizing biases. With advances in XAI, users will have more confidence in AI systems, leading to broader adoption and better integration of AI into decision-making processes across various industries.

Edge AI

Edge AI refers to the shift in AI processing from centralized data centers to local devices such as smartphones, wearables, and IoT devices. This trend significantly improves speed and reduces latency, enabling real-time decision-making and enhanced user experiences. By processing data on-device, edge AI also addresses privacy concerns, as sensitive information does not need to be transmitted to a central server. This makes it particularly appealing for applications where privacy is a critical factor, such as healthcare and personal devices. The rise of edge AI is closely tied to the growth of IoT, where millions of interconnected devices need intelligent, real-time processing capabilities. Moreover, edge AI enhances system efficiency, reducing the reliance on cloud computing and decreasing energy consumption. With the proliferation of mobile devices and IoT sensors, edge AI will play a key role in powering the next generation of smart, responsive, and secure applications.

AI in Cybersecurity

AI is set to revolutionize cybersecurity by enhancing threat detection, prevention, and response. AI-driven systems can analyze vast amounts of data in real-time, identifying patterns and anomalies that indicate potential security threats. These systems can predict, detect, and mitigate cyber threats autonomously, significantly reducing the time between the onset of a threat and the response. Machine learning algorithms enable these systems to continuously improve, adapting to new types of cyberattacks without human intervention. Additionally, AI can automate routine security tasks, freeing up security teams to focus on more complex issues. As cyber threats become more sophisticated, AI's role in cybersecurity will only increase, helping to protect sensitive data, prevent data breaches, and ensure the integrity of digital infrastructures. With proactive AI-driven defense systems, organizations can stay ahead of evolving cyber threats, providing enhanced security for users and businesses alike.

Reinforcement Learning and Autonomous Systems

Reinforcement learning (RL) is driving advancements in autonomous systems, such as self-driving vehicles, drones, and robotics. RL allows machines to learn optimal behaviors through trial and error, improving their performance over time. This is especially important for autonomous systems that need to navigate dynamic and unpredictable environments. RL algorithms can enable vehicles and robots to make better decisions, improving safety, efficiency, and reliability. In the case of autonomous vehicles, RL can help with real-time decision-making, such as when to adjust speed, change lanes, or stop. Similarly, RL is enhancing industrial automation, where robots can learn more efficient ways to perform tasks. As RL algorithms become more advanced, autonomous systems will become increasingly capable, reducing human intervention and enhancing operational efficiency. The ongoing improvements in RL will lead to safer, smarter, and more reliable autonomous systems in various industries, revolutionizing transportation, logistics, and manufacturing.

Multimodal AI Models

Multimodal AI models integrate multiple data types, such as text, audio, images, video, and sensor data, to enhance AI's contextual understanding and human-like interactions. By processing diverse inputs simultaneously, these models can interpret and respond to complex real-world scenarios more effectively than single-modal systems. For example, multimodal AI can understand a video's context by analyzing both the visual content and accompanying audio, improving its ability to recognize objects, actions, and emotions. This makes multimodal AI ideal for applications like virtual assistants, autonomous vehicles, and healthcare, where multiple types of data need to be analyzed together for accurate decision-making. The ability to combine various data sources also enhances the AI's ability to communicate and interact more naturally with humans, improving user experiences. As these models continue to evolve, they will enable more intuitive, intelligent, and context-aware applications across a wide range of industries, from entertainment to healthcare.

Responsible AI and Ethical Considerations

As AI technology becomes more pervasive, responsible AI practices and ethical considerations are increasingly essential. Stricter regulations and ethical standards will guide the development and deployment of AI systems, ensuring that they are used fairly and transparently. Organizations will prioritize reducing bias, improving fairness, and ensuring that AI systems are accountable for their decisions. Ethical AI will focus on minimizing harmful consequences, such as discrimination or unequal access to resources, and ensuring that AI decisions do not adversely affect marginalized communities. Moreover, AI systems will need to be designed with the utmost respect for privacy and data protection, ensuring that sensitive information is handled responsibly. As part of responsible AI, organizations will invest in methods to make AI systems explainable and interpretable, fostering trust among users. By addressing these ethical challenges, AI can be deployed in ways that promote social good, enhance transparency, and support ethical decision-making across industries.

AI-Augmented Workforce

AI is transforming the workforce by automating repetitive tasks and augmenting human capabilities, enabling workers to focus on more strategic, creative, and higher-order cognitive tasks. AI tools can handle routine processes such as data entry, scheduling, and basic customer service, freeing employees to engage in more complex problem-solving and decision-making. This shift leads to increased productivity and innovation, as employees are empowered to use their time and skills more effectively. AI will also provide workers with new capabilities, such as enhanced data analysis and decision-making support, improving their ability to perform tasks with greater precision and insight. While some jobs may be displaced by automation, new roles will emerge in areas like AI management, data science, and system design. As the workforce evolves, AI will serve as a collaborative partner, enhancing human potential and creating new opportunities for growth and skill development.

Quantum Machine Learning

Quantum computing is poised to revolutionize machine learning by drastically accelerating computations and enabling the solution of previously intractable problems. Unlike classical computers, quantum computers can process vast amounts of data simultaneously through quantum bits (qubits), allowing for exponential speedup in complex calculations. In machine learning, this could mean faster training times for models, more accurate predictions, and the ability to tackle highly complex problems in fields like drug discovery, material science, and optimization. Quantum machine learning (QML) could enable AI systems to analyze and process data in ways that were previously impossible with classical computing. However, quantum computing is still in its early stages, and widespread adoption will require overcoming challenges related to hardware, stability, and scalability. Despite these hurdles, the potential of quantum machine learning to accelerate AI research and unlock new capabilities makes it an exciting area of development with transformative potential across various industries.

Personalized Healthcare

AI-driven personalized healthcare is revolutionizing the way medical treatments are designed and delivered. By analyzing vast amounts of patient data, AI can help develop precision medicine, tailoring treatments to an individual's genetic makeup, lifestyle, and health conditions. AI models can assist in diagnosing diseases earlier, predicting patient outcomes, and identifying the most effective treatment plans based on a patient's unique characteristics. Additionally, AI-powered predictive health monitoring tools can track patients' conditions in real-time, enabling early intervention and reducing hospitalizations. AI is also enabling the development of digital therapeutics, where personalized treatment plans are delivered through mobile apps or wearables. These innovations are improving patient outcomes by providing more accurate, timely, and customized care. As AI in healthcare continues to advance, it will increasingly focus on improving access, reducing costs, and ensuring that patients receive the right care at the right time, ultimately leading to healthier populations and more efficient healthcare systems.

Foundation Models and Transfer Learning

Foundation models are large, general-purpose AI models capable of performing multiple tasks, reducing the need for task-specific models. These models can be fine-tuned through transfer learning, allowing them to adapt to new applications quickly and efficiently. For example, a foundation model trained on vast amounts of text data can be adapted for specific tasks such as sentiment analysis, language translation, or customer service, significantly reducing the time and cost required to develop new AI applications. This flexibility makes foundation models highly valuable for businesses seeking scalable and adaptable AI solutions. With transfer learning, organizations can leverage pre-trained models, customizing them to meet their unique needs without starting from scratch. This approach also accelerates the deployment of AI solutions, making them more accessible to a broader range of industries. The development of foundation models and transfer learning will be pivotal in reducing AI development costs and democratizing AI technology.

AI in Sustainability and Climate Change

AI is becoming a critical tool in the fight against climate change and in promoting sustainability. AI-driven models can predict and monitor environmental impacts, helping policymakers and organizations make informed decisions about energy usage, resource management, and conservation efforts. For instance, AI can optimize energy consumption in smart grids, reducing waste and increasing efficiency in power distribution. Additionally, AI can assist in climate modeling, helping scientists predict weather patterns, track climate changes, and develop mitigation strategies for rising global temperatures. AI is also being used to improve the sustainability of industries such as agriculture, where it can optimize resource usage, reduce water consumption, and minimize waste. Through advanced data analytics and optimization techniques, AI can identify opportunities to reduce emissions, enhance recycling processes, and optimize supply chains. As AI technology continues to evolve, its role in addressing global sustainability challenges will become increasingly important, enabling more effective climate action and environmental protection.

Summary

Machine learning (ML) applications have transformed various industries, driving efficiency, accuracy, and innovation. From healthcare, where ML assists in disease prediction and diagnostics, to finance, facilitating fraud detection and algorithmic trading, its impact is profound. In the automotive sector, machine learning underpins autonomous driving systems, significantly enhancing safety and efficiency. Similarly, personalized recommendations powered by ML have reshaped customer experience in e-commerce and entertainment. Despite these advantages, the implementation of ML faces challenges, including data privacy concerns, ethical considerations, biases, and computational resource requirements. Continuous advancements promise to resolve these issues, improving transparency and explainability of ML models. As industries increasingly rely on data-driven decision-making, machine learning's relevance will grow, influencing future developments across multiple sectors. However, ensuring ethical deployment, transparency, and fairness will be essential to maximize societal benefits, making ML a powerful tool for addressing complex real-world problems sustainably and responsibly.

Exercise Questions

- What is machine learning?
- Name two applications of ML in healthcare.
- How does machine learning help in fraud detection?
- What role does ML play in autonomous vehicles?
- Define supervised and unsupervised learning.
- Give an example of ML use in recommendation systems.
- What challenges do organizations face when implementing ML?
- How is ML utilized in image recognition?
- Why is data quality important in machine learning?
- What ethical considerations are associated with ML applications?

7

THEORETICAL FOUNDATIONS OF MACHINE LEARNING

Machine Learning (ML) stands at the confluence of statistics, computer science, and optimization, forming a transformative discipline that enables systems to learn from data and improve over time. While the practical success of ML is evident across diverse domains such as healthcare, finance, natural language processing, and autonomous systems, the theoretical underpinnings of ML provide a critical framework to understand why and how learning from data is possible. Theoretical ML equips practitioners and researchers with the tools to analyze algorithms, assess generalization performance, and determine the limits of learning models. At its core, this field is concerned with formulating learning as a mathematical problem, studying its computational feasibility, and characterizing the trade-offs between model complexity, data availability, and prediction accuracy. One of the most significant contributions of theoretical machine learning is the formalization of learning paradigms. The Probably Approximately Correct (PAC) learning model, introduced by Valiant in the 1980s, provides a formal framework to define learnability and success criteria for hypotheses generated from finite data. This model established the idea that for any target function in a given hypothesis class, a learner should be able to find a hypothesis that performs well on unseen data with high probability, provided sufficient training data. This foundation has been expanded into various learning settings, such as agnostic learning (where no assumption is made about the target function), and online learning (which deals with sequential data). These models have helped clarify conditions under which learning is guaranteed, enabling theoretical evaluation of algorithmic performance.

Another pillar of theoretical machine learning is the concept of generalization — the ability of a model trained on a sample dataset to perform well on unseen data. The study of generalization involves bounding the difference between training error and test error using principles from statistical learning theory. Tools such as Vapnik–Chervonenkis (VC) dimension, Rademacher complexity, and covering numbers help quantify the capacity of hypothesis spaces, allowing one to understand overfitting and underfitting in rigorous terms. For instance, a model with high capacity might fit training data perfectly but fail to generalize, while a model with low capacity might not capture essential patterns. The balance between bias and variance, and the notion of regularization, all stem from these theoretical constructs. In addition to generalization, computational learning theory explores the algorithmic complexity of learning problems. Many learning tasks are shown to be NP-hard or intractable, which implies that even if a function is learnable in principle, finding an efficient algorithm may not be feasible. To address this, the theory classifies algorithms according to their computational demands and convergence guarantees. Convex optimization, for instance, plays a central role in many ML algorithms because convex problems have globally optimal solutions that are computationally tractable. Non-convex optimization, common in deep learning, presents theoretical challenges, motivating research into saddle points, gradient dynamics, and landscape geometry. Thus, the interplay between algorithmic design and theoretical analysis is fundamental in building scalable and reliable ML systems. Furthermore, theoretical foundations address questions of robustness and stability, which have become increasingly relevant in the age of adversarial attacks and noisy data environments. Stability theory examines how small changes in training data affect the output of a learning algorithm — a property intimately linked to generalization. Algorithms with strong stability often exhibit better test performance. Similarly, robustness to adversarial perturbations or missing data is formalized through Lipschitz continuity, adversarial risk bounds, and distributional shifts. These frameworks enable researchers to design models that are not only accurate but also resilient in real-world scenarios, enhancing trustworthiness and deployment readiness. Lastly, the theoretical landscape of machine learning is evolving to accommodate modern advancements such as deep learning and reinforcement learning. While classical theory provides strong tools for linear models, kernel methods, and decision trees, deep neural networks operate in regimes where traditional assumptions often break down. Nevertheless, efforts are ongoing to extend theoretical analysis to these domains through the study of overparameterization, implicit regularization, neural tangent kernels, and the role of stochastic gradient descent. These theoretical insights aim to bridge the gap between the empirical success of large-scale models and a principled understanding of their behavior. The foundations laid by decades of theoretical research remain indispensable in shaping the future of learning algorithms, ensuring they are not only effective but also interpretable, reliable, and grounded in provable guarantees.

Introduction to Learning Theory

Learning theory forms the foundational bedrock of machine learning, cognitive science, and educational psychology. It seeks to understand how systems (biological or artificial) can improve their performance over time through experience. In computational terms, learning is the process by which an algorithm improves its predictions or decisions based on data rather than being explicitly programmed. The theory provides both a mathematical and conceptual framework to analyze and understand learning from data. Learning theory is deeply rooted in fields like statistics, logic, information theory, and computer science. It aims to formalize the concept of learning, develop efficient learning algorithms, and analyze their performance.

Learning Feasible

The feasibility of learning depends on multiple interrelated factors that determine whether a system can effectively learn from data and generalize to unseen scenarios.

Availability of Representative Data

The feasibility of learning is heavily dependent on the availability of representative data. For a model to generalize effectively, it must be trained on datasets that reflect the true distribution of the problem domain. If the data is too sparse, skewed, or noisy, the model may struggle to identify the actual patterns, leading to poor performance on unseen inputs. Bias in data can also result in unfair or inaccurate outcomes. Therefore, the success of any learning algorithm hinges on high-quality, diverse, and sufficiently large datasets that encapsulate the relevant features and variability of the environment or problem space.

Hypothesis Space and Model Complexity

The hypothesis space encompasses all the potential models or functions a learner might choose from. Its size and structure directly influence learning feasibility. If the space is too small, the learner may miss critical patterns (underfitting), failing to capture the complexity of the data. Conversely, if the hypothesis space is too large, it may overfit—capturing noise rather than meaningful trends. Balancing model complexity is essential, often managed through regularization or pruning. The ideal model should be expressive enough to capture true patterns but simple enough to avoid overfitting, embodying the principle of Occam's Razor and the bias-variance trade-off.

Learnability

Learnability refers to whether a concept or function can be learned from data within a reasonable amount of time and sample complexity. The Probably Approximately Correct (PAC) framework provides a theoretical foundation for understanding this. According to PAC theory, a problem is learnable if a learning algorithm can, with high probability, find a hypothesis that is approximately correct, given a sufficient number of training examples. This concept helps identify which problems are tractable and which may be infeasible. It emphasizes that not all learning tasks are solvable with finite resources, guiding the selection of algorithms and problem formulations accordingly.

Computational Resources

The availability of computational resources critically impacts the feasibility of learning. Even if a task is statistically learnable, it may not be practically solvable if the algorithm has high computational or memory demands. Machine learning models, especially deep learning architectures, require significant processing power, storage, and time—particularly during training. Scalability becomes essential when dealing with large datasets or complex models. Efficient algorithms that optimize both training speed and inference latency ensure that learning remains viable within realistic constraints. Thus, computational feasibility plays a central role in the selection and deployment of learning systems in practical environments.

Feedback Mechanism

Feedback mechanisms are central to guiding the learning process. In supervised learning, feedback is provided in the form of labeled data, helping the model adjust its parameters based on error signals. In reinforcement learning, feedback is delivered through rewards or penalties, shaping the agent's behavior over time. The quality, frequency, and clarity of feedback influence how quickly and accurately a model learns. Ambiguous or delayed feedback can hinder learning, leading to slow convergence or suboptimal results. Therefore, a well-designed feedback loop whether through accurate labels or reward structures—is essential for directing learning in a purposeful and effective manner.

Noise Tolerance

Noise tolerance refers to a model's ability to handle irrelevant, corrupted, or misleading data. In real-world scenarios, datasets often contain noise due to measurement errors, missing values, or inconsistent labeling. A feasible learning system must differentiate between meaningful patterns and random fluctuations. Robust algorithms employ techniques like regularization, cross-validation, and data augmentation to mitigate the effects of noise. If a model lacks noise tolerance, it risks overfitting learning spurious correlations that degrade performance on new data. Therefore, the capacity to maintain generalization despite noisy inputs is a critical trait of practical, deployable machine learning systems.

Types of Learning Problems (Inductive vs. Deductive)

Inductive learning is the process of generalizing from specific examples to broader rules or patterns. Most machine learning algorithms fall into this category, where the system learns a function or model from training data.Deductive learning involves applying existing knowledge or rules to derive specific conclusions. It starts with general premises and logically deduces the outcomes in particular cases.Learning problems can be broadly categorized into inductive and deductive learning. These represent two fundamentally different approaches to reasoning and knowledge acquisition in Table 7.1.

Table 7.1: Comparative analysis on inductive versus deductive learning problems.

Aspect	Inductive Learning	Deductive Learning
Definition	Learning general rules or models from specific examples or data	Applying known rules or theories to deduce specific outcomes
Approach	Data-driven; bottom-up reasoning	Rule-driven; top-down reasoning
Goal	Discover patterns, hypotheses, or predictive models	Derive conclusions based on logical inference
Example in ML	Training a classifier from labeled data	Using decision logic or knowledge base to derive predictions
Knowledge Requirement	Does not require pre-defined rules; learns from observations	Requires a predefined set of rules or logic
Output	Probabilistic or generalizable model	Deterministic conclusions
Uncertainty Handling	Handles uncertainty and noise in data	Limited in handling uncertainty unless rules are explicitly defined
Common Algorithms	Decision Trees, Neural Networks, SVM, KNN	Rule-based Systems, Expert Systems, Logic Programming
Real-World Use Cases	Spam detection, image classification, speech recognition	Theorem proving, legal reasoning, automated diagnosis using rules

Bias-Variance Tradeoff

The bias-variance tradeoff is a foundational concept in machine learning and statistical modeling that governs the performance of learning algorithms, especially their ability to generalize to unseen data. It reflects a fundamental tension between two types of errors that affect model accuracy:

- **Bias:** Error due to incorrect assumptions in the learning algorithm.
- **Variance:** Error due to sensitivity to small fluctuations in the training dataset.

Bias

Bias arises when a model is too simple to capture the underlying structure of the data. For instance, using a linear model to fit data generated by a quadratic relationship leads to underfitting. The model performs poorly on both the training and test data.

High Bias → Oversimplified model → Poor training and test performance

Variance

Variance occurs when a model is too complex, capturing noise along with the data's actual patterns. It performs well on the training set but poorly on the test set due to overfitting.The goal of machine learning is to find the sweet spota model that balances bias and variance for optimal performance on unseen data.

High Variance → Overly complex model → Good training but poor test performance

Understanding Model Generalization

Model generalization refers to the ability of a model to perform well on new, unseen data. This is the ultimate objective of any predictive modeling task. The relationship between generalization and the bias-variance tradeoff can be summarized as follows:

- **Underfitting:** High bias, low variance → poor generalization
- **Overfitting:** Low bias, high variance → poor generalization
- **Good generalization:** Moderate bias, moderate variance → optimal performance on new data

Example: Imagine training a model to predict housing prices:

A high-bias model may predict price solely based on square footage, ignoring other relevant features like location or number of bedrooms.A high-variance model might memorize every small fluctuation in historical prices, failing to generalize when market conditions change.Generalization is achieved when the model is neither too simplistic nor too tailored to the training data.

Visualizing Bias and Variance

Visualizing bias and variance help in understanding how different models behave. Here are common ways to illustrate the bias-variance tradeoff:

Prediction Error vs. Model Complexity

This curve typically shows:

Training Error decreases as model complexity increases.Validation/Test Error first decreases (as bias drops), then increases (as variance rises).As model complexity increases, prediction error follows a U-shaped curve. Simple models have high bias and low variance, leading to underfitting and high error on both training and validation datasets. As complexity increases, bias decreases and variance rises, improving the model's ability to fit the training data while increasing the risk of overfitting. At an optimal pointmoderate complexitybias and variance are balanced, minimizing test error and achieving the best generalization. Beyond this point, increasing complexity further reduces training error but leads to higher variance and worse test performance due to overfitting.

Table 7.2: Represent the Prediction Error versus Model Complexity.

Model Complexity	Bias	Variance	Training Error	Validation/ Test Error	Model Behavior
Low (Simple Model)	High	Low	High	High	Underfitting
Moderate	Moderate	Moderate	Moderate	Low (Optimal)	Good Generalization
High (Complex Model)	Low	High	Low	High	Overfitting

Target Function vs. Model Output

The bullseye Table 7.3 helps visualize the interplay between bias and variance in model predictions. When bias is high and variance is low, predictions cluster tightly but far from the target, indicating underfitting. Conversely, low bias and high variance produce predictions scattered widely around the true value, reflecting overfitting. The ideal scenario is low bias and low variance, where predictions are both accurate and consistentclose to the center of the bullseye. The worst case arises when both bias and variance are high, leading to predictions that are neither accurate nor stable, scattered far from the true value in all directions.

Table 7.3: Target Function versus Model Output.

Bias	Variance	Visualization (Bullseye)	Interpretation
High	Low	Predictions far from center but close together	Underfitting
Low	High	Predictions spread widely, but around the center	Overfitting
Low	Low	Predictions close to center and close together	Ideal model
High	High	Predictions far and scattered	Worst case

Learning Curves

Learning curves graphically represent a model's performance over time or with increased data. Typically plotted with training and validation error on the y-axis and the number of training examples on the x-axis, these curves help diagnose issues like underfitting or overfitting. Analyzing the shape and convergence of these curves enables practitioners to determine if the model needs more data, complexity adjustments, or better regularization. They are crucial for understanding how well a machine learning algorithm generalizes to unseen data and guide hyperparameter tuning by revealing whether performance improves with more training or hits a plateau due to model limitations.

High Bias

A high bias model suffers from underfitting, meaning it is too simplistic to capture the underlying patterns in the data. In learning curves, this is evident when both training and validation errors remain high and close together, showing that the model performs poorly even on the training set. The model may be linear when the relationship is nonlinear, or it might lack essential features or complexity. Solutions include using more complex algorithms, increasing model parameters, or engineering better features. Adding more training data typically does not help, as the fundamental issue lies in the model's insufficient capacity.

High Variance

A high variance model exhibits overfitting, where it learns the training data too well, including its noise, but fails to generalize to new data. In the learning curve, this is shown by a low training error but a significantly higher validation error. This indicates that the model is too complex relative to the amount of data or the regularization is insufficient. Common remedies include simplifying the model, applying regularization techniques, or increasing the size of the training dataset. Monitoring learning curves helps determine whether additional data or algorithm tuning can help reduce the gap between training and validation errors.

Balanced

A balanced model demonstrates good generalization, indicated by learning curves where training and validation errors are both low and converge over time. This suggests that the model has learned the data well without overfitting or underfitting. Such a model has appropriate complexity for the task and benefits from sufficient training data and effective regularization. Balanced learning curves reflect a healthy bias-variance tradeoff and suggest that the model is likely to perform well on unseen data. Maintaining this balance involves proper feature selection, regularization, and sometimes ensemble methods. It is the desired state in supervised learning scenarios. The Mathematical View

Total Expected Error = Bias^2 + Variance + Irreducible Error

- **Bias^2:** How far off the average model prediction is from the actual output.
- ***Variance:*** How much the model predictions vary for different training sets.
- **Irreducible Error:** Noise in the data that cannot be explained by any model.

Probably Approximately Correct (PAC) Learning

PAC learning, introduced by Leslie Valiant in 1984, is a foundational theoretical framework in computational learning theory. It formalizes the concept of learning a function from a set of examples in a way that ensures the learned function is probably (with high probability) approximately correct (within a small error margin). The PAC model bridges probability theory, combinatorics, and computational complexity, and it underlies many machine learning algorithms.

Formal Definition of Learnability

PAC Learnability

Let:

- X: input space
- C: concept class — a set of Boolean functions c:X→ {0,1}
- H: hypothesis class — the set of functions the learning algorithm can output
- D: an unknown probability distribution over X
- L(h): true error = $\Pr_{x \sim D}[h(x) \neq c(x)]$
- L_S(h): empiricalerror = fraction of training examples where h(x)≠c(x)

A concept class C is **PAC-learnable** by a hypothesis class H if there exists a learning algorithmA and a polynomial functionpoly (·) such that for any:

- ϵ∈ (0,1): desired accuracy (error tolerance)
- δ∈ (0,1): desired confidence (failure probability)
- distribution D over X
- target concept c∈C

then for sample size m≥poly(1/ϵ,1/size(c), size(x)),the algorithm A, when given m i.i.d. samples (x1, c(x1)),…,(x_m,c(x_m))outputs a hypothesis h∈H such that:

$$\Pr_{S \sim D^m}[L(h) \leq \epsilon] \geq 1 - \delta$$

This means that with probability at least 1−δ, the hypothesis h will have error at mostϵ.

Sample Complexity

Sample complexity refers to the number of training examples required to ensure that the hypothesis learned by a learning algorithm satisfies the PAC condition.

Realizable Case

In the *realizable* case, where there exists a hypothesis h∈Hsuch that h(x)=c(x)for all x, the number of samples mmm needed to ensure that with probability at least 1−δ, the error is at most ϵ, is given by:

$$m \geq \frac{1}{\epsilon}\left(\ln|\mathcal{H}| + \ln\frac{1}{\delta}\right)$$

This bound tells us that the more complex the hypothesis class (i.e., the larger |H|), the more samples are needed to learn.

Agnostic Case

In the agnostic setting (where the target function may not belong toH), the required sample complexity becomes:

$$m \geq \frac{1}{2\epsilon^2}\left(\ln|\mathcal{H}| + \ln\frac{1}{\delta}\right)$$

Here, error is measured with respect to the best possible hypothesis in

VC Dimension

The Vapnik-Chervonenkis (VC) dimension of a hypothesis class H, denoted VC(H), is a measure of its capacity or complexity. It is defined as the cardinality of the largest set of points that can be shattered by H.A set of points $x_1, x_2..., x_n\}$ is shattered by H if, for every possible binary labeling of the points, there exists a hypothesis h∈H that correctly classifies the points under that labeling.

Intuition

A higher VC dimension means that the hypothesis class can represent more complex patterns, but it also increases the risk of overfitting and requires more data to generalize well.

Sample Complexity with VC Dimension

In terms of VC dimension, for binary classification, the sample complexity required to PAC-learn is:

$$m \geq \frac{1}{\epsilon}\left(4 \cdot VC(\mathcal{H}) \cdot \log\left(\frac{2e}{\epsilon}\right) + \log\left(\frac{2}{\delta}\right)\right)$$

This shows that:

- **Lower VC dimension:** easier to learn with fewer samples.
- **Higher VC dimension:** more expressive hypothesis class but requires more data.

No Free Lunch Theorem

The No Free Lunch Theorem, first formalized by David Wolpert and William Macready in the 1990s, asserts that no single optimization algorithm performs best for all possible problems. In the domain of machine learning, this theorem implies that no learning algorithm is universally superior when averaged over all possible data-generating distributions. More formally, if one algorithm performs better than another on a particular set of problems, it must perform worse on a different set of problems. Hence, the performance of algorithms is problem-dependent. The theorem challenges the notion of a "one-size-fits-all" solution in AI, and it reinforces the importance of understanding the problem space, the data characteristics, and the objectives before choosing or designing an algorithm.

Implications for Algorithm Selection

No Universal Best Algorithm

The No Free Lunch Theorem highlights that no single algorithm performs best across all machine learning problems. This means that the choice of algorithm must be problem-specific, considering factors like dataset size, feature types, data distribution, and the complexity of relationships within the data. For example, a neural network might excel in image recognition tasks, while a logistic regression model may be more efficient for binary classification on small tabular datasets. Consequently, algorithm selection should not be based on popularity or prior success alone, but rather on the contextual demands and constraints of the task at hand.

Importance of Problem-Specific Tuning

Beyond choosing the right algorithm, optimizing its performance through hyperparameter tuning and model customization is essential. Different algorithms have distinct strengths depending on the problem type. Decision trees are effective for handling categorical variables and non-linear patterns, while support vector machines (SVMs) are powerful in high-dimensional, continuous data scenarios. Hyperparameters like tree depth, regularization coefficients, or learning rates must be carefully adjusted to fit the specific problem. Without this tuning, even a theoretically suitable algorithm may underperform, underscoring the importance of aligning model characteristics with the structure and demands of the dataset.

Need for Benchmarking and Empirical Evaluation

Relying solely on theoretical assumptions about algorithm performance can be misleading; empirical validation is essential. Benchmarking involves testing multiple models using techniques like cross-validation, precision-recall analysis, and error metrics such as F1-score, RMSE, or AUC-ROC. This process helps identify which algorithm performs best under real-world conditions, given the actual data. By analyzing validation results and comparing outcomes, developers gain practical insight into model suitability and can avoid overfitting or underfitting. Empirical evaluation thus plays a pivotal role in refining the algorithm selection process through evidence-based decision-making.

Algorithm Portfolios

Rather than relying on a single model, practitioners often experiment with an array of algorithms to build an effective solution. This approach, known as using algorithm portfolios, includes testing individual models and leveraging ensemble methods like bagging, boosting, and stacking. For instance, Random Forest combines multiple decision trees to reduce variance, while Gradient Boosting iteratively corrects errors to enhance accuracy. These ensemble techniques benefit from the diversity of underlying models, reducing the risk of poor generalization. The strategy acknowledges that different algorithms capture different data patterns, and their combination can lead to superior performance.

AutoML and Meta-Learning

To address the challenge of model selection and tuning, AutoML (Automated Machine Learning) systems and meta-learning frameworks are increasingly adopted. AutoML automates the search for optimal algorithms and hyperparameters, reducing the need for manual intervention. Meta-learning, or "learning to learn," uses knowledge from prior tasks to inform choices in new but related problems. These approaches streamline the machine learning pipeline, especially for non-experts or large-scale applications. While they do not replace domain knowledge, they significantly accelerate experimentation and discovery, reinforcing the idea that no single algorithm suffices across all tasks and that automation can support more informed selections.

Tradeoffs in Model Performance

Given the No Free Lunch Theorem, model performance is inherently tied to tradeoffs:

Bias-Variance Tradeoff

The bias-variance tradeoff represents a core dilemma in model performance. High-bias models, like linear regression, simplify assumptions to generalize better but may miss underlying data patterns, leading to underfitting. In contrast, high-variance models, such as deep neural networks, fit training data closely and can capture intricate trends but risk overfitting and poor generalization. The key lies in balancing the two—reducing variance without inflating bias and vice versa. Achieving this balance depends on the specific dataset's size, noise level, and complexity. Cross-validation and regularization techniques help mitigate these risks by ensuring that the model neither underfits nor overfits.

Accuracy vs. Interpretability

Model selection often demands a tradeoff between accuracy and interpretability. High-performing models like deep neural networks or ensemble methods typically yield superior accuracy but act as "black boxes," offering little insight into how predictions are made. On the other hand, interpretable models like logistic regression or decision trees allow for clear explanation of results but may fall short in capturing complex data relationships. The appropriate choice depends on the application domain. For instance, in healthcare or finance, model transparency and explainability are vital, whereas in recommendation systems or image classification, accuracy often outweighs interpretability in priority.

Generalization vs. Specialization

Generalization and specialization define another critical model performance tradeoff. A general model is designed to perform adequately across various tasks and datasets but may not excel in any single one. Conversely, a specialized model is optimized for a narrow domain or dataset and can outperform generalized models in that context, yet it may fail when exposed to new or slightly altered scenarios. This tradeoff is particularly relevant in dynamic environments where adaptability is key. Practitioners must assess the variability of input data and the stability of task requirements when deciding whether to pursue generalization or domain-specific specialization.

Computation Time vs. Performance

Complex models often promise superior accuracy and learning capacity but at the expense of increased computation time and resource usage. Training large neural networks or ensemble models can be time-consuming and require powerful hardware. In contrast, simpler models like Naive Bayes or linear classifiers train and infer rapidly, making them ideal for real-time or resource-constrained applications. In practical deployments—such as mobile devices, embedded systems, or time-sensitive environments—prioritizing computational efficiency may justify a minor compromise in predictive performance. Thus, model selection must consider not only accuracy but also latency, scalability, and the available computational infrastructure.

Overfitting vs. Underfitting

Overfitting and underfitting are common pitfalls that arise when a model's complexity is misaligned with the training data. Overfitting occurs when a model captures noise along with the signal, performing well on training data but poorly on unseen data. This is typical of very complex models with insufficient regularization or limited data. Underfitting, by contrast, happens when a model is too simple to learn the underlying structure of the data, resulting in poor performance across both training and test sets. Proper data preprocessing, model selection, and techniques like cross-validation, regularization, and early stopping are crucial to achieving the right balance.

Occam's Razor and Model Simplicity

Occam's Razor is a fundamental philosophical principle that has found profound relevance in machine learning and statistical modeling. It asserts that among competing hypotheses that explain known observations equally well, the simplest one should be selected. In the context of machine learning, this translates into a preference for simpler models that achieve comparable performance to more complex alternatives. Overly complex models tend to "memorize" the training data, resulting in overfitting, while simpler models often generalize better to unseen data. The principle encourages us to avoid unnecessary assumptions and to seek elegance and clarity in model construction.

Principle of Parsimony

The Principle of Parsimony, closely tied to Occam's Razor, is a guideline that promotes simplicity in the formulation of models. In statistics and machine learning, this principle argues that one should not increase model complexity without necessity. Simpler models are typically more interpretable, more robust to noise, and easier to validate.

For example: In linear regression, adding too many predictors can inflate the model's variance without significantly improving predictive performance. In decision trees, deep trees with many branches may perfectly fit the training data but perform poorly on new samples. The parsimony principle emphasizes that each additional model parameter should be justified by a significant improvement in performance or interpretability. This leads to better generalization, reduced computation, and often enhanced insight into the underlying process being modeled.

Regularization as Practical Occam's Razor

While Occam's Razor is a philosophical guideline, regularization implements it in practice. Regularization techniques constrain model complexity by adding a penalty term to the loss function used during training. This discourages the model from fitting the noise in the data and effectively applies a computational version of the parsimony principle. Two common forms of regularization are:

L1 Regularization (Lasso)

- Adds the absolute value of coefficients as a penalty.
- Encourages sparsity by driving some coefficients to zero.
- Ideal for feature selection in high-dimensional data.

L2 Regularization (Ridge):

- Adds the square of coefficients as a penalty.
- Shrinks coefficients but rarely zeroes them.
- Promotes smoothness and discourages large parameter weights.

The regularized objective can be represented as:

$$\text{Loss}_{\text{total}} = \text{Loss}_{\text{data}} + \lambda \cdot \text{Penalty}$$

where λ controls the trade-off between data fidelity and model simplicity.

Regularization embodies Occam's Razor by systematically balancing the model's fit to data with its complexity. It ensures that the model doesn't merely chase the lowest possible error on training data but instead strives for a structure that is both accurate and simple enough to generalize effectively.

Role of Assumptions in Learning Algorithms

Learning algorithms rely on a set of foundational assumptions to make sense of the data and generalize well to unseen instances. These assumptions help constrain the hypothesis space, determine how models learn patterns, and guide the selection of appropriate algorithms for specific problems. If these assumptions are violated or poorly aligned with the real-world data, model performance can degrade significantly. Two critical areas where assumptions play a central role are: data distributions and independence, and noise and label imperfections.

Independent and Identically Distributed (i.i.d.) Assumption

Most machine learning algorithms operate under the assumption that data samples are independent and identically distributed (i.i.d.). This means:

- Independent: Each data point is not influenced by any other.
- Identically distributed: All data points are drawn from the same underlying probability distribution.

This assumption is crucial for theoretical guarantees like convergence, generalization, and stability. For instance, the performance of supervised learning models like logistic regression or neural networks often hinges on the expectation that training and test data come from the same distribution.

Violations of i.i.d. and Real-World Data

In practice, many datasets violate the i.i.d. assumption:

- Time-series data (e.g., stock prices) exhibit temporal dependencies.
- Sensor data from IoT devices may be correlated.
- Data drift occurs when the distribution changes over time due to external factors.

These violations can lead to:

- Overfitting on temporally correlated data.
- Poor generalization when models trained on one domain are applied to another (domain shift).

Mitigation strategies include:

- Time-aware cross-validation for time-series.
- Domain adaptation and transfer learning to bridge distributional gaps.
- Data augmentation to introduce variation and reduce over-reliance on static distributions.
- Feature Independence (Naive Bayes Assumption)

Some algorithms, such as Naive Bayes, explicitly assume feature independence given the class label. While rarely true in real-world scenarios, this assumption simplifies computations and often provides surprisingly good results in applications like spam filtering or document classification. However, its effectiveness diminishes when strong feature correlations exist.

Types of Noise in Learning

Noise in datasets can originate from various sources and affect both the input features and the output labels:

Feature Noise

Feature noise arises when input variables (features) are distorted or corrupted due to various reasons, such as measurement errors, environmental fluctuations, hardware sensor inaccuracies, or rounding errors in data preprocessing. This type of noise alters the actual values of features, potentially confusing the learning algorithm. For example, a temperature sensor might occasionally report incorrect values due to hardware limitations. In supervised learning, such noise can reduce model accuracy, mislead feature importance analysis, and result in overfitting if the model tries to capture the noise instead of the true pattern. Effective preprocessing and robust algorithms are essential to mitigate feature noise.

Label Noise

Label noise refers to inaccuracies in the target variable or class labels, commonly caused by human annotation errors, ambiguous class definitions, or inconsistent labeling guidelines. This is especially problematic in supervised learning, where the model relies on correct labels to learn patterns. For instance, in medical imaging datasets, different experts might label the same image differently due to subjective interpretation. Label noise can significantly degrade model performance, confuse classification boundaries, and hinder generalization. Strategies to address label noise include label smoothing, noise-tolerant loss functions, or relabeling through consensus-based or model-based approaches to improve dataset reliability.

These imperfections can severely hinder learning algorithms, particularly those sensitive to outliers (e.g., decision trees, SVMs with hard margins).

Impact of Label Noise

Label noise can lead to:

Model Confusion

Model confusion occurs when a learning algorithm captures incorrect or misleading relationships in the data, often due to small or noisy datasets. In such scenarios, the model struggles to distinguish relevant patterns from irrelevant or coincidental associations. This can result in poor generalization, where the model performs well on training data but fails on unseen examples. Model confusion can also arise from ambiguous or overlapping classes, poor feature selection, or label noise. Addressing this issue often requires larger, cleaner datasets, better feature engineering, and robust cross-validation techniques to help the model learn accurate and meaningful mappings.

Reduced Accuracy

Reduced accuracy is a common consequence when a machine learning model fails to capture the underlying patterns in the data effectively. This typically happens due to insufficient or poor-quality data, model complexity issues, or inappropriate training strategies. As a result, the model's predictions on both training and test data degrade, making it unreliable for real-world applications. When true patterns are obscured by noise or bias, the model learns irrelevant details instead of the actual signal. Techniques such as data augmentation, feature selection, regularization, and proper model tuning are essential to mitigate accuracy loss and improve performance.

Increased Variance

Increased variance refers to a model's tendency to perform well on training data but poorly on test data due to overfitting. This occurs when the model learns noise or random fluctuations in the training dataset as if they were meaningful patterns. Such overfitting results in a highly sensitive model that lacks generalization capability. High variance is particularly problematic with complex models trained on limited or noisy data. Cross-validation, pruning, regularization (like L1/L2), and simplifying the model architecture are common strategies used to reduce variance and achieve a better balance between fitting the training data and performing well on unseen data.This is particularly problematic in high-stakes domains such as healthcare or finance, where even small labeling errors can mislead learning.

Robustness to Noise

Some models and techniques are inherently more robust to noise:

- Regularization (L1, L2) helps in preventing overfitting to noise.

- Ensemble methods like bagging (e.g., Random Forests) average out errors.
- Noise-aware models, such as those using label smoothing or loss correction, explicitly incorporate noise into their loss functions.
- Probabilistic models (e.g., Bayesian approaches) account for uncertainty and help quantify confidence in predictions.

Detecting and Correcting Label Noise

Label noise—errors in the labels assigned to training data—can significantly degrade the performance of machine learning models. Detecting and correcting such noise is crucial for building robust systems. Techniques include analyzing model confidence, disagreement among classifiers, and instance hardness to flag potential mislabeled data. Statistical methods like confusion matrices and loss-based ranking also help identify label inconsistencies. Once identified, correction can involve relabeling, removing noisy data, or using noise-robust algorithms. These steps enhance model reliability, especially in domains like healthcare or finance where data quality is paramount. Overall, managing label noise is essential for trustworthy predictive modeling. Common strategies to handle label imperfections include:

Human-in-the-loop Validation

Human-in-the-loop validation integrates human expertise into the data labeling process to improve accuracy and reliability. In cases where machine-generated or crowd-sourced labels may be erroneous, domain experts review and verify questionable labels flagged by automated systems. This approach is especially valuable in specialized fields like medical imaging, legal document analysis, or scientific research, where expert insight ensures label correctness. By strategically involving humans to validate a subset of critical or uncertain data points, this method reduces label noise, enhances training data quality, and leads to more robust and generalizable machine learning models.

Data Cleaning Algorithms

Data cleaning algorithms automatically identify and address label noise using techniques such as clustering, outlier detection, and noise filtering. These methods assess inconsistencies in data patterns or distances between feature vectors to detect mislabeled instances. For example, if a data point is assigned a class label but clusters with a different class, it may be considered suspicious. Algorithms like Edited Nearest Neighbors (ENN), Condensed Nearest Neighbor (CNN), and LOF (Local Outlier Factor) can be used for noise detection. Such tools reduce human intervention, scale well with large datasets, and improve model accuracy by enhancing the reliability of the training data.

Semi-supervised Learning

Semi-supervised learning combines a small set of labeled data with a large volume of unlabeled data to reduce the dependency on potentially noisy labels. Algorithms like self-training, co-training, or graph-based models propagate labels from clean examples to similar unlabeled instances. This technique leverages the structure in the data to build models that generalize well, even in the presence of imperfect labels. It's particularly effective when obtaining clean labels is expensive or time-consuming. By minimizing reliance on noisy data and utilizing the abundant unlabeled examples, semi-supervised learning offers a practical way to build accurate models under labeling uncertainty.

Curse of Dimensionality

The term "Curse of Dimensionality", coined by Richard Bellman in the context of dynamic programming, refers to the various phenomena that arise when analyzing and organizing data in high-dimensional spaces that do not occur in low-dimensional settings. As the number of dimensions (features) increases, the volume of the space increases exponentially, causing data to become sparse. This sparsity is problematic for many machine learning algorithms and statistical techniques which rely on data density and proximity.

Impact on Distance Metrics and Learning

In high-dimensional spaces, intuitive notions like distance, volume, and proximity become counterintuitive and less meaningful. This affects several core aspects of machine learning:

Loss of Discriminative Power in Distance Metrics

Most machine learning algorithms use distance-based metrics (e.g., Euclidean, Manhattan, Cosine) to measure similarity between data points. In high dimensions, the distance between all pairs of data points tends to converge, meaning the ratio between the nearest and farthest neighbors approaches 1. This makes it difficult for models like K-Nearest Neighbors (KNN), clustering (like K-Means), and kernel-based methods (e.g., SVM) to distinguish between different data points. Mathematically, for uniformly distributed data in an n-dimensional unit hypercube, the contrast between the minimum and maximum distance reduces with increasing n.

Increased Computational Complexity

As dimensionality increases, the volume of the data space grows exponentially, leading to significant increases in computational cost. Algorithms that rely on pairwise comparisons, such as nearest neighbor searches or similarity matrix computations, face performance degradation due to the need for massive storage and processing resources. This is often referred to as the "curse of dimensionality" in terms of time and memory complexity. Even with modern hardware, such operations can become infeasible in high-dimensional settings. This issue severely limits the scalability of machine learning models and data analysis methods when working with large and complex feature spaces.

Overfitting and Generalization

In high-dimensional spaces, the number of features can far exceed the number of training samples, leading to an increased risk of overfitting. Models may memorize noise or irrelevant details instead of learning meaningful patterns, which compromises their ability to generalize to new data. This situation elevates the VC-dimension of the hypothesis space, indicating a greater capacity to fit data but also requiring substantially more training data to achieve robust performance. Consequently, without sufficient data, models trained on high-dimensional datasets tend to perform well on training data but poorly on unseen data, highlighting weak generalization.

Sparse Data

As dimensions grow, data points become increasingly sparse, meaning they are far apart in the feature space. This sparsity undermines the reliability of statistical estimates such as mean, variance, or density, which are foundational to many algorithms. Methods that depend on local neighborhoods—such as clustering, density estimation, or manifold learning—struggle in such environments because meaningful neighborhoods cease to exist. The lack of nearby points diminishes the ability to infer structure from data, which can lead to inaccurate models and reduced predictive performance. Thus, sparsity becomes a major obstacle in high-dimensional data analysis.

Computational Learning Theory and Algorithmic Efficiency

Computational Learning Theory (CLT) is a theoretical framework for understanding the capabilities and limitations of learning algorithms. It provides formal models to analyze how well machines can learn from data, how much data is needed, and what computational resources (time and memory) are required. This field bridges computer science and statistical learning by offering guarantees on algorithm performance under certain assumptions. A central goal of CLT is to identify the feasibility and efficiency of learning, especially when constrained by finite data and computational power. Algorithmic efficiency in machine learning is critical for designing systems that can scale with large datasets, adapt in real time, and perform well within hardware limitations. It focuses on the time and space complexity of learning algorithms and investigates trade-offs between accuracy, speed, and resource usage.

Time and Space Complexity in ML

In the context of machine learning (ML), time complexity refers to the computational time required to train a model or make predictions, while space complexity denotes the amount of memory consumed during these processes. These complexities are generally expressed in Big-O notation (e.g., O(n), O(n^2)), where n is a function of the dataset size or model parameters.

Time Complexity

Time complexity in ML varies with the algorithm:

Linear Models (e.g., Linear Regression, Logistic Regression): O(n·d)

Linear models are efficient and widely used for both regression and classification tasks. The training time complexity is O(n·d), where n is the number of data samples and d is the number of features. This linear time complexity arises because these models typically involve calculating the dot product of each feature vector with a weight vector and adjusting weights using gradient-based methods or closed-form solutions. Their simplicity and scalability make them suitable for large datasets with a relatively small number of features, though they struggle with nonlinear patterns unless extended with techniques like polynomial features.

Decision Trees: Training is O(n·d·log n); prediction is usually O(log n)

Decision trees partition the data recursively based on feature values to construct a tree-like structure. The training complexity is O(n·d·log n), driven by the need to sort the data at each node to find optimal splits across d features and log-scaled depth. The prediction time, once the tree is built, is O(log n) for balanced trees since only a single path from root to leaf is traversed per query. Their interpretability and ability to handle both categorical and numerical features are advantageous, though they can overfit if not pruned or regularized.

Support Vector Machines (SVM): O(n^2) to O(n^3) depending on the kernel used

Support Vector Machines are powerful for classification, particularly with clear margins between classes. Their training complexity ranges from O(n^2) to O(n^3), especially for nonlinear kernels, because they require solving a convex quadratic optimization problem involving all n training samples. For large datasets, this becomes computationally intensive, particularly with kernels like RBF. Linear SVMs, using approximations like stochastic gradient descent, offer better scalability. While effective in high-dimensional spaces and robust to overfitting, the high computational cost of kernelized SVMs makes them less suitable for very large datasets without optimization techniques.

Neural Networks: O(e·n·d·m), where e is epochs and m is the number of parameters

Neural networks are highly flexible models capable of capturing complex patterns through multiple layers of computation. Their training complexity is O(e·n·d·m), where e is the number of epochs, n is the number of training samples, d is the number of features, and m represents model parameters including weights and biases. Each epoch involves forward and backward passes through the network for all samples, scaling with depth, width, and batch size. While neural networks excel in tasks like image recognition and natural language processing, their training can be resource-intensive, requiring GPUs and careful tuning to prevent overfitting or vanishing gradients.

Space Complexity

Space complexity accounts for:

- Storing model parameters (weights, biases),
- Temporary variables during training (e.g., gradients in backpropagation),
- Dataset size in memory.

For example, deep neural networks may require hundreds of megabytes to gigabytes of memory during training due to the need to store activations and gradients for backpropagation.

Efficient algorithm design often involves:

- Reducing redundant computations (e.g., caching results),
- Using data structures like sparse matrices,
- Batch processing to manage memory.

Feasibility of Learning with Finite Resources

The feasibility of learning under resource constraints—such as limited time, memory, and data—is central to computational learning theory. This feasibility is explored through the following concepts:

PAC Learning Framework

Probably Approximately Correct (PAC) learning, introduced by Valiant, formalizes the idea of feasible learning. A hypothesis is PAC-learnable if, given a sufficient number of samples and time, the learning algorithm can find a hypothesis that is close to the true function with high probability.

Resource-Bounded Learning

Resource-bounded learning focuses on developing machine learning systems that can operate effectively within strict computational, memory, or time constraints. These constraints often arise in real-world applications where devices or systems have limited processing power, storage capacity, or energy availability. The goal is to optimize algorithms and model architectures to ensure they perform adequately without exceeding resource budgets. This includes adopting strategies such as model pruning, quantization, and knowledge distillation. Resource-aware learning is especially critical in scenarios such as edge computing, real-time applications, and large-scale distributed systems where efficiency, speed, and scalability are just as important as model accuracy. Many real-world learning tasks must be executed under finite resources:

Edge Devices

Edge devices like smartphones, sensors, and IoT modules operate under severe limitations in memory, computational power, and energy consumption. Machine learning models deployed on these devices must be lightweight and efficient. Techniques such as model compression, quantized neural networks, and mobile-specific architectures (e.g., MobileNet, TinyML) are employed to enable real-time inference while minimizing energy usage. These models are designed to perform essential tasks—such as object detection, speech recognition, or anomaly detection—locally without relying on continuous cloud communication, thus reducing latency and preserving data privacy. Resource-bounded learning on edge devices ensures AI capabilities are accessible even in constrained environments.

Real-Time Systems

Real-time systems, such as autonomous vehicles, medical monitoring tools, or fraud detection systems, demand immediate and accurate decision-making. In such environments, machine learning models must offer low-latency inference while maintaining high accuracy. Computational efficiency becomes a top priority, often requiring optimized model architectures, reduced input dimensionality, or the use of specialized hardware like GPUs or FPGAs. These systems cannot afford long processing delays, so they benefit from techniques like early exit models, real-time scheduling, and prioritization strategies. Resource-bounded learning ensures that real-time systems can perform complex analysis rapidly, making AI viable for safety-critical and time-sensitive applications.

Cloud-scale Systems

Cloud-scale systems are responsible for training and deploying massive machine learning models across large, distributed infrastructures. These systems must manage vast datasets, high-throughput pipelines, and compute-intensive operations efficiently. Resource-bounded learning in this context emphasizes distributed training, parallel computing, and energy-efficient architecture design. Frameworks such as TensorFlow, PyTorch with Horovod, and parameter server models enable scalability and faster convergence. Challenges like network bottlenecks, load balancing, and memory optimization are addressed to ensure the system operates within cost and energy budgets. By leveraging cloud-scale resource efficiency, organizations can develop and deploy state-of-the-art models at industrial scale.

Algorithmic Approaches to Enhance Feasibility

To maintain feasibility, modern ML uses:

Stochastic Gradient Descent (SGD)

Stochastic Gradient Descent is an optimization technique that enhances the feasibility of machine learning by significantly reducing computational overhead. Unlike traditional gradient descent that computes gradients over the entire dataset, SGD updates model parameters using small, random subsets of data called mini-batches. This approach accelerates convergence and lowers memory requirements, making it practical for large-scale datasets. It allows real-time and adaptive learning in dynamic environments. Despite its noisy updates, proper tuning of learning rates and batch sizes can lead to robust performance. SGD is widely used in deep learning frameworks due to its efficiency and scalability.

Transfer Learning

Transfer Learning improves the feasibility of machine learning by reusing knowledge from pre-trained models on new but related tasks, thereby reducing the demand for extensive computational resources and large labeled datasets. Instead of training models from scratch, which is time and resource intensive, transfer learning allows fine-tuning of existing models, accelerating development and deployment. This is especially useful in domains with limited data, such as medical imaging or low-resource languages. Pre-trained architectures like ResNet or BERT serve as strong foundations, significantly shortening training time and enabling high performance with minimal additional data and computation.

Model Compression

Model compression techniques aim to reduce the computational and memory footprint of machine learning models while preserving their predictive accuracy. These methods—such as pruning, quantization, and knowledge distillation—make models smaller, faster, and more suitable for deployment on edge devices with limited resources. Pruning eliminates redundant parameters, quantization lowers the precision of weights, and knowledge distillation transfers knowledge from a large teacher model to a smaller student model. These techniques are especially valuable in mobile and embedded applications, where energy efficiency and low-latency inference are crucial. Model compression thus enhances real-world feasibility without compromising performance.

Online Learning

Online learning is a machine learning paradigm designed for environments where data arrives in a sequential manner, making it ideal for applications with limited memory or real-time constraints. Instead of processing the entire dataset at once, the model is updated incrementally with each new data point. This reduces storage requirements and enables adaptive learning, which is beneficial in scenarios like stock market prediction, recommendation systems, or IoT sensor networks. Online learning algorithms, such as stochastic gradient descent variants or passive-aggressive methods, ensure feasibility by maintaining lightweight models capable of quick updates and responsiveness to concept drifts.

Summary

Beginning with an overview of learning theory, we explored what makes learning feasible under real-world constraints, examining both inductive and deductive paradigms. Key concepts such as the bias-variance tradeoff, generalization, and Probably Approximately Correct (PAC) learning were introduced to highlight the inherent challenges in achieving accurate, robust models. Formal notions like sample complexity, VC dimension, and learnability provided mathematical grounding for evaluating algorithmic performance.Critical philosophical principles such as Occam's Razor and the principle of parsimony emphasized the balance between simplicity and predictive power. We also examined the role of regularization as a practical embodiment of these principles, reinforcing the value of restraint in model complexity. Computational learning theory framed machine learning in terms of time and space efficiency, drawing attention to the feasibility of learning under finite resources. Finally, real-world concerns such as data noise, independence assumptions, and the curse of dimensionality were addressed, along with effective strategies for dimensionality reduction.By understanding these theoretical foundations, practitioners can make informed choices about algorithm selection, data preprocessing, and model optimization, ultimately guiding the development of more accurate, efficient, and generalizable learning systems.

Exercise Questions

- Explain the difference between inductive and deductive learning approaches. Provide a practical example of each in machine learning.
- Define the bias-variance tradeoff. How does it affect model generalization in supervised learning?
- What is Probably Approximately Correct (PAC) learning? Describe its significance in determining the learnability of a hypothesis.
- Describe the concepts of sample complexity and VC (Vapnik–Chervonenkis) dimension. How do they relate to overfitting and underfitting?
- State and explain the "No Free Lunch" theorem in the context of algorithm selection. Why is it important in ML model development?
- Discuss the principle of Occam's Razor. How is regularization a practical implementation of this principle in modern ML algorithms?
- What is the curse of dimensionality? Explain its impact on distance-based algorithms and how it can be mitigated.

- Differentiate between model simplicity and model performance. How can one achieve a balance using theoretical concepts?
- What are the implications of noisy labels and non-i.i.d. (independent and identically distributed) data on learning algorithms?
- Explain how time and space complexity influence the feasibility of machine learning models in resource-constrained environments.

8

INFORMATION THEORY AND STATISTICAL FOUNDATIONS OF MACHINE LEARNING

The field of machine learning is fundamentally rooted in the ability of systems to derive patterns and make predictions from data. To achieve this, it must quantify and manage uncertainty, which is where the principles of information theory and statistics become essential. Information theory, originally developed by Claude Shannon in the context of communication systems, provides a framework for measuring the amount of information and understanding entropythe degree of uncertainty in a data distribution. Simultaneously, statistics provides the theoretical backbone for inference, estimation, and hypothesis testing, enabling learning models to draw valid conclusions from sample data. These two disciplines converge to form the theoretical substrate upon which modern machine learning algorithms are built, offering insight into how systems interpret, compress, and generalize from information. One of the central concepts in information theory, entropy, quantifies the unpredictability in a random variable and serves as a measure of disorder or surprise. In machine learning, entropy becomes a pivotal metric for evaluating the impurity of data partitions, particularly in decision trees and classification problems. Algorithms like ID3 and C4.5 utilize information gain, derived from entropy, to select features that best reduce uncertainty and enhance predictive power. This idea of minimizing entropy extends to clustering, anomaly detection, and even deep learning, where information-theoretic objectives influence regularization and feature learning. Understanding how information is distributed and how it can be efficiently extracted is vital to designing intelligent algorithms.

Machine learning models operate under the premise of uncertainty, making probabilistic modeling and statistical inference essential. Probability theory enables algorithms to model complex distributions, while inferential statistics allows them to estimate parameters and make predictions from finite samples. Techniques like Maximum Likelihood Estimation (MLE), Bayesian inference, and hypothesis testing are critical in constructing robust learning systems. Statistical tools help evaluate model performance, select features, and detect overfitting. Moreover, they guide the interpretation of outputs, assigning confidence scores, p-values, and credible intervals to predictions thereby enhancing transparency and trust in machine learning systems. Bayesian methods introduce a powerful probabilistic approach to learning by treating model parameters as random variables with prior distributions. This approach contrasts with frequentist methods, which view parameters as fixed but unknown quantities. Bayesian inference updates prior beliefs based on observed data through Bayes' Theorem, enabling models to naturally handle uncertainty and incorporate prior knowledge. In machine learning, Bayesian techniques underpin algorithms such as Gaussian Naive Bayes, Bayesian networks, and probabilistic graphical models. Moreover, they play a key role in advanced topics like Bayesian deep learning, where uncertainty estimation in predictions is critical for applications in medicine, autonomous systems, and finance.

The statistical learning theory framework, pioneered by Vapnik and Chervonenkis, formalizes the process of learning from data. It defines key constructs such as hypothesis spaces, risk functions, and generalization error, providing mathematical rigor to model evaluation and selection. Concepts like the VC dimension, PAC (Probably Approximately Correct) learning, and uniform convergence help explain why some models generalize better than others, despite having similar training performance. This theoretical foundation bridges the gap between empirical results and theoretical guarantees, giving practitioners tools to reason about trade-offs such as bias versus variance, model complexity versus accuracy, and underfitting versus overfitting. As machine learning evolves to tackle more complex, real-world challenges, the synergy between information theory and statistical foundations becomes increasingly vital. From data preprocessing and model training to evaluation and deployment, the theoretical underpinnings ensure that machine learning systems are not only accurate but also interpretable, efficient, and reliable. Information theory provides strategies for optimal coding, feature selection, and data compression, while statistics offers rigor in inference, validation, and uncertainty quantification. Together, they guide the design of principled learning algorithms, enable robust decision-making under uncertainty, and support the development of intelligent systems that can learn, adapt, and thrive in dynamic environments

Information Theory in ML

Information theory, pioneered by Claude Shannon in 1948, provides a mathematical framework for quantifying, encoding, and communicating information. Originally conceived to address problems in data transmission and compression, information theory has become instrumental in machine learning (ML), particularly in algorithms that require assessing uncertainty, optimizing decision-making processes, and selecting the most informative features from datasets. Central concepts such as entropy, information gain, and uncertainty play pivotal roles in refining predictive models, guiding algorithmic decisions, and enhancing interpretability.

Entropy, Information Gain, and Uncertainty

Entropy

Entropy is a fundamental measure in information theory that quantifies the uncertainty or impurity inherent in a dataset. Mathematically, entropy H of a discrete random variable X, taking possible values $x_1, x_2 ..., x_n$ with probabilitiesp(xi), is defined as:

$$H(X) = -\sum_{i=1}^{n} p(x_i) \log_2 p(x_i)$$

Entropy is maximized when the probability distribution is uniform, reflecting maximum uncertainty (i.e., all outcomes equally likely), and minimized when the distribution is peaked (i.e., certain outcomes). In machine learning, entropy is critical in evaluating datasets, where higher entropy indicates greater disorder and unpredictability, whereas lower entropy implies structured and predictable data.For instance, in classification tasks, entropy provides insight into the purity of a subset of data—low entropy indicates homogeneous classes, making predictions straightforward, whereas high entropy indicates heterogeneous classes, complicating accurate predictions.

Information Gain

Information gain measures the reduction in entropy that occurs when a dataset is partitioned based on a specific feature or attribute. Formally, information gain (IG) for a featureA is expressed as:

$$IG(D, A) = H(D) - \sum_{v \in Values(A)} \frac{|D_v|}{|D|} H(D_v)$$

where:

H(D) is the entropy of the original dataset,

Dv is the subset of data with feature A having value v,

|Dv|/|D| represents the proportion of instances with the given feature value.

A higher information gain indicates that the feature provides substantial information about the outcome, effectively reducing uncertainty. In contrast, features with low or zero information gain contribute little or nothing towards predictive accuracy.

Uncertainty

Uncertainty in information theory refers to the degree of unpredictability or randomness within the data. It relates closely to entropy, serving as a practical measure of how uncertain an algorithm is about making correct predictions based on available information. High uncertainty corresponds to high entropy, implying that predictions made by models without sufficient distinguishing information are unreliable. Conversely, reduced uncertainty correlates with low entropy, indicating well-defined patterns and higher predictive confidence.

Relevance to Decision Trees and Feature Selection

Decision Trees

Decision trees leverage concepts from information theory, particularly entropy and information gain, to construct predictive models that recursively partition datasets into increasingly homogeneous subsets. At each node, the decision tree selects the feature that provides the highest information gain, effectively reducing the uncertainty about the predicted outcome. The decision-making process involves:

- Calculating entropy for the initial dataset.
- Evaluating the information gain for each potential feature.
- Choosing the feature that maximizes information gain to split the dataset into subsets.

Repeating this process iteratively until stopping criteria (such as minimum entropy or maximum depth) are satisfied. Thus, information gain serves as a criterion for splitting nodes and ensures that decision trees efficiently identify the most informative features, thereby optimizing predictive accuracy.

Feature Selection

Information theory plays a pivotal role in feature selection by determining the relevance of features based on their capacity to reduce uncertainty and improve predictive performance. Features contributing significantly to decreasing entropy (high information gain) are considered informative and valuable for model building. Conversely, features that yield negligible reductions in entropy provide minimal predictive value and may introduce noise, computational overhead, or complexity, negatively impacting model performance. By quantifying the informativeness of features through information gain, feature selection algorithms (e.g., Information Gain-based Feature Selection, Mutual Information) effectively reduce dimensionality, enhance model generalization, prevent overfitting, and improve computational efficiency. Consequently, information theory provides a robust theoretical basis for systematic, informed feature selection, crucial for building accurate and interpretable machine learning models.

Kullback-Leibler Divergence and Cross-Entropy

Kullback–Leibler Divergence is a statistical measure used to quantify how one probability distribution diverges from a second, expected distribution. It is defined as the sum over all possible events of the true distribution times the logarithm of the ratio between the true and estimated probabilities.

Measuring Distance Between Distributions

In information theory, probability theory, and machine learning, measuring how two probability distributions differ from one another is crucial. Two central concepts frequently employed for this purpose are Kullback–Leibler (KL) divergence and cross-entropy. Although related, each provides unique insights into the differences between probability distributions.

Kullback–Leibler Divergence

The Kullback–Leibler divergence, or KL divergence, is a statistical measure used to quantify how much one probability distribution diverges from a second, reference distribution. For discrete probability distributions P(x) and Q(x), the KL divergence from Q(x) to P(x) is defined as:

$$D_{KL}(P \parallel Q) = \sum_{x} P(x) \log \frac{P(x)}{Q(x)}$$

For continuous distributions, the summation is replaced with integration:

$$D_{KL}(P \parallel Q) = \int_{-\infty}^{\infty} p(x) \log \frac{p(x)}{q(x)}\, dx$$

Key properties of KL divergence include:

- **Non-negativity:** DKL(P||Q) ≥0, with equality if and only if P(x)=Q(x)for all x. However, it is not symmetric: DKL(P||Q) ≠DKL(Q||P).
- **Interpretation:** KL divergence is often interpreted as the expected logarithmic difference between the probabilities according to the true distribution P and the approximation Q.
- **Asymmetry:** The direction matters, which implies the measure captures differences based on how one distribution is approximating another.

In essence, KL divergence is a measure of "information lost" if Q is used to approximate the true distribution P.

Cross-Entropy

Cross-entropy is another metric closely associated with KL divergence, frequently used in contexts like classification tasks in machine learning. Cross-entropy quantifies the difference between two probability distributions, specifically highlighting the discrepancy between the true distribution P(x) and an estimated distribution Q(x):

$$H(P, Q) = -\sum_{x} P(x) \log Q(x)$$

When distributions are continuous, the summation again becomes integration:

$$H(P,Q) = -\int_{-\infty}^{\infty} p(x) \log q(x)\, dx$$

Cross-entropy has several critical attributes:

- It measures the average number of bits required to represent data from distribution P when encoded with distribution Q.
- It becomes minimal (equal to the entropy of P) when the two distributions match exactly (P=Q).
- It is widely employed as a loss function (known as cross-entropy loss) for classification tasks in neural networks, particularly due to its effectiveness in evaluating probabilistic predictions.

Relationship Between KL Divergence and Cross-Entropy

KL divergence and cross-entropy are related concepts. Specifically, KL divergence can be expressed as the difference between the cross-entropy and the entropy of the true distributionP(x):

$$D_{KL}(P \parallel Q) = H(P,Q) - H(P)$$

Here:

H(P) is the entropy of the true distribution

P(x), measuring uncertainty or inherent randomness.

H (P, Q) quantifies how much additional uncertainty (or error) is introduced by approximating

P(x) with Q(x).

Thus, minimizing cross-entropy with respect to Q is equivalent to minimizing KL divergence, since the entropy of the true distribution P is constant for a given data distribution.

Applications in Classification and Neural Networks

KL divergence and cross-entropy play pivotal roles in machine learning, particularly in classification tasks and neural network training.

Applications of Cross-Entropy in Neural Networks

Classification Loss Functions

Cross-entropy is commonly used as the loss function in multi-class classification tasks, where the network outputs a probability distribution across classes.

For instance, in a classification problem with ground truth P(x) (often one-hot encoded) and predicted distribution Q(x), the cross-entropy loss is defined as:

$$\text{Loss} = -\sum_{x} P(x) \log Q(x)$$

Minimizing this loss function guides the neural network to align its predictions closely with the true data distribution.

Gradient Optimization

Cross-entropy is highly compatible with optimization methods like gradient descent because it generates gradients that effectively reduce the difference between predicted and actual distributions. Neural network training commonly uses stochastic gradient descent (SGD) or variants like Adam to iteratively minimize cross-entropy loss.

KL Divergence in Neural Networks

Regularization and Variational Autoencoders (VAEs)

KL divergence serves as a regularization term, ensuring that learned probability distributions in latent spaces closely match prior distributions. Variational Autoencoders explicitly use KL divergence to constrain learned latent distributions to a predefined distribution (often a Gaussian) in Table 8.1.

Knowledge Distillation

KL divergence is essential in knowledge distillation, a technique where knowledge from a complex "teacher" neural network is transferred to a smaller, simpler "student" network. Minimizing the KL divergence between the output distributions of the teacher and student networks allows the student model to closely replicate the teacher's behavior.

Model Evaluation and Comparison

KL divergence is frequently used to measure and compare how different models' approximate distributions, enabling researchers to objectively assess improvements and differences between various model structures.

Table 8.1: Summary of Differences and Use Cases.

Aspect	Kullback-Leibler Divergence	Cross-Entropy
Symmetry	Asymmetric ((D_{KL}(P	
Minimum Value	0 (if distributions match exactly)	Equal to entropy of true distribution (when distributions match exactly)

Use in ML	Regularization, latent distribution matching, knowledge distillation	Primary loss function for neural network classification tasks
Interpretation	Information loss in approximation	Expected message length required to encode data from one distribution using another distribution

Maximum Likelihood Estimation (MLE) and Maximum a Posteriori (MAP)

Maximum Likelihood Estimation (MLE) is a statistical approach used to estimate the parameters of a probabilistic model by finding values that maximize the likelihood of observing the given data. It focuses solely on the observed dataset and assumes that the data is independently and identically distributed (iid).

Mathematical Formulation

Given observed data D= $\{x_1, x_2 ..., x_n\}$and a parameterized model defined by parameter θ, the likelihood function L(θ)is expressed as:

$$L(\theta) = P(x_1, x_2, ..., x_n \mid \theta)$$

Assuming independence, this becomes:

$$L(\theta) = \prod_{i=1}^{n} P(x_i \mid \theta)$$

MLE seeks to find the optimal parameters θ^ that maximize this likelihood:

$$\hat{\theta}_{MLE} = \arg\max_{\theta} L(\theta)$$

To simplify calculations, usually the log-likelihood is maximized instead:

$$\hat{\theta}_{MLE} = \arg\max_{\theta} \log L(\theta) = \arg\max_{\theta} \sum_{i=1}^{n} \log P(x_i \mid \theta)$$

Maximum A Posteriori Estimation (MAP)

Maximum A Posteriori (MAP) estimation is a Bayesian extension of MLE. It incorporates prior knowledge about parameters in the form of a prior probability distribution. Unlike MLE, MAP estimation not only maximizes the likelihood of observing the data but also considers prior beliefs or knowledge about parameters.

Mathematical Formulation

MAP incorporates Bayes' theorem, which relates the posterior probability P(θ|D) to likelihood P(D|θ)and the prior probability P(θ):

$$P(\theta \mid \mathcal{D}) = \frac{P(\mathcal{D} \mid \theta)P(\theta)}{P(\mathcal{D})}$$

The MAP estimate maximizes the posterior probability:

$$\hat{\theta}_{MAP} = \arg\max_{\theta} P(\theta \mid \mathcal{D}) = \arg\max_{\theta}[P(\mathcal{D} \mid \theta)P(\theta)]$$

Using logarithms, this optimization typically becomes simpler:

$$\hat{\theta}_{MAP} = \arg\max_{\theta}[\log P(\mathcal{D} \mid \theta) + \log P(\theta)]$$

Probabilistic Modeling in Learning

Probabilistic modeling involves specifying a model through probability distributions to represent uncertainty explicitly. In machine learning, both MLE and MAP form the core methods for fitting probabilistic models to data:

- MLE provides a purely data-driven approach, ideal for large datasets where prior information is minimal or irrelevant.
- MAP leverages Bayesian inference, effectively incorporating external knowledge or domain expertise, making it advantageous in smaller datasets or highly uncertain environments.
- Probabilistic models built through these estimation methods provide powerful ways to capture uncertainty, make predictions, assess model confidence, and optimize decision-making.

Frequentist vs. Bayesian Interpretations

The frequentist interpretation views probability as a long-run frequency. Parameters are fixed, unknown constants to be estimated solely based on observed data in Table 8.2.Example: Frequentists interpret an MLE-estimated parameter as the value most frequently supported by observed samples if data collection were repeatedly conducted.

Table 8.2: Frequentist versus Bayesian Interpretations.

Aspect	Frequentist Interpretation (MLE)	Bayesian Interpretation (MAP)
Definition of Probability	Probability as long-run frequency of events from repeated experiments.	Probability as a measure of uncertainty or degree of belief, updated with evidence.
Parameters	Unknown but fixed constants estimated solely from data.	Random variables characterized by probability distributions expressing prior beliefs.
Role of Prior Information	No prior beliefs or distributions about parameters; estimation relies solely on observed data.	Explicit incorporation of prior beliefs through prior distributions, updated by observed data.
Inference	Uses confidence intervals and hypothesis tests that reflect repeated sampling behavior.	Utilizes posterior distributions, providing probabilistic interpretations of parameter uncertainty.
Estimation Method	Maximum Likelihood Estimation (MLE) based on maximizing the likelihood of observed data.	Maximum A Posteriori (MAP) estimation, maximizing the posterior probability (combining likelihood and prior).
Interpretation of Results	Estimates reflect properties of repeated sampling; e.g., 95% confidence intervals contain the true parameter in 95% of repeated experiments.	Posterior probabilities represent updated beliefs about parameters; credible intervals reflect probability that parameters lie within given ranges.
Example	An MLE-estimated parameter is interpreted as the value most frequently supported by the data if the experiment were repeated indefinitely.	A MAP-estimated parameter is viewed as the most probable value given prior beliefs and observed evidence.

Bayesian Interpretation (MAP Approach)

The Bayesian approach interprets probability as a measure of uncertainty or degree of belief. Parameters are considered random variables described by probability distributions, reflecting our uncertainty and prior knowledge:

- Parameters have probability distributions reflecting uncertainty.
- Beliefs about parameters are updated in response to new evidence (data).
- Results are inherently interpretable as posterior distributions, providing full distributions rather than point estimates.

Example: Bayesian interpretation of MAP-estimated parameters explicitly includes the prior distribution. Parameters are continuously updated as new data is observed, integrating prior beliefs with observed evidence.

Bayesian Inference in Machine Learning

Bayesian inference provides a rigorous probabilistic framework for updating beliefs based on evidence. It is fundamentally rooted in Bayes' theorem, which allows for combining prior knowledge with new observations to obtain updated probabilities. At its core, Bayesian inference systematically quantifies uncertainty, making it a powerful tool in various machine learning tasks.

Concepts: Prior, Likelihood, and Posterior

Bayesian inference revolves around three essential concepts: prior, likelihood, and posterior, interconnected through Bayes' theorem:

$$P(\theta|X) = \frac{P(X|\theta) \cdot P(\theta)}{P(X)}$$

Prior (P(θ))

The prior probability represents initial beliefs or assumptions about parameters or hypotheses before observing any data. Priors can be informative (based on expert knowledge or historical data) or non-informative (reflecting maximum uncertainty, such as uniform distributions). Example: If modeling the effectiveness of a drug, a prior might reflect existing knowledge or literature, indicating a belief that the drug has an 80% chance of effectiveness.

Likelihood (P(X|θ))

Likelihood describes the probability of observing the given data X, assuming a particular parameter value θ. It represents how well specific parameter values explain the observed data. Example: Given clinical trial results, the likelihood quantifies how probable it is to observe the collected health outcomes if the drug indeed has a specific effectiveness rate.

Posterior (P(θ|X))

Posterior probability integrates the prior and the likelihood, updating the initial belief after incorporating the observed data. It represents the refined probability of a parameter after observing evidence. *Example:* After analyzing clinical trial data, the posterior might update the initial belief from an 80% effectiveness (prior) to a revised estimate of 90%, indicating strengthened confidence due to observed positive outcomes.

The denominator: P(X), known as the marginal likelihood or evidence, acts as a normalization constant ensuring probabilities sum up to one:

$$P(X) = \int_{\theta} P(X|\theta)P(\theta)d\theta$$

Applications of Bayesian Inference in Machine Learning

Bayesian inference underpins multiple popular algorithms and models in machine learning. Two prominent examples are the Naïve Bayes classifier and Bayesian networks.

Naïve Bayes Classifier

Naïve Bayes is a probabilistic classifier based on applying Bayes' theorem with strong independence assumptions between features. Despite its simplicity, Naïve Bayes is highly effective, especially in text classification, spam filtering, and sentiment analysis.

Bayesian Framework:

Given a set of features X= $(x_1, x_2..., x_n)$and class labels CCC, the posterior probability for each class is computed as:

$$P(C|X) = \frac{P(X|C)P(C)}{P(X)}$$

Assuming conditional independence between features, the likelihood simplifies to:

$$P(X|C) = \prod_{i=1}^{n} P(x_i|C)$$

- Prior: The prior P(C) typically represents the proportion of each class in the training data.
- Likelihood: The likelihood P(X|C) captures the probability of observing the feature set given each class.
- Posterior: The posterior P(C|X) reflects updated class probabilities after considering observed features, used directly for classification decisions.

Example Application

In email spam classification, priors reflect the general proportion of spam emails, likelihoods represent word frequencies within spam versus legitimate emails, and the posterior gives the probability that an email is spam after observing its words.

Bayesian Networks

A Bayesian Network (also known as a belief network) is a graphical model that represents probabilistic relationships among random variables using directed acyclic graphs (DAGs). Each node in the network corresponds to a variable, and edges encode conditional dependencies.

Structure and Conditional Probability Tables (CPTs):

Bayesian Networks represent joint probability distributions compactly by factorizing them into conditional probability distributions:

$$P(X_1, X_2, ..., X_n) = \prod_{i=1}^{n} P(X_i | \text{Parents}(X_i))$$

- **Prior:** Priors are captured within initial probability tables (nodes without parents) or conditional distributions (nodes with parents).
- **Likelihood:** Observed evidence updates the likelihood of different variable configurations across the network.
- **Posterior:** Bayesian inference propagates evidence through the network, updating the posterior probabilities at each node. This allows for querying the network to answer probabilistic questions.
- **Inference:** Algorithms like exact inference (Variable Elimination, Junction Tree) or approximate inference methods (Markov Chain Monte Carlo, Gibbs sampling) compute posterior distributions over queried variables.

Example Application: In medical diagnosis, a Bayesian network represents relationships between diseases and symptoms. Given symptoms as evidence, Bayesian inference updates probabilities for possible diseases, facilitating diagnostic decision-making.

Likelihood Functions and Log-Loss

The concepts of likelihood functions and log-loss are fundamental in statistics and machine learning, specifically in probabilistic modeling and classification tasks. Understanding these concepts deeply involves examining their mathematical foundations, optimization behaviors, and practical applications in models such as logistic regression and deep neural networks.

Likelihood Function

The likelihood function quantifies the probability of observing a set of data given specific model parameters. Formally, given a set of data points $X = \{x_1, x_2 ..., x_n\}$and parameters θ, the likelihood function is defined as:

$$L(\theta|X) = P(X|\theta) = \prod_{i=1}^{n} P(x_i|\theta)$$

In the context of classification, each data point xi is associated with a label y_i, and the likelihood measures how well the model parameters explain the observed labels.

Log-Loss (Cross-Entropy Loss)

The log-loss (also known as cross-entropy loss) is derived directly from the negative log-likelihood, widely used as a loss function in classification tasks, especially binary and multi-class problems. Given actual labels y_i and predicted probabilities y^i, the log-loss is defined for binary classification as:

$$\text{Log-loss} = -\frac{1}{n}\sum_{i=1}^{n}[y_i \log(\hat{y}_i) + (1 - y_i)\log(1 - \hat{y}_i)]$$

Minimizing log-loss is equivalent to maximizing the likelihood of observing the given data.

Convexity and Optimization Behavior

Convexity: Convexity refers to a mathematical property of functions where, for any two points, the line segment joining them lies above or on the function's graph. The log-loss function, particularly for logistic regression, is convex. Convexity is critical because:

- **Guaranteed Global Minimum:** A convex loss function ensures a unique global minimum, meaning optimization algorithms consistently converge to an optimal solution.
- **Ease of Optimization:** Gradient-based optimization methods, such as Gradient Descent or Newton's method, are more effective and computationally stable on convex functions.
- **Optimization Behavior:** The optimization of log-loss is typically achieved via gradient-based algorithms (e.g., Gradient Descent, Stochastic Gradient Descent, Adam). The properties of log-loss lead to the following beneficial optimization behaviors
- **Stable and Efficient Convergence:** Due to the smooth and convex shape of log-loss in logistic regression, gradient-based methods converge steadily and predictably toward the global optimum.
- **Sensitivity to Probability Estimates:** Log-loss heavily penalizes predictions far from actual labels. This encourages models to produce accurate probabilistic outputs rather than just correct classifications, improving confidence calibration.

- **Gradient Magnitude and Learning Dynamics:** The gradients of log-loss are well-defined and continuous, facilitating efficient computation. However, very confident incorrect predictions result in large gradients, strongly correcting model parameters, guiding the model towards improved predictions.

Use in Logistic Regression

Logistic regression is one of the simplest yet most effective binary classification algorithms. It explicitly utilizes log-loss (cross-entropy) for parameter estimation.

Formulation:

Logistic regression assumes that the probability of belonging to a class follows a sigmoid function of linear combinations of features X:

$$P(Y=1|X;\theta)=\sigma(\theta^T X)=\frac{1}{1+e^{-(\theta^T X)}}$$

The likelihood function in logistic regression is thus defined as:

$$L(\theta|X,y)=\prod_{i=1}^{n} P(y_i|x_i,\theta)=\prod_{i=1}^{n}[\sigma(\theta^T x_i)]^{y_i}[1-\sigma(\theta^T x_i)]^{(1-y_i)}$$

Optimization in Logistic Regression

By taking the negative log of this likelihood, we derive the standard cross-entropy loss used for parameter estimation:

$$\text{Log-loss}=-\sum_{i=1}^{n}[y_i\log(\sigma(\theta^T x_i))+(1-y_i)\log(1-\sigma(\theta^T x_i))]$$

Gradient-based optimization (like Gradient Descent) adjusts parameters to minimize this loss, thus maximizing the likelihood of observed outcomes.

Use in Deep Learning

Deep learning models, particularly neural networks for classification tasks, extensively employ cross-entropy (log-loss) as a primary optimization objective.

Rationale in Deep Learning

Differentiable and Efficient Gradient Computation: Neural networks depend on backpropagation and gradient computations. The smooth differentiability of log-loss makes it ideal for training neural network parameters efficiently.

Multi-class Classification Generalization:

For multi-class classification (with classes c), log-loss generalizes naturally to categorical cross-entropy:

$$\text{Log-loss (multi-class)} = -\frac{1}{n}\sum_{i=1}^{n}\sum_{c} y_{i,c}\log(\hat{y}_{i,c})$$

Here, yi,crepresents the ground-truth indicator variable (1 for the true class, 0 otherwise), andy^i,c is the predicted probability of class c.

Behavior and Optimization in Deep Networks

- Combating Vanishing Gradients: Using log-loss in conjunction with activation functions like softmax stabilizes training. It helps to maintain meaningful gradient values even when predictions approach the correct outcomes, ensuring robust backpropagation.
- Encouraging Confident and Calibrated Predictions: The sensitivity of cross-entropy loss encourages neural networks to output probabilities closer to ground truth, thus achieving calibrated probabilistic interpretations rather than just discrete decisions.
- Regularization and Generalization: Through penalizing overly confident wrong predictions harshly, log-loss implicitly helps reduce overfitting, promoting generalization on unseen data.

Role of Statistical Decision Theory

Statistical decision theory provides a structured framework for decision-making under uncertainty. It systematically analyzes situations in which decisions must be made based on uncertain or probabilistic information. Within machine learning, statistical decision theory forms the theoretical foundation underpinning predictive modeling, particularly in classification problems. The primary objective is to optimize decision-making by quantifying uncertainties, potential outcomes, and associated risks through mathematical and probabilistic formulations. This facilitates selecting the best actions or models to minimize expected losses and maximize overall prediction accuracy or utility.

Risk Minimization and Loss Functions

In statistical decision theory, risk minimization involves selecting models or decision rules that minimize the expected loss, reflecting the cost associated with incorrect or suboptimal decisions. A fundamental component of risk minimization is the loss function, a quantitative measure defining the cost incurred when predictions deviate from true outcomes. Formally, for a prediction problem, a loss function L(y,y^) measures the cost of predicting y^ when the actual outcome is y. Different tasks utilize diverse loss functions depending on their objectives:

- 0–1 Loss: Widely used in classification tasks, it assigns a loss of 0 for correct predictions and 1 for incorrect predictions:

$$L(y, \hat{y}) = \begin{cases} 0 & \text{if } y = \hat{y} \\ 1 & \text{if } y \neq \hat{y} \end{cases}$$

- Squared Error Loss (Quadratic Loss): Commonly applied in regression tasks, penalizing predictions proportionally to the squared difference between the actual and predicted values:

$$L(y, \hat{y}) = (y - \hat{y})^2$$

- Absolute Error Loss: Another loss measure often used in regression, defined as the absolute difference between actual and predicted values:

$$L(y, \hat{y}) = |y - \hat{y}|$$

The expected risk, or average risk R(h) associated with a prediction rule h, is computed by averaging the loss over the distribution of the data:

$$R(h) = \mathbb{E}_{X,Y}[L(Y, h(X))] = \int_x \int_y L(y, h(x))\, p(x, y)\, dy\, dx$$

Risk minimization thus involves finding the decision rule h*that minimizes the expected risk:

$$h^* = \arg\min_{h \in \mathcal{H}} R(h)$$

Bayes Optimal Classifier

The Bayes optimal classifier represents the theoretically optimal decision rule under statistical decision theory. It minimizes the probability of classification error (or equivalently, the expected risk under the 0–1 loss) by selecting the class with the highest posterior probability, given observed data. Suppose a classification task involves predicting a class label y∈ {c1, c2..., ck}, based on observed input xxx. According to Bayesian decision theory, the optimal decision rule is defined as follows:

$$h_{\text{Bayes}}(x) = \arg\max_{c_j} P(Y = c_j \mid X = x)$$

In other words, given a feature vector x, the Bayes optimal classifier assigns the instance to the class with the highest posterior probability.

Derivation and Intuition

The Bayes optimal classifier directly minimizes the expected loss when using the 0–1 loss function. Formally, the expected conditional risk given a data instance x is:

$$R(h|X = x) = \sum_{j=1}^{k} L(c_j, h(x))P(Y = c_j|X = x)$$

Under the 0–1 loss function, this reduces to the probability of making an incorrect classification:

$$R(h|X = x) = 1 - P(Y = h(x)|X = x)$$

Thus, to minimize this conditional risk, one must choose the class that maximizes the posterior probability:

$$h_{\text{Bayes}}(x) = \arg\max_{c_j} P(Y = c_j|X = x)$$

Significance in Practice

- Benchmark for Performance: Although the Bayes optimal classifier provides the theoretical lower bound on classification error, it is rarely directly computable in practice, as exact posterior probabilities are typically unknown. However, it sets an important theoretical benchmark for the performance of practical classifiers.
- Model Comparison and Evaluation: Practical classifiers are evaluated relative to this theoretical optimum, and improvements in classifier accuracy often aim to approximate the performance of the Bayes optimal classifier.

Information Bottleneck Principle

The Information Bottleneck (IB) principle is a theoretical framework originating from information theory, introduced by Tishby, Pereira, and Bialek (1999). It provides a systematic method for extracting compact yet informative representations from data. At its core, the IB principle aims to compress an input signal X into a reduced representation T, ensuring this compressed representation retains maximum relevant information about a target variable Y. Formally, the IB problem seeks a balance between compressing the data (reducing redundancy) and preserving predictive utility, mathematically expressed by optimizing the following functional:

$$\min_{p(t|x)} I(X;T) - \beta I(T;Y)$$

Here, I (X; T)denotes mutual information between the input X and the representation TTT, capturing the degree of compression. Meanwhile, I (T; Y) represents mutual information between T and the target variable Y, reflecting sufficiency or predictive relevance. The hyperparameter β controls the trade-off between compression and prediction: a smaller β leads to greater compression at the potential cost of losing predictive accuracy, whereas a larger βprioritizes prediction at the expense of less compression.

The IB principle has become influential in various areas of machine learning, particularly in feature extraction, clustering, and representation learning. Its appeal lies in its explicit balancing act, clearly linking information theory concepts to practical learning scenarios.

Learning Compact and Sufficient Representations

Learning compact and sufficient representations is fundamental in machine learning, particularly for tasks involving high-dimensional and complex data. Compactness refers to reducing the dimensionality or complexity of representations, making them computationally efficient and easier to interpret. Sufficiency denotes that the representation must retain all essential information needed for accurate predictions or reconstructions. The IB principle elegantly formalizes these goals, highlighting two desirable yet often conflicting properties:

- Compression (Compactness): A compressed representation discards irrelevant or redundant information from the raw data. This property enhances generalization by removing noisy features, reducing computational complexity, and mitigating the risk of overfitting.
- Sufficiency (Predictive Accuracy): Representations must encapsulate critical predictive features required to accurately infer the target variable. An overly compressed representation might exclude important predictive cues, impairing model performance.

In practice, applying IB involves finding a representation TTT that minimizes redundancy (by limiting I (X; T) while simultaneously maximizing relevance (by maximizing I (T; Y). This optimal trade-off leads to meaningful representations that are neither overly simplified nor excessively complex, providing an efficient foundation for downstream predictive tasks such as classification, regression, or clustering.

Deep Learning and Representation Compression

Deep learning models, particularly deep neural networks, naturally lend themselves to representation compression guided by the IB principle. In deep learning, intermediate layers progressively transform input data into increasingly abstract representations. Recent research has revealed that neural networks implicitly approximate IB-like trade-offs, progressively compressing input representations while preserving relevant predictive information. During the training of deep networks, early layers generally retain more detailed, high-dimensional information, whereas later layers compress representations, emphasizing task-relevant features. Empirical studies indicate that, as training progresses, neural network representations undergo two distinct phases:

- Fitting Phase: The early stage of training, where networks maximize I (T; Y), improving predictive accuracy and reducing training error. Here, neural representations expand and become richer in detail.
- Compression Phase: Subsequent training iterations drive networks toward reducing I (X; T), eliminating redundant features, thereby enhancing generalization and robustness. This phase is particularly visible in deeper neural architectures, where high-dimensional inputs (e.g., images, audio, text) are distilled into compact representations that capture essential patterns relevant to the output task.

The IB framework thus provides theoretical insights into the optimization behavior of deep networks, suggesting that successful deep models implicitly achieve optimal information-theoretic trade-offs. Furthermore, it inspires explicit regularization strategies, such as Variational Information Bottleneck (VIB), which integrates the IB objective directly into neural network training. VIB promotes robust and generalizable representations by explicitly penalizing the flow of unnecessary information. Overall, the IB principle significantly enhances our understanding of deep learning, clarifying how and why deep networks learn efficient and powerful representations. By explicitly connecting compression and prediction, the IB principle provides both theoretical justification and practical methodologies to design and interpret sophisticated deep learning models.

Fisher Information and Cramér-Rao Bound

Fisher Information and the associated Cramér-Rao bound are fundamental concepts in statistical inference, specifically in parameter estimation theory. These concepts quantify the theoretical limits to the precision of parameter estimates, revealing how accurately parameters of a statistical model can be determined from observed data.

Fisher Information

Fisher Information (FI) measures the amount of information an observable random variable X carries about an unknown parameter θ upon which the probability distribution of X depends. Formally, if X is a random variable with probability density function (PDF) f(x|θ), the Fisher Information I(θ) is defined mathematically as:

$$I(\theta) = E\left[\left(\frac{\partial}{\partial \theta} \ln f(X|\theta)\right)^2 \middle| \theta\right] = -E\left[\frac{\partial^2}{\partial \theta^2} \ln f(X|\theta) \middle| \theta\right]$$

The Fisher Information quantifies how quickly the log-likelihood function changes as the parameter θ varies. Intuitively, a large Fisher Information means that small changes in the parameter value will significantly alter the distribution of the data, thereby making the parameter easier to estimate precisely. Conversely, smaller Fisher Information indicates a flatter log-likelihood surface, implying greater uncertainty and less precision in estimation. For vector parameters θ= (θ_1, θ_2..., θ_k), the Fisher Information extends to an information matrixI(θ), whose elements are given by second derivatives of the log-likelihood function:

$$[I(\boldsymbol{\theta})]_{ij} = -E\left[\frac{\partial^2}{\partial \theta_i \partial \theta_j} \ln f(X|\boldsymbol{\theta}) \middle| \boldsymbol{\theta}\right]$$

This Fisher Information matrix is crucial for evaluating the simultaneous estimation accuracy for multiple parameters.

Cramér-Rao Bound

The Cramér-Rao bound (CRB) is a direct consequence of Fisher Information, establishing a theoretical lower bound on the variance of unbiased estimators. Specifically, for any unbiased estimator θ^ of a parameter θ, the variance of the estimator satisfies the following inequality:

$$\text{Var}(\hat{\theta}) \geq \frac{1}{I(\theta)}$$

In the multidimensional case, where multiple parameters θ are simultaneously estimated, this bound generalizes to the matrix inequality:

$$\text{Cov}(\hat{\boldsymbol{\theta}}) \geq I(\boldsymbol{\theta})^{-1}$$

Thus, the inverse of the Fisher Information matrix sets a fundamental limit on the covariance matrix of parameter estimators. No unbiased estimator can achieve a variance smaller than this theoretical lower bound. An estimator achieving this bound with equality is termed an efficient estimator, and it represents the optimal estimator within the unbiased class.

Limits of Parameter Estimation Accuracy

The Fisher Information and Cramér-Rao bound have direct implications for the accuracy achievable by any statistical estimation procedure:

- Lower Bound on Estimation Variance: Fisher Information sets a fundamental limit to precision. High Fisher Information indicates that the parameter can be estimated with low variance, while low Fisher Information leads to inherently less accurate estimates. Thus, the Fisher Information directly defines the "best-case scenario" for parameter estimation precision.
- Impact of Sample Size: Fisher Information typically scales linearly with sample size n. As sample size increases, the precision of estimation improves proportionally. Specifically, the variance of optimal unbiased estimators typically decreases proportionally to $1/n$.
- Efficient Estimators: Estimators that reach the Cramér-Rao bound are termed efficient. Maximum Likelihood Estimators (MLEs) often attain this bound asymptotically, meaning that as the sample size becomes large, the MLE becomes optimal in terms of minimum achievable variance.
- Practical Constraints: Practical estimators might not always reach the CRB due to finite-sample effects, nonlinearities in parameterization, or the absence of unbiased estimators. Thus, the CRB provides a benchmark for evaluating estimator performance rather than a universally achievable target.

Implications for Model Sensitivity

Fisher Information plays a pivotal role in assessing a model's sensitivity to parameter variations. When Fisher Information is high, even minor changes in a parameter result in significant shifts in the likelihood function, indicating that the parameter has a strong influence on model outputs. This sensitivity implies that accurate estimation of such parameters is crucial for reliable model performance. On the other hand, low Fisher Information suggests that the model is relatively insensitive to that parameter, making it harder to estimate accurately. This information helps researchers identify which parameters are most critical for precise model calibration and prediction.

Experimental Design Optimization

Fisher Information provides a quantitative foundation for optimizing experimental designs. By selecting experimental conditions that maximize Fisher Information, researchers can ensure that collected data contains the most informative signal about model parameters. This optimization reduces estimation variance and increases confidence in parameter values. The Cramér-Rao Bound (CRB), which depends inversely on Fisher Information, serves as a benchmark to compare different design strategies. Designs that result in lower CRB values are preferred, as they provide higher estimation accuracy. Thus, Fisher Information supports the creation of efficient, targeted, and cost-effective experimental protocols for model refinement.

Parameter Identifiability

Fisher Information also highlights issues related to parameter identifiability. If a parameter consistently yields low Fisher Information across data scenarios, it may be structurally non-identifiable, meaning that no amount of data can accurately estimate it. This insight suggests potential flaws in the model's structure or the parameter's formulation. Such findings prompt critical reassessment, such as reparametrizing the model, modifying data collection strategies, or incorporating prior knowledge. Detecting weak identifiability early prevents misinterpretation of results and helps ensure that statistical inference is based on parameters that can be estimated reliably and meaningfully from available data.

Model Robustness and Stability

Fisher Information analysis serves as a diagnostic tool for assessing model robustness and stability. A model where critical parameters possess high Fisher Information is typically more resilient to small changes in data or model inputs, resulting in stable and consistent predictions. Conversely, if key parameters have low Fisher Information, the model may exhibit unstable behavior under minor perturbations, leading to unreliable or erratic outputs. This can compromise decision-making based on model predictions. Therefore, evaluating Fisher Information across parameters helps in stress-testing the model, identifying fragile components, and guiding efforts to enhance overall model reliability and interpretability.

Summary

The critical interplay between information theory and statistical foundations in machine learning, emphasizing how these concepts guide learning, prediction, and decision-making under uncertainty. It began with an introduction to entropy, information gain, and uncertainty, which are foundational in feature selection and decision tree construction. The chapter detailed how divergence measures like Kullback-Leibler and cross-entropy quantify differences between distributions and support classification models. Probabilistic modeling, through Maximum Likelihood Estimation (MLE) and Maximum A Posteriori (MAP), highlighted differing views in parameter inference, with a comparison between frequentist and Bayesian interpretations. Concepts like priors, likelihood, and posteriors were contextualized within Naïve Bayes and Bayesian Networks. The importance of likelihood functions and log-loss in optimization was reinforced through their application in logistic regression and deep learning. Statistical decision theory and loss functions were presented as tools for formalizing learning objectives, culminating in the Bayes Optimal Classifier. The chapter also discussed the

Information Bottleneck principle, linking information compression to efficient representation learning in deep networks. Finally, Fisher Information and the Cramér-Rao Bound underscored the theoretical limits of estimation precision, shedding light on model sensitivity and robustness. Collectively, this chapter bridges theoretical rigor and practical modeling, laying a strong foundation for advanced learning systems.

Exercise questions

- Define entropy and explain its significance in measuring uncertainty in machine learning models.
- How is information gain used in decision tree algorithms for feature selection?
- What does Kullback-Leibler (KL) divergence measure, and why is it asymmetric?
- Differentiate between Maximum Likelihood Estimation (MLE) and Maximum A Posteriori (MAP) estimation.
- Explain the roles of prior, likelihood, and posterior in Bayesian inference.
- What is the log-loss function, and how is it applied in logistic regression?
- Describe the Information Bottleneck Principle and its relevance in deep learning.
- How does cross-entropy relate to classification problems in neural networks?
- What is the purpose of the Cramér-Rao Bound, and how does it relate to Fisher Information?
- Compare and contrast the frequentist and Bayesian approaches in statistical modeling.

BIBLIOGRAPHY

Anwar, K., Siddiqui, J., & Saquib Sohail, S. (2019). Machine Learning Techniques for Book Recommendation: An Overview. *SSRN Electronic Journal*. https://doi.org/10.2139/ssrn.3356349

Anwar, K., Siddiqui, J., & Sohail, S. S. (2020). Machine learning-based book recommender system: A survey and new perspectives. In *International Journal of Intelligent Information and Database Systems*. https://doi.org/10.1504/IJIIDS.2020.109457

Azhaguramyaa, V. R., Janet, J., Madhavan, G. R., Balakrishnan, S., & Arunkumar, K. (2022). Sentiment Analysis on Book Reviews Using Machine Learning Techniques. *8th International Conference on Advanced Computing and Communication Systems, ICACCS 2022*. https://doi.org/10.1109/ICACCS54159.2022.9785311

Brownlee, J. (2020). Probability for Machine Learning : Discover how to harness uncertainty with Python. *Machine Learning Mastery*.

Burkov, A. (2019). The Hundred-Page Machine Learning Book-Andriy Burkov. In *Expert Systems*.

Burkov, A. (2021). Hundred-The Page Machine Learning Book. In *Expert Systems*.

Chen, C. H., Yang, S. J. H., Weng, J. X., Ogata, H., & Su, C. Y. (2021). Predicting at-risk university students based on their e-book reading behaviours by using machine learning classifiers. *Australasian Journal of Educational Technology*. https://doi.org/10.14742/ajet.6116

Correia, M., & Rodrigues, L. (2024). Security and Privacy. In *Law, Governance and Technology Series*. https://doi.org/10.1007/978-3-031-41264-6_5

Daimari, D., Mondal, S., Brahma, B., & Nag, A. (2023). FAVORITE BOOK PREDICTION SYSTEM USING MACHINE LEARNING ALGORITHMS. *Journal of Applied Engineering and Technological Science*. https://doi.org/10.37385/jaets.v4i2.1925

Daimari, D., Narzary, M., Mazumdar, N., & Nag, A. (2021). A Machine Learning Based Book Availability Prediction Model for Library Management System. *Library Philosophy and Practice*.

Dong, C., & Zhang, F. (2023). Book Review: Machine Learning and Human Intelligence: The Future of Education for the 21st Century. *Policy Futures in Education*. https://doi.org/10.1177/14782103221117655

Douglass, M. J. J. (2020). Book Review: Hands-on Machine Learning with Scikit-Learn, Keras, and Tensorflow, 2nd edition by Aurélien Géron. *Physical and Engineering Sciences in Medicine*. https://doi.org/10.1007/s13246-020-00913-z

Gogula, S. D., Rahouti, M., Gogula, S. K., Jalamuri, A., & Jagatheesaperumal, S. K. (2023). An Emotion-Based Rating System for Books Using Sentiment Analysis and Machine Learning in the Cloud. *Applied Sciences (Switzerland)*. https://doi.org/10.3390/app13020773

Goldberg, Y. (2017). Neural Network Methods for Natural Language Processing. *Synthesis Lectures on Human Language Technologies*. https://doi.org/10.2200/S00762ED1V01Y201703HLT037

Goulet, J.-A. (2020). Probabilistic Machine Learning for Civil Engineers. *MIT Press*.

Grant, T. D., & Wischik, D. J. (2020). On the path to AI: Law's prophecies and the conceptual foundations of the machine learning age. In *On the Path to AI: Law's Prophecies and the Conceptual Foundations of the Machine Learning Age*. https://doi.org/10.1007/978-3-030-43582-0

Han, J., Hong, J., & Sutardja, N. (2015). Machine learning techniques for price change forecast using the limit order book data. *ArXiv*.

Hastie, T., Tibshirani, R., & Friedman, J. (2009). machine learning book. *Elements*.

Hiray, P. S. R. (2021). Book Recommendation System Using Machine Learning. *International Journal for Research in Applied Science and Engineering Technology*. https://doi.org/10.22214/ijraset.2021.39658

Ji, Q. (2022). Readability Evaluation of Books in Chinese as a Foreign Language Using the Machine Learning Algorithm. *Mobile Information Systems*. https://doi.org/10.1155/2022/5957566

Koprowski, R., & Foster, K. R. (2018). Machine learning and medicine: book review and commentary. *Biomedical Engineering Online*. https://doi.org/10.1186/s12938-018-0449-9

Lee, S., Ji, H., Kim, J., & Park, E. (2020). What books will be your bestseller? A machine learning approach with Amazon Kindle. *Electronic Library*. https://doi.org/10.1108/EL-08-2020-0234

Lee, S., Kim, J., & Park, E. (2023). Can book covers help predict bestsellers using machine learning approaches? *Telematics and Informatics*. https://doi.org/10.1016/j.tele.2023.101948

Mueller, J., & Massaron, L. (2016). Machine learning for dummies. In *For dummies*.

Natarajan, B. K. (1993). A reply to Hellerstein's book review of Machine Learning: A Theoretical Approach. In *Machine Learning*. https://doi.org/10.1007/BF00993108

Nawar, A., Toma, N. T., Al Mamun, S., Kaiser, M. S., Mahmud, M., & Rahman, M. A. (2021). Cross-Content Recommendation between Movie and Book using Machine

Learning. *15th IEEE International Conference on Application of Information and Communication Technologies, AICT 2021*. https://doi.org/10.1109/AICT52784.2021.9620432

Ntakaris, A., Magris, M., Kanniainen, J., Gabbouj, M., & Iosifidis, A. (2018). Benchmark dataset for mid-price forecasting of limit order book data with machine learning methods. *Journal of Forecasting*. https://doi.org/10.1002/for.2543

Nugraha, E., Ardiansyah, T., Junaeti, E., & Riza, L. S. (2020). Enhanced digital library with book recommendations based on collaborative filtering. *Journal of Engineering Education Transformations*. https://doi.org/10.16920/JEET/2020/V34I0/157882

Panesar, A. (2021). Machine Learning and AI for Healthcare. In *Machine Learning and AI for Healthcare*. https://doi.org/10.1007/978-1-4842-6537-6

Pattern Recognition and Machine Learning. (2007). *Journal of Electronic Imaging*. https://doi.org/10.1117/1.2819119

Richert, W., & Coelho, L. P. (2015). Building Machine Learning Systems with Python, Second Edition. In *Book*. https://doi.org/10.1007/s13398-014-0173-7.2

Sarma, D., Mittra, T., & Hossain, S. (2021). Personalized Book Recommendation System using Machine Learning Algorithm. *International Journal of Advanced Computer Science and Applications*. https://doi.org/10.14569/IJACSA.2021.0120126

Sethy, A., Rout, A. K., Uriti, A., & Yalla, S. P. (2023). A comprehensive machine learning framework for automated book genre classifier. *Revue d'Intelligence Artificielle*. https://doi.org/10.18280/ria.370323

Shanmugam, R. (2018). Elements of causal inference: foundations and learning algorithms. *Journal of Statistical Computation and Simulation*. https://doi.org/10.1080/00949655.2018.1505197

Starmer, J. (2022). The StatQuest Illustrated Guide to Machine Learning. *Rhns*.

Thangam, D. (2024). Predictive Analytics Using Statistics and Big Data: Concepts and Modelling. *Journal of the Royal Statistical Society Series A: Statistics in Society*. https://doi.org/10.1093/jrsssa/qnad089

Vemuri, V. K. (2020). The Hundred-Page Machine Learning Book. *Journal of Information Technology Case and Application Research*. https://doi.org/10.1080/15228053.2020.1766224

Wu, H. (2022). Book Review: Supervised machine learning for text analysis in R by EmilHvitfeldt and JuliaSilge . *Biometrics*. https://doi.org/10.1111/biom.13674

REFERENCES BOOKS

- Introduction to Machine Learning with Python by*Andreas C. Müller & Sarah Guido*
- Understanding Machine Learning: From Theory to Algorithms by *Shai Shalev-Shwartz and Shai Ben-David*
- Machine Learning by *Saikat Dutt, Subramanian Chandramouli and Amit Kumar Das*
- Data Science and Machine Learning: Mathematical and Statistical Methods by *Dirk P. Kroese, Zdravko I. Botev, Thomas Taimre, Radislav Vaisman*
- Introduction to Machine Learning by *Alex Smola and S.V.N. Vishwanathan*
- Foundations of Machine Learning by *Mehryar Mohri, Afshin Rostamizadeh, and Ameet Talwalkar*
- Introduction to Machine Learning by *Nils J. Nilsson and Robotics Laboratory*
- Information Science and Statistics by *Christopher M. Bishop*
- Machine Learning for Absolute Beginners: A Plain English Introduction by*Oliver Theobald*
- Machine Learning Crash Course for Engineers by *Eklas Hossain*
- Machine Learning and Its Application: A Quick Guide for Beginners by*Indranath Chatterjee*